WHEN THAT ROUGH GOD GOES RIDING

WHEN THAT ROUGH GOD GOES RIDING

LISTENING TO VAN MORRISON

GREIL MARCUS

PublicAffairs
New York

Published in the United States by PublicAffairs™,
a member of the Perseus Books Group.
All rights reserved.
Printed in the United States of America.

"It's All in the Game" lyrics by Carl Sigman,
music by Charles Gates Dawes. Copyright © 1951 (renewed) by
Music Sales Corporation. International copyright secured.
All rights reserved. Used by permission.

PublicAffairs books are available at special discounts for bulk purchases in
the U.S. by corporations, institutions, and other organizations. For more
information, please contact the Special Markets Department at the Perseus
Books Group, 2300 Chestnut Street, Suite 200, Philadelphia, PA 19103, call
(800) 810-4145, ext. 5000, or e-mail special.markets@perseusbooks.com.

Designed by Trish Wilkinson
Text set in 11.5 Minion

Library of Congress Cataloging-in-Publication Data

Marcus, Greil.
    When that rough god goes riding : listening to Van Morrison / Greil
Marcus. — 1st ed.
        p.   cm.
    Includes bibliographical references and index.
    ISBN 978-1-58648-821-5 (alk. paper)
    1. Morrison, Van, 1945– —Criticism and interpretation. 2. Rock
music—History and criticism. I. Title.
ML420.M63M37 2010
782.42164092—dc22
2010001656

First Edition

10 9 8 7 6 5 4 3 2 1

CONTENTS

For Dave Marsh

NORTHERN MUSE. GREEK THEATRE, BERKELEY.
3 MAY 2009

The fourteen-piece band assembled for a concert in which Van Morrison was to perform the whole of his forty-one-year-old album *Astral Weeks* so dominated the stage you might not have even noticed the figure seated at the piano; the sound Morrison made when he opened his mouth seemed to come out of nowhere. It was huge; it silenced everything around it, pulled every other sound around it into itself—Morrison's own fingers on the keys, the chatter in the crowd that was still going on because there was no announcement that anything was about to start, cars on the street, the ambient noise of the century-old open-air stone amphitheatre, where in 1903 President Theodore Roosevelt spoke, where in 1906 Sarah Bernhardt appeared to cheer on San Francisco as it dug out of its ruins, where in 1964 the student leader Mario Savio rose to speak to the whole of the university gathered in one place and was seized by police the instant he stood behind the podium as the crowd before him erupted in screams, where Senator Robert F. Kennedy spoke in 1968, days before he was shot. The first word out of Morrison's mouth that night, if it was a word, not just a sound, something between a shout and a moan, was, you could believe, as big as anything that ever happened on that stage.

INTRODUCTION

In 1956, the stiff and tired world of British pop music was turned upside down by Lonnie Donegan's "Rock Island Line," a skiffle version of a Lead Belly song, played on guitar, banjo, washboard, and homemade bass. Like thousands of other teenagers, John Lennon put together his own skiffle band in Liverpool that same year; Van Morrison, born George Ivan Morrison in 1945 in East Belfast, in Northern Ireland, formed the Sputniks in 1957, the year the Soviet Union put the first satellite into orbit and John Lennon met Paul McCartney. Morrison would never find such a comrade, and, unlike the Beatles, he would never find his identity in a group. Whether in Ireland, England, or the United States, he would always see himself as a castaway.

East Belfast was militantly Protestant, but Morrison's parents were freethinkers; even after his mother became a Jehovah's Witness for a time in the 1950s, his father remained a committed atheist. The real church in the Morrison household was musical. There was always the radio ("My father was listening to John McCormack"); more obsessively, there was "my father's vast record collection," 78s and LPs by the all-American Lead Belly, and within the kingdom of his vast repertoire of blues, ballads, folk songs, protest songs, work songs, and party tunes that dissolved all traditions of race or place, the minstrel and bluesman Jimmie Rodgers, cowboy singers of the likes of Eddy Arnold and Gene Autry, the balladeer Woody Guthrie, the hillbilly poet Hank Williams, the songsters Sonny Terry and Brownie McGhee, the gospel blues guitarist Sister Rosetta Tharpe—and later Muddy Waters, Howlin' Wolf, Little Walter, John Lee Hooker, Big Joe Williams, all of them magical names. Thus when the thirteen-year-old singer, guitar banger, and harmonica player Van Morrison went from the Sputniks to Midnight Special, named for one of Lead Belly's signature numbers—and after that from Midnight Special to the Thunderbolts, a would-be rock 'n' roll outfit that tried to catch the thrills of Jerry Lee Lewis and Little Richard, and from the Thunderbolts to the Monarchs Showband, a nine-man outfit with a horn section, choreographed shuffles, and stage suits that would play your company dinner, your Christmas party, your wedding, and which in the early '60s toured Germany offering Ray Charles imitations to homesick GIs, only a patch of the map Morrison carried inside himself had been scratched.

In 1964, in Belfast, with the band Them, Morrison began to find his style: the blues singer's marriage of emotional extremism and nihilistic reserve, the delicacy of a soul singer's presentation of a bleeding heart, a folk singer's sense of the uncanny in the commonplace, the rhythm and blues band-leader's commitment to drive, force, speed, and excitement above all. The group's name, calling up the 1957 horror movie about giant radioactive ants loose in the sewers of Los Angeles, was full of teenage menace:

WHO ARE? WHAT ARE? THEM

ran ads in the Belfast *Telegraph*. With Morrison pushing the combo through twenty minutes of his own "Gloria," night after night in the ballroom of a seamen's mission called the Maritime Hotel, Them began to live up to its name.

Cut to three minutes or less on 45s, the band's songs would soon bring Morrison a taste of fame. In 1965, in London—"Where," the liner notes to Them's second album quoted Morrison, "it all happens! . . ."—the group crumbled, but Morrison recorded under their name with a few members of the band and a clutch of studio musicians. Though Morrison would disavow them as the most paltry reductions of what had happened at the Maritime—"It wasn't even Them after Belfast," Morrison told me one afternoon in 1970, as he told others before and since—Them made two unforgettable albums, harsh in one moment, lyrical in the next. In 1965 and 1966 Them scored modest hits on both sides of the Atlantic: "Gloria" (covered by the Chicago band the Shadows of Knight, who had the bigger hit in the U.S.A., except on the West Coast), "Here Comes the Night," "Baby Please Don't Go," "Mystic Eyes."

To those who were listening, it was clear that Van Morrison was as intense and imaginative a performer as any to have emerged in the wake of the Beatles and the Rolling Stones—who, he claimed of the latter band in angry, drunken moments, stole it all from him, from *him*! Yet it was equally clear, to those who saw Them's shows in California in 1966—at the Fillmore Auditorium in San Francisco, and at the Whisky A-Go-Go in Los Angeles in 1966, where the group headlined over Captain Beefheart one week and the Doors the next—that Morrison lacked the flair for pop stardom possessed by clearly inferior singers, Keith Relf of the Yardbirds, Eric Burdon of the Animals, never mind Mick Jagger, who in those days were seizing America's airwaves like pirates, if not, as with Freddie and the Dreamers or Wayne Fontana and the Mindbenders, conning the nation's youth like the King and the Duke bamboozling Huck and Jim. Morrison communicated distance, not immediacy; bitterness, not celebration. His music had power, but too much subtlety for its power not to double back into fear, loss, fury, doubt.

What he lacked in glamour he made up in strangeness—or rather his strangeness made glamour impossible, and at the same time captivated some who felt strange themselves. Morrison never covered Randy Newman's "Have You Seen My Baby?"—"I'll talk to strangers, if I want to / 'Cause I'm a stranger, too"—he didn't have to. He was small and gloomy, a burly man with more black energy than he knew what to do with, the wrong guy to meet in a dark alley, or backstage on the wrong night. He didn't fit the maracas-shaking mode of the day. Instead, in 1965, he recorded a ghostly version of "It's All Over Now, Baby Blue" that outran Bob Dylan's original, and then turned the fey Paul Simon rewrite of Edward Arlington Robinson's 1897 poem "Richard Cory" into a bone-chilling fable of self-loathing and vengefulness.

In 1966 Morrison abandoned the last remnant of Them—its name—and put himself altogether under the wing of the legendary New York record man Bert Berns, renowned for writing or producing Solomon Burke's "Cry to Me," Erma Franklin's "Piece of My Heart," Garnett Mimms's "Cry Baby," and the Isley Brothers' "Twist and Shout," not to mention "Here Comes the Night." In 1967 they made the single "Brown-Eyed Girl," after which Berns, working from sometimes unfinished recordings, rushed out a dark, cracked-blues album called *Blowin' Your Mind!* (the phrase was already as out-of-date as the soupy psychedelic jacket); the signature number was the nearly ten-minute "T. B. Sheets," which was exactly what it was about. Who wanted to listen to an endless cynical number about a woman dying of tuberculosis, closer to a bilious stand-up routine than a song, when the air was filled with "San Francisco (Be Sure to Wear Flowers in Your Hair)"?

The bright, bouncy "Brown-Eyed Girl" was Morrison's least convincing recording and his first top-ten hit single—and, except for "Domino" in 1970, so far his last. Though "Brown-Eyed Girl" has stayed on the radio ever since, at the time Morrison himself was quickly forgotten; he had both trivialized himself and blown himself up. His career was all but destroyed. When Nik Cohn's *Pop from the Beginning*, the first good rock 'n' roll history, appeared in 1969, even when a revised edition came out in 1973, neither Them nor Morrison were even mentioned.

Consumed by resentment over the swindle of stardom, fame, records, money, debt, and oblivion, caught in a trap of performing and publishing contracts after Berns's death at the end of 1967, Morrison found himself in Boston, where late-night DJs soon got used to a character with an incomprehensible Irish accent drunkenly pestering them for John Lee Hooker music. One night Morrison was booed off the stage when Peter Wolf, then the leader of a local band called the Hallucinations, brought him out of the audience to front their version of "Gloria." "Don't you know who this is?" Wolf shouted at the hissing crowd. "This man *wrote the song!*" But they didn't know. In 1967, when you said Morrison you meant the Doors, who, one could have read at the time, were at work on "their new masterpiece": *their* version of "Gloria."

Morrison returned to Belfast, apparently a burnt-out victim of the pop wars. There he wrote a set of songs about childhood, initiation, sex, and death, which finally took form as *Astral Weeks*. It was as serious an album as could be imagined, but it soared like an old Drifters 45, "When My Little Girl Is Smiling" or "I Count the Tears." From there Morrison's music opened onto the road it has followed since: a road bordered by meadows alive with the promise of mystical deliverance and revelation on one side, forests of shrieking haunts and beckoning specters on the other, and rocks, baubles, traps, and snares down the middle. With his wife, he moved to the musicians' pastoral bohemia of Woodstock, then to the San Francisco Bay Area, celebrated a domestic paradise, and pledged to walk down Broadway in his hot pants. Then his paradise fell to pieces, and his music shot back and forth between false promises and affirmations too hard-won to deny, from upstate New York to Marin County under a Belfast cloud, idyll and civil war, inspiration and boredom, the platitudes of a New Age seeker and the bad news of someone convinced that no one is listening, down ten, twenty, thirty, forty years, by now almost half a century, to find a man now brooding in his present-day redoubt in Bath, dreamy site of Roman spas, John Wood's eighteenth-century Druidic power spot Bath Circus, and Morrison's own Exile Productions. "The only thing that matters is whether you've got it or not," he once said. "The only thing that counts is whether you're still around. I'm still around." Yes, and so what? As a physical fact, Morrison may have the richest and most expressive voice pop music has produced since Elvis Presley, and with a sense of himself as an artist that Elvis was always denied. But what is that voice for?

Van Morrison's music as I hear it holds a story—a story made of fragments. There is in his music from the very first a kind of quest: for the moment when the magic word, riff, note, or chord is found and everything is transformed. At any time a listener might think that he or she has felt it, even glimpsed it, a realm beyond ordinary expression, reaching out as if to close your hand around such a moment, to grab for its air, then opening your fist to find a butterfly in it—but Morrison's sense of what that magic moment is must be more contingent. For him this quest is about the deepening of a style, the continuing task of constructing musical situations in which his voice can rise to its own form.

"When I was very young," the late Ralph J. Gleason wrote in 1970 in a review of Morrison's album *Moondance*, "I saw a film version of the life of John McCormack, the Irish tenor, playing himself. In it he explained to his accompanist that the element necessary to mark the important voice off from the other good ones was very specific. 'You have to have,' he said, 'the yarragh in your voice'"—and to get the yarragh, for Morrison, you may need a sense of the song as a thing in itself, with its own brain, heart, lungs, tongue, and ears. Its own desires, fears, will, and even ideas: "The question might really be," as he once said, "is the song singing you?" His music can be heard as an attempt to surrender to the yarragh, or to make it surrender to him; to find the music it wants; to bury it; to dig it out of the ground. The yarragh is his version of the art that has touched him: of blues and jazz, for that matter of Yeats and Lead Belly, the voice that strikes a note so exalted you can't believe a mere human being is responsible for it, a note so unfinished and unsatisfied you can understand why the eternal seems to be riding on its back.

Morrison will take hold of the yarragh, or get close to it, raise its specter even as he falls back before it, for the moment defeated, with horns, volume, quiet, melody and rhythm and the abandonment of both, in the twist of a phrase or the dissolution of words into syllables and syllables into preverbal grunts and moans. He will pursue it perhaps most of all in repetition, railing or sailing the same sound ten, twenty, thirty times until it has taken his song where he wants it to go or failed to crack the wall around it. The yarragh is not, it seems, something Morrison can get at will, or that in any given year or even decade he is even looking for; the endless stream of dull and tired albums through the 1980s and '90s, carrying titles like warning labels—*Beautiful Vision*; *Poetic Champions Compose*; *Avalon Sunset*; *No Guru, No Method, No Teacher*; *Inarticulate Speech of the Heart*; *A Sense of Wonder*; *Enlightenment*—attest to that. So do a string of records where Morrison seems to attempt to reduce whatever might be elusive, undefinable, and sui generis in his music to parts that can never recombine into a whole, as he recorded jazz and jump blues with his sometime accompanist Georgie Fame, country with Linda Gail Lewis, Jerry Lee's sister, traditional Irish songs with the Chieftains, and, most touchingly, even skiffle with Lonnie Donegan himself, back in Belfast, two old men standing up to the crowd to sing "Midnight Special," not so far from where, once, one of them named a band after it. Those are episodes in a career. It's the fragments of music as broken and then remade by the yarragh that this book is looking for. "The only time I actually work with words," Morrison said in 1978, "is when I'm writing a song. After it's written, I release the words; and every time I'm singing, I'm singing syllables. I'm singing signs and phrases."

The quest for the yarragh—for moments of disruption, when effects can seem to have no cause, when the sense of an unrepeatable event is present, when what is taking place in a song seems to go beyond the limits of respectable speech—is also a performer's quest to evade and escape the expectations of his audience. It's a struggle to avoid being made irrelevant and redundant, a creature tied as if by chains to his hits of forty, thirty, twenty years earlier, even to the song that hit last month—forbidden, by the laws of the pop mind and the pop market, from ever saying anything he hasn't said before. The result is a distrust of the audience, coming out, on any given night, in anger, insult, drunkenness, disdain directed at the singer's own songs as much as toward whatever crowd might be present. From the time of his first hits Morrison has, in a way, set himself against any possible audience: he does his work in public, but with his back turned, sometimes literally so—and it might go back to those nights in the Maritime Hotel in 1964. "Out of nowhere, these kids began showing up," Morrison said in 1970, and I remember the way his eyes sparkled in a set, stolid face as he talked: "Sometimes, when it all worked, something would happen, and the audience and musicians would be as one." That was because no one knew what might happen—and no one knew what was supposed to happen. Before a song is recorded, there is no right way; afterward, especially in the pop glare, audiences know what to expect and expect what they know.

Van Morrison, then, is a bad-tempered, self-contradictory individual whose work is about freedom. How do you get it? What do you do with it? How do you find it when it disappears—and what is it? Is the yarragh the means to freedom, or is it, when you can find it, the thing itself? When Morrison reaches the moments of upheaval, reversal, revelation, and mirror-breaking that are this book's subject—in his music and, sometimes, in what other people have done with his music, finding, as Neil Jordan would do with Morrison's music in his film *Breakfast on Pluto*, a yarragh behind the yarragh, or dramatizing it as Morrison might not—all of those questions are thrown into relief.

It becomes plain that any summing up of Morrison's work would be a fraud. That is what makes his failures interesting and his successes incomplete; it's what allows the most valuable instances of his music to exist less in relation to other instances in his career in any historical sense than in a kind of continual present. It's that territory I will try to map.

Ralph J. Gleason, "Rhythm: A Young Irishman Haunted by Dreams," *San Francisco Chronicle*, 1 March 1970.

"My father was listening": interview with Dave Marsh, "Kick Out the Jams" (Sirius XM Radio, 8 March 2009).

"The only time": Jonathan Cott, "Van Morrison: The *Rolling Stone* Interview," *Rolling Stone*, 30 November 1978, 52.

Mario Savio's oratory can be heard on *Is Freedom Academic? A Documentary of the Free Speech Movement at the University of California at Berkeley* (KPFA-Pacifica Radio, LP, 1965). See also Robert Cohen, *Freedom's Orator* (New York: Oxford, 2009).

The Heart and Soul of Bert Berns (UMVD, 2002). Includes Berns's productions of "Everybody Needs Somebody to Love" and "Cry to Me" by Solomon Burke, "Cry Baby" by Garnett Mimms, "Piece of My Heart" by Erma Franklin, and "Twist and Shout" and "I Don't Want to Go On Without You" by the Isley Brothers. *The Bert Berns Story Volume 1: Twist and Shout 1960–1964* (Ace, 2008) features an end-of-the-journey-to-the-end-of-the-night composite photo of Solomon Burke and

Berns facing the abyss in the studio while Little Esther Phillips, in a gleaming white dress, looks on; it includes "A Little Bit of Soap" by the Jarmels, the obscure "If I Didn't Have a Dime (to Pay the Jukebox)" by Gene Pitney, "Gypsy" by Ben E. King, "Look Away" by Garnett Mimms, "Mojo Hannah" by Little Esther Phillips, "Killer Joe" by the Rocky Fellas, and "Here Comes the Night" by Lulu. *Sloopy II Music Presents the Songs of Bert Russell Berns* (B00, no date, but going for $399 on eBay) collects forty-four tracks on two CDs, including "Here Comes the Night" by both Them and (in his unhinged *PinUps* version) David Bowie, "Are You Lonely for Me Baby" by both Freddie Scott and Otis Redding & Carla Thomas, "Baby Come On Home" by Solomon Burke and Led Zeppelin, "Cry Baby" by Garnett Mimms and Janis Joplin, "Goodbye Baby (Baby Goodbye)" by Solomon Burke and Janis Joplin, "I Want Candy" by the Strangeloves and Bow Wow Wow, "Piece of My Heart" by Erma Franklin and Janis Joplin, and "Tell Him" and "Run Mascara Run" by the Exciters.

Van Morrison, *Blowin' Your Mind!* (Bang, 1967).

————*Astral Weeks* (Warner Bros.–Seven Arts, 1968).

PART ONE

A GRIMY CINDERELLA
IN A PURPLE STAGE SUIT

MYSTIC EYES. 1965

It came barreling out of car radio speakers like a flood on a black night. Surrounded by some of the best and most tuneful pop music ever made—the Beach Boys' "I Get Around," Petula Clark's "Downtown," the Supremes' "Stop! In the Name of Love," Wilson Pickett's "In the Midnight Hour," the Beatles' "Eight Days a Week," the Miracles' "The Tracks of My Tears," Bob Dylan's "Like a Rolling Stone," Otis Redding's "I've Been Loving You too Long (to Stop Now)," the Byrds' "Turn! Turn! Turn!"—even up against Sam the Sham and the Pharaohs' "Wooly Bully"; even up against Them's own "Gloria" or "Here Comes the Night"—this made no sense. You couldn't see through it, you couldn't see into it. What was happening?

It starts in the middle, as if you've switched stations halfway through some other song without realizing it. It's moving so fast you feel as if you'll never catch up. The band—guitar, drums, bass, an organ hovering in the background—can't catch up with the harmonica that's leading the charge, Little Walter as a nightrider; suddenly they do, and then they take a step ahead. You realize that the last thing you want is for the harmonica—high, implacable, uncaring, a body without a mind, it seems to be its own force, not some mere instrument played by some particular person who has to get up in the morning and go to sleep at night—to lose this race. It doesn't; it cuts in front of the stampeding combo, playing a swirling pattern that focuses the band. There's a call and response, a joining of forces, no longer one against the others, but a whole against a part, and the part is whoever's listening. You're the target. You're about to be left behind, to the wasteland this flood will leave in its wake.

When lyrics appear in the song—as the Them guitarist Billy Harrison once put it so perfectly, when Morrison begins to "throw words at it"—you notice for the first time that there haven't been any. Suddenly what was chaos, unformed, threatening, thrilling, a giant, gaping mouth—is now a story. There's a singer and he's going to tell you about something, something about walking down by the old graveyard and looking into the eyes of the dead. But then that breaks up, too. "Eyes," he says again and again, the word fraying with each repetition, slipping the "mystic" that stands at its head, except when it doesn't. Morrison seems to turn away from the word, from words altogether, as if only fools actually believe that phonemes can signify, that a word is what it names, that there's any chance of understanding anything at all. The moment doesn't have the force, the desire—the termite instinct, as the critic Manny Farber unearthed it, of "doing go-for-broke art and not caring what comes of it"—of the first rampage of the music, which is like the harshest instrumental passage of Howlin' Wolf's 1951 "How Many More Years" turning into its own monster and turning against its own song. But the moment has its own humanity, which everywhere else is abstract: that half-second when the particular person singing the song's words gives up on words, in frustration, in disgust, in triumph, fully entering the music as himself and nobody else, throwing a single "eyes" against the wall with the knowledge that neither it nor any other words will ever catch a half of what he means. You're caught up in an irresolvable adventure that is taking place as you listen, in the notion that you can drop someone into the middle of a story and then jerk him or her out of it as if it were nothing more than a few minutes on the radio, now a bad dream you're certain is yours alone.

Them, "Mystic Eyes" (Parrot, US, Decca, UK, 1965). Included on *Them* (Parrot, 1965) and *The Angry Young Them* (Decca, 1965). Collected on *The Story of Them Featuring Van Morrison* (Polydor, 1998).

TUPELO HONEY, 1971

Florida Tupelo Honey is one of the rarest honeys with an exquisite buttery flavor and light color. Tupelo trees thrive along the rivers and creeks of the Florida panhandle and have delicate fragrant blossoms that can produce wonderful tupelo honey crops.

The Florida Tupelo flower is very delicate and blooms for only a very short time every year. Our beekeepers go through great lengths to keep our Florida tupelo honey pure by taking all the honey boxes off the hives and putting on clean empty beeswax combs right as the first tupelo flowers bloom. After about two weeks of bloom, we go out and take the honey boxes off the hives and spin it out to get the rare tupelo honey.

The Tupelo blossoms have very delicate little pistols that secrete the nectar. A strong wind or hard rain can rip the blossoms from the trees.

The blossoming period generally starts about the 20th of April every year and lasts about 3 weeks.

The honeybees are very eager to visit the blossoms, as the nectar can be quite abundant in good years.

Tupelo trees thrive in the river and creek bottoms where it is very wet. ˑ

—Sleeping Bear Farms, Beulah, Mississippi, 2009

Tupelo Honey was Van Morrison's gorgeous Woodstock album. It featured tinted photos of Morrison, his wife, and horses, including one of Morrison dressed like a country squire, all woodsy splendor. At the time, the record was like propaganda for the notion of leaving the strife of the previous decade behind and starting a new life, free of care. One of the songs was even called "Starting a New Life." There was "Old, Old Woodstock," "When That Evening Sun Goes Down," "You're My Woman," "I Wanna Roo You" ("Scottish Derivative," read the parenthetical subtitle, not that you needed a translation), "Moonshine Whiskey." Like "Wild Night," the single that leaped onto the radio in a flash and lost its luster almost as quickly, constant airplay making its celebration of kids out on the street feel tinsel cheap, a record anybody could have made and hundreds of people already had, the songs were cartoons. Today they make me think of the "War Free Edition" of the *New York Times* people buy in Jonathan Lethem's novel *Chronic City*. They make me think even more of something Dominique Robertson, then Robbie Robertson's wife, said to me when not long after *Tupelo Honey* appeared I went to Woodstock to talk to Robertson about the Band. I was seduced by the bucolic ease of this little corner of upstate New York, a world apart, but she wasn't. "Look at all this," she said, her hand waving toward the window opening onto the mountains, the forests, the sun. "It's everything people ought to want, and I hate it." "'This country life is killin' me,'" she sang, making up a song likely no one else in town would have thought of in that moment in history. "There's nothing here but dope, music, and beauty. If you're a woman, and you don't make music and you don't use dope, there's nothing here at all."

Maybe you could have heard that leaking through the cracks of Morrison's songs; a place where even the chirping of the birds seemed to bless your love was too good to be true. But the most gorgeous number on the album was the title song, and it was too good not to be true.

At almost seven unfolding minutes, it was a kind of odyssey. The constant invocation of "Tupelo honey" couldn't not invoke Elvis Presley; he too was smiling over the song's golden couple, as if they were living out all the best hopes of "Can't Help Falling in Love." It began with the most reassuring organ sound, gently picked notes on a guitar, a vocal that caressed the first verse, then ached through the chorus. You could miss the scrambled imagery of freed slaves and Camelot, "the road to freedom" and "knights in armor bent on chivalry"; you could catch it and feel part of a drama whose beginnings were lost in time and that would never end. "She's an angel," Morrison sang. "She's an angel," repeated the male voices behind him, the big, friendly sound of men who are jealous only of the fact that they're not as deserving as the singer has proven himself to be.

Morrison's voice grew bigger as the song went on, his singing more expansive, words turning into gestures, his arms spread wide, a finger pointing to the sky. "Yes she is," he almost whispered back at the chorus, as if answering himself in his own mind. "Yes she is!" he'd say elsewhere, banishing all doubt. The music went forward in steady steps, the knights sure in their mission, King Arthur with Excalibur in his hands.

The song had opened with an odd four lines, an old saying that seemed to come out of nowhere and go back there. "You can take. All the tea in China. Put it in a big brown bag for me. Sail right round all the seven oceans. Drop it straight into the deep blue sea." As Morrison smoothed the words, they struck a balance that gave the song as it moved on both its lightness and its weight—but finally there comes a point when all of this comes to a halt. Morrison has been all but kissing his words, lolling over them; then his clearwater tone breaks, and he takes a breath. The band drops back. "You can take," Morrison says, "all the tea in Chiney"—and with "Chiney," the vulgar word capsizing the ship, the scene shifts from the Woodstock hills and the open seas of the seven oceans to a Belfast wharf where an ugly old man is trying to sell you something you know you shouldn't want, and someone else over there in the shadows is waiting for a chance to expose himself. "Drop it, smack dab, in the middle of the deep blue sea," Morrison says, with the "smack dab" hit hard, the first word percussive, like a slap in the face, the "Drop it" instantly producing the image not of a bag of tea but of a gun, the singer daring anyone to stop him, to question him, and a smell of violence rises to the surface of the line.

"*Because*—" he announces: because she's as sweet as Tupelo honey, even if, for a second, the face that gets slapped by smack is hers. Literally, the words say that it doesn't matter what the world is or what it throws at me: love conquers all.

But as music, as words changing as they're spoken, they say nothing clearly. "All the tea in Chiney," then that "*Because—*" those words as they jump out of the song and bang up against each other make as true a yarragh, a breach, as any other. They can mean "Top of the world"—with James Cagney's murderous, self-immolating "Ma!" right on top of that. They can be funny. They can be crafty, inveigling, secretive, illegal. They can say, as the song says elsewhere, "You can't stop us." They can say *fuck it.* But whatever they say, that so strangely confiding "Chiney," a single word carrying a whole world of old movies up its sleeve, Charlie Chan prowling an opium den, Marlene Dietrich telling you "It took more than one man to change my name to Shanghai Lily," the peremptory, dismissively final "Drop it, smack dab, in the middle," they all take what appeared to be the song away from itself. In the middle of "Tupelo Honey" you can feel the rumble of "Mystic Eyes."

The first time I heard the song, this passage was like a bump in the road, and I drove right over it. Ever since, it's been the whole song, the part of the story that I wait for, like a punch line that no matter how many times you've heard it before never loses its sting.

Jonathan Lethem, *Chronic City* (New York: Doubleday, 2009).
Van Morrison, "Tupelo Honey," on *Tupelo Honey* (Warner Bros., 1971).

BABY PLEASE DON'T GO. 1965

In 1965, Them's "Baby Please Don't Go"—usually cited as a rock 'n' roll update of a song first recorded by the Mississippi blues singer Joe Williams—had the virtue of sounding as if it had emerged full-blown from Van Morrison's forehead. After a twenty-five-second lead-in—knife-edge notes on a guitar, following footsteps from a bass, drums and organ kicking up noise, harmonica curving the rhythm—Morrison leaps into the song as if he hasn't noticed the musical horde racing ahead, and as with "Mystic Eyes" in an instant the band is chasing him. There's a desperation in his hurry that all but rewrites the song: he's singing "Well, your man done gone," but you can hear it as "Your mind done gone" and believe it.

"It's so frantic," said my friend Phil Marsh, a guitarist in Berkeley in 1965, at a time when the country blues—the likes of Joe Williams' Washboard Blues Singers' 1935 original, a rickety, windblown number with fiddle and washboard that was like a shack, or Williams's 1940 remake with John Lee Williamson, the first Sonny Boy, on harmonica, which was like a fishing skiff on a lake, rocking every time a man cast but still when he waited—was a religion: a religion of fatalism, in which there was no hurry. But Them's "Baby Please Don't Go" isn't frantic. Just as you don't see Morrison coming, you're not ready when the music empties out. The band, at first onto the song like a flare shot in the air, begins to fragment. As the bassist pushes against the beat, poking it, the guitarist, the session player Jimmy Page or not, seems to be feeling his way into another song, flipping half-riffs, high, random, distracted metal shavings. Though the excitement of the music doesn't flag for a second, silence—anticipation— seems in command. Something is going to happen. You don't know what.

All sorts of people had recorded "Baby Please Don't Go," or the song inside it, "Alabama Bound," before Them seized it.* Lead Belly's 1940 "Alabama Bound," with the Golden Gate Jubilee Quartet, could be a bunch of guys with their arms around each other exiting a bar. ("I'm going back tomorrow," one man says. "Me, too, boy," says another.) Lightnin' Hopkins's glowing 1948 recording of "Baby Please Don't

---

* And after: Morrison recorded "Alabamy Bound" with Lonnie Donegan and Chris Barber as part of *The Skiffle Sessions*, the album recorded at Whitla Hall in Belfast in 1998. Donegan starts slowly, not hiding his English accent, Barber hiding his even less so when he takes the song, but when Morrison comes in, first singing background, then swallowing the song whole, he sounds like a sea monster, and his accent seems to have been something the song was searching for all along.

Go," with the Texas singer accompanying himself on electric guitar, was full, open, and endlessly suggestive of what Hopkins was deliberately leaving out of the piece, for the wind that whistled around the notes he hung in the air.

Morrison would have known these records; so likely would Jimmy Page, or, assuming Morrison was borrowing his father's 78s or bringing his friends around, even Them guitarist Billy Harrison.

What did it mean for young people to discover the old country blues in the early 1960s? For some, like Phil Marsh, it meant the reverence due a religion, and they played the old songs to capture their notes, their melodies, their flourishes, as precisely as possible, as if to pass down the truth unadulterated and uncorrupted. But others heard the radicalism of the country blues: the ferocity, the way in which within the structures of an all but unalterable musical form there were no limits at all to the demands one might make on himself or herself, on those around them, on life as such. Others were drawn to the statements of black men and women who if they acted in everyday life as they acted in their songs would have had groundhogs delivering their mail. What they wanted to capture was the spirit of singers who somehow summoned the nerve to sing about the world as if it remained to be made, or as if it could be unmade. Thus Van Morrison's "Baby Please Don't Go" is harsh, the whole performance slashing through paper walls.

Quickly, there's nothing between the singer and the song: no reverence, no respect, no hesitation in taking the fruits of someone else's culture. If one's own response to that culture—the culture as set down by a small number of people in Mississippi and elsewhere in the American South from the late 1920s to the early '40s—is as strong as Van Morrison's plainly was, how can that culture not be in the deepest sense one's own? One learns the language in order to speak the song—in order to speak out loud in the world. In 1965, Them's "Baby Please Don't Go" was out loud, on the radio, and its yarragh was its heedlessness.

Joe Williams' Washboard Blues Singers, "Baby Please Don't Go" (Williams, guitar; Dad Tracy, one-string fiddle; Chasey Collins, washboard, Chicago, 1935, Bluebird), collected on *Harry Smith's Anthology of American Folk Music, Volume Four* (Revenant, 2000).

Joe Williams, "Please Don't Go" (Williams, guitar; John Lee "Sonny Boy" Williams, harmonica; Alfred Elkins, bass cano, Chicago, 1941, Bluebird), included on *The Roots of Van Morrison* (Complete Blues, 2008).

Lead Belly and the Golden Gate Jubilee Quartet (Willie Johnson, William Langford, Henry Owens, Arlandus Wilson, Chicago, 1940, Victor), "Alabama Bound," on Lead Belly, *Alabama Bound* (RCA, 1988).

Lightnin' Hopkins, "Baby Please Don't Go" (Houston, 1948, 1949, Gold Star), on *Mojo Hand: Lightnin' Hopkins Anthology* (Rhino, 1993).

Them, "Baby Please Don't Go" (Parrot, US, Decca, UK, 1965). Collected on *The Story of Them Featuring Van Morrison* (Polydor, 1998). Flipside of "Gloria," the band's first single.

Van Morrison with Lonnie Donegan and Chris Barber, "Alabamy Bound," *The Skiffle Sessions* (Virgin, 2000).

JOHN BROWN'S BODY. 1975

The sense of a search is alive in this fugitive recording, even if the recording itself never comes to life. Sometimes Morrison's failures stick faster than the successes of countless other honorable singers.

It's a rehearsal, or a warm-up for what the people present are actually there to do. Someone snaps strings on an old guitar. Someone else plays the kind of war-movie harmonica notes that the comedian Robert Klein describes as being played in every Civil War picture, "around the campfire," before the next massacre: "Boy?" "Yes, sir?" "Ever been in a battle before?" "No, sir—but I'm aimin' to." "Better stop playin' that goddamn harmonica!" A piano keeps time.

"John Brown body lie molding in a grave," Morrison begins, as if not quite remembering the words, and in a voice so creaky you're not immediately sure it's his. The piece comes through as a lost song, an air that hasn't been sung for generations, that's survived in the common imagination only in bare fragments: "Glory, glory, hallelujah, his truth go marching on." Morrison tries to pump it as a drummer bashes cymbals—"Yeah! Mmm-hmm. I like it. Oh! Look out! Brand new thang!"—but the exclamations sound like vocal exercises.

Then the song sucks him back. He's singing as someone panning for gold, finding nothing but sand, running his hands through the water. He crouches there, waiting for the song to give itself up, to surrender its secrets. But an unidentified violinist—probably not Toni Marcus, the violinist who will appear with Morrison on his *Into the Music* four years later, but I like to think so, so I'll pretend it's her—has been there all along, following Morrison's slow footsteps, looking for a theme—and finally, you might hear, she's had enough. This song is not a secret to her, and she begins to sing it, on her strings, with more blood, loss, and an embrace of a right cause than Morrison can, or will. It's all in the high notes, with an urgency that says she's hearing hidden strains in the song no one has heard before—but as she begins to light up the sky the song as it was composed always reached for, the sky comes down to earth, and for a last moment Morrison steps up to claim the song as if he knew it all along.

Robert Klein, "In Praise of the Harmonica," on *Mind Over Matter* (Rhino, 1974).

Van Morrison, "John Brown's Body," collected on *Catalog Strays 1965–2000* (Wild Card bootleg).

CARAVAN. *THE LAST WALTZ*. 1976

"If he had much stage presence it'd be hard to take," a friend said after seeing Van Morrison perform this song, not long after its release on *Moondance*, in 1970, Morrison's first album after *Astral Weeks*. He'd stand still on stage to sing it, needing only "Now the caravan, is on its way," the first line, to bring him into the setting of the song—a hillside in the country, you could imagine, a line of wood-covered vans or trailers, filled with gypsies or their would-be middle-class inheritors, whoever it might have been with the destiny or the choice to live on the road getting a moment in history through the way the song pushed out of it. You might feel the Impressions' "Gypsy Woman" behind Morrison's song—a long way behind it, dubious, Curtis Mayfield wondering if any song that mentioned gypsies could really summon up the campfires that in his song really did seem to flicker in the listener's eye. Morrison would point his head down with his eyes closed, as if he were trying to answer Mayfield's doubt. "Turn up your radio," he'd whisper the first time the line appeared in the song; the second time it would be a plea, desperate and enthralled, and now there was an answer. It was on the radio. You just had to turn it up, so you didn't miss it. It's easy to miss something on the radio; you turn your head, say "Did you hear that" or "Listen to this," and it's gone, and the DJ isn't going to understand when you call to ask what it was whoever the singer was did right before the instrumental break. "Turn it up"—but not too much, not so the curls in the singer's voice on the radio are flattened with volume and the soul is gone: "That's enough!" Morrison would always shout, just when the perfect level was reached, like someone who has to be touched just this way. Do it right, and it's heaven; squeeze a little too hard, move your hand an inch in the wrong direction, and love turns to ashes. All of that is happening in "Caravan," in the instant.

By the time Morrison recorded his first live album, " . . . *It's Too Late to Stop Now . . .* " from 1974, the song had become a rave-up, almost a set-closer—a crowd favorite—but that night it couldn't find its voice. Curtis Mayfield turned his head. The tempo was too fast—the oldest musician's trick in the oldest book to spark false excitement in a familiar number. Then it stopped, to insist on drama; you could see the levers and pulleys. The music is ornamented, filigreed, the song buried in so many layers of orchestration that the choruses, the heart of the song—"TURN IT UP! TURN IT UP!"—never did more than shout. Morrison took time to introduce the band, then seemed to drift off, murmuring "Now for the best, later for the garbage," as if talking to himself, and it might have been the most true and least forced moment in the performance.

Two years later, at the Last Waltz, the Band's Thanksgiving night farewell concert at Winterland in San Francisco, with the bill heavy with guest stars, the show, which produced a certain streak of tedium that lifted only for two or three numbers at a time, had come nearly to a halt. After a few mountain turns of a runaway train—the Band playing inside out for "Mystery Train" with Paul Butterfield, for "Who Do You Love" with their old mentor, the 1950s rockabilly flash Ronnie Hawkins, and then, titanically, almost seven minutes of "Mannish Boy" led by Muddy Waters— the show lost its breath. Waters was followed by Eric Clapton, Neil Young, Joni Mitchell, and Neil Diamond; the sense of I'll-never-forget-this-night the crowd had brought with them and the Band itself had insisted on (an unheard-of ticket price, a full Thanksgiving dinner, curtains from the opera house, chandeliers flown in from Los Angeles) began to disappear, replaced by mere stargazing. People in the audience began to speculate about who else might show up. One fan predicted that Buddy Holly would appear precisely at midnight. Another person claimed to have seen Murry Wilson—the then recently deceased father of three-fifths of the Beach Boys—backstage. Someone yelled out for "Free Bird."

Morrison was next—the last guest before the very last, Bob Dylan—and he turned the night around. "I always go by what gets the most house," said Dr. John, himself one of the first Last Waltz guests, flat on his own "Such a Night," a haunt on "Liza Jane" with the New Orleans singer Bobby Charles. "To me, Van Morrison got the most house, of anything. I was checkin' the gig," he said in his crawly voice, the gutter growl of a man who hasn't been impressed by anything since 1957, "and it was like, the whole gig, it got house. 'Cause mostly, you know, it's like famous people . . . But nuttin' was like that. Nuttin' got that much house. That was way above anything else. That was a hard act to follow."

At the rehearsal the night before, where Martin Scorsese, who was filming the concert, or rather directing it—with every song plotted, every shot blocked, lighting designed to vary what would appear on a screen—"Caravan" was already a showstopper, and there wasn't even a show. Morrison stepped right into it, the Band playing easily behind him, staying out of his way, Allen Toussaint's horn section working from arrangements that were fixed in meter but still had room in them. "Now the caravan is on its way," Morrison sang, not a word rushed, no melodramatic pause, simply the first line of an old story everybody knows. You say "Once upon a time," not "Once—upon a time," unless you're full of yourself, or you don't trust the audience. Morrison may not trust his audience, but this night there wasn't one.

At the show itself you could imagine that the song grew bigger than it ever had before. Again and again there is an increase in pressure, then release. You are constantly aware of the back of the throat. Nothing is abstract, nothing is taken for granted. "Turn up your radio": "radio" becomes "RAD-IO"—

RAADIO

—and suddenly it's not a radio, it's a Flash Gordon death ray. The horn section locks into a pattern, *dah* da da *dah*, drawn out more every time,

DAHHHH da da *DAH!*

Again and again, there's a freer theme to highlight the hard count, and as the horn section pushed back, louder each time, Morrison matching it in volume, he began to kick his right leg into the air like a Rockette. He shot an arm up, a dynamo, the movements repeated, repeated, repeated, and shocking every time. Finally as he left the stage he was swaying from side to side, his body all vehemence, his face in the placid, self-circled expression of someone who hears nothing but the song playing in his head. All in all it signified that finally he had taken everything the song had to give, he had left nothing out, making you stare and ask, where did this person come from, why is he here? It was always a song that demanded to be made a testimony—*this is the last song I'm ever going to sing in my life*—and that's what Morrison gave back. Edwyn Collins, the singer for the Glasgow band Orange Juice, once remembered his manager crying after a performance: "The big moments are never as good as you think they're going to be." This night they were—but before any of this happened there was a rupture that broke the ground for the performance, and it had nothing to do with music.

"At rehearsal, when we went over this," Robbie Robertson said in commentary for the video release of *The Last Waltz*, "he came in and he had just flown in from somewhere. I guess he'd come right from the airport, and he was wearing a raincoat, maybe it had been raining, I don't remember now, but he had on this Mickey Spillane–looking raincoat. And I thought, you know what? This detective thing, this Humphrey Bogart detective thing, is working for me. And I said to Van, 'I like this, I like this Mike Hammer thing you got going here—you should wear this outfit tonight.' And he said, 'You think so? You really like it?' 'It works. It's definitely working.' And he said, 'Oh, ok.' And that night, when it came time for the show, as you can see, he felt more the need to dress for the occasion."

As the dishes were being cleared from the Thanksgiving tables, I'd seen Morrison wandering the still mostly empty aisles in Winterland, dressed in his raincoat, scowling. He was thirty; he looked older, pudgy and losing his hair. It was surprising to see him appear onstage like a grimy Cinderella in a purple stage suit: a spangled bolero jacket, sausage pants with contrasting lacing up the crotch, a green top with a scoop neck that produced what could only be called cleavage. *God*, you thought—*where did he get this thing?* Who drugged him, knocked him out, dragged him into a costume store, and put this on him and said, *Well, here you are, you look* great, *Van, you look just terrific!* It was as if he was daring the audience, or for that matter the Band, not to see past the ludicrousness of his costume ("I remember a couple of times becoming completely distracted and felt like I was in the audience," Robertson said), not to see what he was doing, not to hear the music.

"Van always looked to me like a half-homicidal leprechaun who lived under the bridge," the critic Jay Cocks likes to say. For a night he came out from under the bridge. Then he went back. It was stunning; no one remarked on the slime dripping from his elbows, the bits of dead rats on his shoes.

Quotes from *The Last Waltz* (MGM DVD, 1978/2002).

Edwyn Collins, "This Much I Know," interview with Michael Odell (2008), in *Best Music Writing 2009*, ed. GM (New York: Da Capo, 2009), 287.

Impressions, "Gypsy Woman" (ABC-Paramount, 1961).

Van Morrison, "Caravan," *Moondance* (Warner Bros., 1970).

———"Caravan," on "*. . . It's Too Late to Stop Now . . .*" (Warner Bros., 1974).

———"Caravan" (rehearsal and performance), included on the Band, *The Last Waltz* box set (Warner Bros./Rhino, 2002), and on DVD as above.

IT'S ALL OVER NOW, BABY BLUE. 1966

When Bob Dylan first began performing "It's All Over Now, Baby Blue," the song that would close his album *Bringing It All Back Home*, released in the spring of 1965, no one had heard it before. It would come at the end of a concert, and it would be a shock—not for its melody, or its words, or its tinge of finality (in the summer of that year, at the Newport Folk Festival, Dylan would sing it as his farewell to those in the crowd who had booed him for appearing with a band), but for what Dylan was doing with his arms.

He would bend over his guitar, thrust his arms out from it akimbo, and begin to flap them up and down, as if he were a puppet and the strings were his own rhythm, and the rhythm in the song was big, loose, dramatic, and unsatisfied. No matter how hard Dylan pumped, there was something missing, and that seemed to be the point. Performing solo for the last season before he began, first with pickup groups and then with the Arkansas-Canadian quintet the Hawks, to present his songs as he was hearing them in his head—hearing them, you can imagine, as the Beatles or the Rolling Stones or the Animals might have done them, but not as well, he had to know, as he would—what the performance dramatized was the absence of the power the song itself wanted.

"It's All Over Now, Baby Blue" cried out for a band. At the Avalon Ballroom in San Francisco in 1966, the Grateful Dead were among the first to try, barely—Jerry Garcia's lead guitar was still light with respect. It was still a folk song; for that matter it was less rock 'n' roll than Dylan's own recording, with Bruce Langhorne's distant, milky electric guitar notes shadowing the themes Dylan was stating on his own strings.

What was missing, perhaps, was a sense that the song was taking place in a world that was not quite the real world, and that the person to whom the song was addressed was in danger; that was what the song said when Van Morrison recorded it with Them late in 1965. When it appeared in 1966 on the group's second album, *Them Again*, it was first of all strange. As they listened to Them, people who already knew the song by heart weren't certain they had ever heard it before. You can imagine Bob Dylan might have felt the same— or at least as he might have when he first heard Sam Cooke sing "Blowin' in the Wind." It's one thing to send a song out into the world on the strength of a voice made of conviction; it's another to have it come back to you as an eagle.

"The feeling that music can create in a listener doesn't come from our opinion or image of the artist who makes the music, if our response is at all genuine," Jon Landau wrote of the Doors and the Memphis soul duo Sam and Dave in 1968. "It doesn't come from the artist telling us what he's trying to do or acting it out. It is there in the way he says the words more than in what the words say. And if Jim Morrison screams at us to 'Break on through to the other side,' well, Sam and Dave don't have to tell us about it because their music is *on* the other side." That's where Them is with "It's All Over Now, Baby Blue."

It begins like the first page of a detective novel, with three clipped, odd bass patterns, like a knock on the door, but with an odd fatalism: the cadence says that the person knocking is going in whether anyone opens the door or not, or that he already knows what he's going to find. "I knocked two longs and two shorts as instructed," the notes say, as Raymond Chandler says in *The Little Sister*. "Nothing happened. I felt jaded and old. I felt as if I'd spent my life knocking at doors in cheap hotels that nobody bothered to open. I tried again. Then turned the knob and walked in," but this time when Philip Marlowe walks in he finds that behind the door of Room 332 in the Van Nuys Hotel is a black hole.

It's a scene set by dark and shapeless notes from an electric piano; they sweep you off your feet. As Morrison comes in, singing deliberately, there are sharp, bright notes from an acoustic guitar, a deepening of the piano sound from an electric guitar, what could be a single chord from an organ sustained for the whole performance, but what's uncanny is

that while the emotional pressure of the performance continues to rise, Morrison bearing down harder verse by verse,
the overwhelming sense of displacement, of being in the
wrong place at the wrong time, comes entirely from the
piano, and the way that throughout the performance it remains altogether on the same plane. It's this that creates an
atmosphere of unrelieved suspense and jeopardy.

You're catching no more than a glimpse of an ongoing
drama. The detective walks right in, but then he vanishes,
and the people in the room—the person speaking, the person he or she is speaking to—are not leaving, and not because, as with the person Marlowe finds—

Beyond the little hallway the room widened towards a pair of windows through which the evening sun slanted in a shaft that reached
almost across the bed and came to a stop under the neck of the man
that lay there. What it stopped on was blue and white and shining
and round. He lay quite comfortably half on his face with his hands
down at his sides and his shoes off. The side of his face was on the
pillow and he seemed relaxed. He was wearing a toupee. The last time
I had talked to him his name had been George W. Hicks. Now it was
Dr. G. W. Hambleton. Same initials. Not that it mattered anymore. I
wasn't going to be talking to him again. There was no blood. None at
all, which is one of the nice things about an expert ice-pick job

—they're dead. They're in a limbo Dylan's recording hardly
hints at, which is why in his performance "Drawing crazy
patterns on your sheets" is unsurprising and why when
Morrison sings the line it's frightening.

It wasn't a story for the asking. Invited on stage for an encore at a Bob Dylan show at Wembley Arena in London in 1984, Morrison took up the song once more. "After it's written, I release the words"—that can be true for anything Morrison sings. It doesn't matter whose words they are. But with Dylan's band locked into a hand-clapping beat, a wail that lifted "crying" out of "Crying like an orphan in the sun" only gave the word an instant's flight. Even against Chrissie Hynde's high, keening shouts on the title phrase at the end of every verse the singalong crowd's insistence that the song not only couldn't but shouldn't speak anything other than a dead language ruled.

Jon Landau, "Soul Men," *Rolling Stone*, 20 January 1968, 18.

Raymond Chandler, *The Little Sister* (1949; New York: Pocket Books, 1963), 36, 38.

Bob Dylan, "It's All Over Now, Baby Blue," on *Bringing It All Back Home* (Columbia, 1965).

Them, "It's All Over Now, Baby Blue," on *Them Again* (Parrot, US, Decca, UK, 1966), included on *The Story of Them Featuring Van Morrison* (Polydor, 1998).

Van Morrison, "It's All Over Now, Baby Blue," London, 7 July 1984, on *Whenever Bob Sheds His Light on Van* (bootleg).

PART TWO

I'M GOING TO MY GRAVE WITH THIS RECORD

ASTRAL WEEKS. 1968

From the sightlines in Berkeley, California, where I lived then and live now, I recall 1968 as a year of horror and bad faith, fervor and despair. Most of all there was the sense of knowing that when you drew a breath you were breathing history along with the air, or the smoke—but that doesn't mean you knew what history was, or would be. History was being made in the instant, which said nothing about what would be included in the books yet to be written, or left out of them, as if what goes in and what goes out stays the same. These names made history in 1968: John Carlos, Bob Beamon, Tommie Smith. They were shouted around the world. Which still echo, which is barely a name at all? "Still the spirit of '68," John Lydon, born to the world as Johnny Rotten, sang in 1979 with his band PiL, when 1968, not a concept but a year, a real time, seemed much farther away than, in this era of media anniversaries, it does now. The song was "Albatross"; the singer sounded beaten down by history, 1968 a huge bird around his neck, but he also sounded as if he knew the beating wings were the wind at his back.

Berkeley was a lookout and a hideout. The great storm of student protest that would convulse the U.S.A. and nations around the world had begun there in 1964 with the Free Speech Movement. It was three months of daily speeches, marches, building occupations, and finally, played out in a Greek Theatre, high drama. That drama—a university in convocation with itself, everyone present, the leaders of the institution speaking quieting words, then a single student, standing to speak, immediately tackled and dragged out of sight, an act of violence actually revealing the face of power behind the face of reasonableness—brought that moment to a close and opened a field that in the years to come would be crossed by thousands. But in 1968 the spirit that animated a simple demand for the free exercise of rights students had assumed were theirs—because they had learned such a story in their classrooms and then, as if by instinct, began to put them into practice—had in the most familiar arena long since turned cheap and rote.

When in May of 1968 a rally was held in Berkeley to celebrate the poorly understood but exciting revolt taking place in France, activists distributed leaflets denouncing the police violence that had dispersed the rally before the rally took place. When students at Columbia University in New York, protesting what they saw as the university's colonialist appropriation of property in Harlem, shut the school down—

with the novel technique of occupying one building, and then, when the police arrived, filing out, only to seize another building, and then another, and another—Berkeley radicals called on their fellows to "Do a Columbia": not for any reason, not in the face of any injustice or insult, but for lack of anything better to do.

With the Vietnam War all but rolling back across the Pacific to poison the United States itself, it was as if people turned to spectacular lies and glamorous trivialities to hide from themselves the fact that their imaginations had turned to ice. Truly enormous events taking place elsewhere did not travel. Word of Prague Spring, even the meaning of the Soviet invasion that crushed it, arrived only in fragments, and no speaker stood up to put the pieces together. News of the massacre of hundreds of students in Mexico City, just before the Olympic Games were to begin there, was suppressed from the start, and so profoundly that the facts would take nearly forty years to come out of the ground. But in the United States few if any looked; curiosity about the world withered.

It's clear now that the signal song of that year, the song with which all through the 1990s and into the twenty-first century Bob Dylan closed his concerts, was "All Along the Watchtower"—a modest, querulous song that ended with words that were anything but quiet, regardless of how simply they were sung: "Two riders were approaching / The wind began to howl." The song occupied the moral center of Dylan's album *John Wesley Harding*, which was released in the last week of 1967; like the rest of the music, those words of warning made their way onto and out of the radio slowly, like a rumor. Too slowly: when Martin Luther King, Jr., was assassinated in Memphis in April, and then, in June, in Los Angeles, Robert F. Kennedy, running for president, was shot and killed, the song did not play, even in the minds of those who watched the funerals on television. It did not give voice to the awful sense of disease, ruin, and damnation that seized the country so fully it could only be channeled into pathetic calls for gun control and a ludicrous riot in Chicago against a presidential nominating convention where, had he lived, Kennedy would have almost certainly lost. To play against these events, to play into them, the song needed the harsher, louder, wilder, even triumphant treatment Neil Young would give it in 1992—an arrangement Dylan himself immediately adopted—and that Van Morrison could have fashioned at any time.

The Mexican government wanted a clean Olympics, a clean show, and so did the world. That is why the massacres took place, why the government buried the event literally and figuratively, and why the cover-up was a complete success, with witnesses disappeared or conventionally murdered for years afterward to keep the peace. So the games went on as planned—except for John Carlos and Tommie Smith of San Jose State in California, American entrants in the two hundred–meter dash. Inspired by Harry Edwards's Olympic Project for Human Rights, which had originally called for a boycott of the Olympics by all black athletes, they had a plan. They would run the race; they would win; they would mount the victory stand; and then, as the band played "The

Star-Spangled Banner," before the eyes of the entire world
they would bow their heads and raise black-gloved fists in
salutes of black power and black unity. With beads around
their necks they would signify the deaths of those leaders like
King who had been assassinated, and the nameless thousands gone who had been lynched and thrown from slave
ships; with shoeless feet they would signify poverty; in their
silence they would speak out. On October 16 the plan was realized: Smith finished first, tying the world record, and took
the gold medal, Carlos finished third and took the bronze. As
Peter Norman of Australia, who took the silver medal—and
who, that night, would wear an Olympics Project for Human
Rights badge in solidarity—stared straight ahead, Smith and
Carlos gestured.

They marked, or scarred, their national anthem as de-
finitively as Jimi Hendrix would a year later at Woodstock.
Though no one, as far as I know, drew the connection at
the time, Hendrix's furiously, exultantly distorted, bottom-
lessly complex recasting of "The Star-Spangled Banner"
was not only a version of what Smith and Carlos did with
it, his version may have been inspired by theirs.

This event has never been forgotten. Carlos and Smith
were treated as terrorists, as if their fists were guns and they
had fired them. They were expelled from their team, sent
home, and covered in obloquy. Though they never backed
down, as the years passed neither man's affirmation of what
he had done matched the other's. There were disagreements
over whose idea the act was, over who owned it. As they do
still, across the decades interviewers worked to draw out

resentment and betrayal, to find a crack in the image of the two men on the stand that for all of the confusion added to it after the fact remains indelibly plain.

On October 18, two days after Smith and Carlos were removed from the games, the American long-jumper Bob Beamon launched himself. He had never jumped farther than twenty-seven feet and four inches; he would never again jump farther than twenty-six feet and eleven and three-quarter inches. But this day, when he landed, he had become the first person in history to jump twenty-eight feet; he had become the first person in history to jump twenty-nine feet. He had traveled twenty-nine feet and two and one-half inches through the air. From 1935 to 1968 the world record in the long jump had increased by eight and a half inches; this day Bob Beamon broke the world record by almost two feet. When he saw his mark on the scoreboard, he fell to his knees and covered his face in shock.

It was an act for which there are no parallels and no metaphors. There can be no statue for it, as, in 2005, at San Jose State University, a statue was unveiled celebrating the act performed in 1968 by John Carlos and Tommie Smith: figures of the two men on the victory stand, with Peter Norman's place empty, so that, as Norman said when the statue was unveiled, "Anybody can get up there and stand up for something they believe in." "We felt a need to represent a lot of people who did more than we did and had no platform," Smith said. It was about human rights, Norman said: "The issue is still there today and they'll be there at Beijing and we've got to make sure we don't lose sight of that."*

Bob Beamon's name is little mentioned today. For twenty-three years, jumpers edged closer to his record, inch by inch; mathematically, it was finally broken by Michael Powell in 1991, but in the way that his act has never been matched, even in imagination it was never really surpassed. In 1968, almost everything became part of history even before people realized what had happened, and for the rest of their lives, they and

---

* Andrew Das, "Obama Fever on the Field," *New York Times*, 8 November 2008: "On Thursday night . . . after scoring the winning touchdown against the Browns with 1 minute and 22 seconds to go, [Denver Broncos receiver Brandon] Marshall reached into his pants and pulled out a glove before his teammates quickly surrounded him.

"Marshall told the NFL Network postgame crew: 'When we look at the 44th president, Barack Obama, he inspired me. And not just me and my teammates, but the nation.'

"Marshall said his planned celebration—which was stopped by teammate Brandon Stokely, who worried that a 15-yard penalty could cost the Broncos in a see-saw game—had its roots in the black power salutes of John Carlos and Tommie Smith at the 1968 Olympics.

"Carlos and Smith each wore a black glove for their salutes, but Marshall said his was black and white.

"'I wanted to create that symbol of unity because Obama inspires me, our multicultural society,' he told reporters after the game, stopping several times during his news conference as emotion overwhelmed him. 'And I knew at the 1968 Olympics in Mexico, Tommie Smith and John Carlos raised the black glove in that fist as a silent gesture of black power and liberation. Forty years later, I wanted to make my own statement and gesture to represent the progress we made.'

"Marshall probably would have been fined if he had carried out his salute, but he said, 'Social landmarks are bigger than fines to me, especially two days after the election.'"

others, many not born at the time, would argue over what they had done. But what Bob Beamon did was in a queer and ineradicable way outside of history, where it remains—and in that sense, in a way different from all the banners raised in 1968, it is an image of freedom against which there can be no argument at all.

As I hear it now, and as I think I heard it then, *Astral Weeks*, recorded in three days in September and October 1968 in New York City, and released on the Warner Bros.–Seven Arts label in November, caught the same spirit. In historical terms it didn't make sense. It didn't, in the small-minded way art and politics are so often linked, reflect the great events of the day, any more than Dylan's *John Wesley Harding*, *Astral Weeks*' true kin, did. *John Wesley Harding* might have been a testament that, as Jon Landau put it in 1968, "Dylan has felt the war," but in its quiet, its lack of hurry, its insistence on setting its own pace, its refusal even to acknowledge that the person whose name was on the album cover had ever done anything before, it like *Astral Weeks* refused to speak the language of the time, and in the way that the time has been rewritten into a single rotting cliché of VIETNAM STUDENT RIOTS LBJ LSD SEXUAL REVOLUTION BLACK POWER NIXON neither *John Wesley Harding* nor *Astral Weeks* can be translated back into that language. "It did come out at a time when a lot of things a lot of people cared about passionately were beginning to disintegrate, and when the self-destructive undertow that always accompanied the great sixties party had an awful lot of people in its maw and was pulling straight down," Lester Bangs wrote in 1978 about *Astral Weeks*. "So, as timeless as it finally is, perhaps *Astral Weeks* was also the product of an era." But it wasn't any yearning for the strife and revelations of another time that accounted for the fact that a few years ago, in a class I was teaching, four students out of sixteen, none of them older than twenty-one, named it as the album they most loved. How did it reach these people, just in the sense of from here to there, of round-about? How did it enter their lives, music that was made well before they were born and yet spoke a common language? The record spoke to these people then; as far as they cared it was made for them, they understood its language as soon as they heard it. No one had to translate it for them, no one had to contextualize it, no one had to offer them any lectures about the music or the politics of the late sixties or the career of Van Morrison.

If *Astral Weeks* caught the spirit of Bob Beamon's event, then it also partook of it. As I understand history, Bob Beamon's jump would not have happened as it did if the skies had been different that day in Mexico City, if he had received a call from his wife that morning, or a different call than he did, or if that day's paper that morning had carried a different story, and the same must have been true when the producer Lewis Merenstein brought Van Morrison into a studio with a few New York City jazzmen: the bassist Richard Davis, the drummer Connie Kay, the guitarist Jay Berliner, the percussionist and vibraphonist Warren Smith, Jr., and the flautist and soprano saxophonist John Payne. The music that resulted wasn't jazz. It wasn't blues. It wasn't rock 'n' roll in any ordinary or hyphenated manner, but it fit perfectly on the radio in between Jimi Hendrix's "Little Wing" or Otis Redding's "Try a Little Tenderness." It was closer to folk music, and closer to "Barbara Allen" or the Irish ballad "Raglan Road" than "We Shall Overcome" or even "Goodnight Irene."

Merenstein had received a call from Warner Bros.: *We've signed Van Morrison, go up to Boston, see what he's got.* Pretty much all anybody knew, and all anybody wanted, was "Brown-Eyed Girl," from *Blowin' Your Mind!* which my friend Barry Franklin described at the time as "two minutes and twenty-six seconds of 'Sweet Pea' and thirty-two minutes of 'T. B. Sheets.'" ("Is the B. in 'T. B. Sheets,'" he asked, "the same B. which appeared in 'Johnny B. Goode'?") Morrison played Merenstein his song "Astral Weeks": "thirty seconds into it," Merenstein told Hank Shteamer in 2009, "my whole being was vibrating." And the moment could not have been any different, Merenstein said, not the call going to Tom Wilson, the producer of "Like a Rolling Stone," who was standing nearby when the phone rang, not Connie Kay catching Napoleon's cold: "Something as timeless as forty years had to happen because it had to happen. I had to be the one to do it. Not that producer, not that producer, regardless of their accomplishments. It had to be Richard, not that bass player. I don't want to sound existential, but there was Van, and that was it; there was no band . . . there were no arrangements . . . the direction was him singing and playing—that was where I followed. That's why it came out the way it did. If I would've gone somewhere else, it wouldn't have come out the way it did. So there obviously was a direction from somewhere in the sky." "This is not an exaggeration, this is not just trying to be poetic," Brooks Arthur, the recording engineer for *Astral Weeks*, said in 2009. "A cloud came along, and it was called the Van Morrison sessions. We all hopped upon that cloud, and the cloud took us away for a while, and we made this album, and we landed when it was done."

They recorded live, Morrison saying nothing to the musicians in terms of banter or instruction, and saying everything in the cues of his chords, hesitations, lunges, silences, and in those moments when he loosed himself from words and floated on his own air. But that's too simple. When you listen, you hear the musicians talking to each other; more than that, you hear them hearing each other.

In the first notes of "Sweet Thing," Morrison opens the tune with his acoustic guitar; as soon as a listener has something to grab onto, Richard Davis restates Morrison's theme, with the barest increase in force that makes all the difference. Davis was born in Chicago; he was a veteran of sessions with Eric Dolphy and Roland Kirk. This day it's as if Davis is sweeping into the song to dance Morrison even farther into it—into *Astral Weeks'* great swirl. Someone other than Morrison is now leading the listener into the bower of the song, a hillside where you can tumble down like Jim and little Sabine in *Jules and Jim*; that gives Morrison the freedom to forget the shape of the song, what it needs, what it wants, and trust himself. He'll sing the song; someone else will play it.

After the sessions were finished, Merenstein, with Morrison and the conductor Larry Fallon consulting, overdubbed strings and horn parts. Sometimes the songs are unimaginable without them, and the added sounds so layered into the original instruments as to be part of them, as on "Sweet Thing"; sometimes they're gratuitous, especially the strings on "Cyprus Avenue" and the gypsy violin on "Madame George," but after forty years they tune themselves out. When the music is at its most contingent—when Merenstein's argument about how the record might never have happened at all becomes an awareness that the fate of a song, whether or not it will achieve the finality you in fact know it will, rests on the way Richard Davis steps out of a rest and whether or not Morrison will know what Davis has just done and what he himself can now do to live up to it— it's scary, because the inevitability of the music is also its unlikeliness. Early on, there's a rupture in "Sweet Thing" when Morrison hollers—a long, happy *hoyyyyyyyy*, the singer shot out of the cannon of his own breath—and the scene the sound makes is so complete, the musicians around Morrison filling in the "gardens all wet with rain" he's already described, that you realize no one has to go back to the song at all. Near the end of "Madame George"—almost two minutes from its actual end, but at the end of the song as a written piece, a story told in lines and verses, one after the other—there's a pause, and then, at seven minutes thirtyfour seconds, a single thick, weighted bass note from Davis that is as final a sound as any song could hold without dropping dead on the spot. The story is over, the note says; everything that is going to happen has happened; everyone has been left behind; everyone is dead, and all that remains is looking back. Morrison goes on, drawing a seemingly endless loop of loss, regret, reverie, and escape around himself— as he does so, you are actually hearing him change from a child into a creature who may not yet be a man but who is not a child, who may no longer even be human, rather a figment of his own false memories—but Davis is finished. Every note he plays after that last one is sweeping up, closing the windows, locking the door. At this point the song is as much his as Morrison's; both have their own ideas about what it's for, what it's about, who Madame George is, and why anyone should care: why in their different ways they are going to make you care. At its highest pitch, the album has become a collaboration between Morrison and Davis, or a kind of conspiracy, one that takes advantage of the producer and the other musicians but excludes them from the real conversation—excludes them, but somehow not the listener. In the blues term for the shadow self that knows what the self refuses to know, here Davis is Morrison's second mind; there Morrison is Davis's. You are listening in, but you can never be sure you heard what you thought you heard.

There is death all over the music—an acceptance of death. Save for one couplet, the last words on the album are a farewell, in the form of a closing door: "I know you're dying— and I know, you know it too." Davis rattles the door in its frame. But usually death is not so close. It's something you see in someone's face, maybe years off, but already looming. You freeze up—or you realize you have no time to waste. You begin asking what it is you really want. In the title song the singer asks to be born again—"There you go," he says to himself in the mirror, or to the person who he expects will save him, "talking to Hudie Ledbetter." Lead Belly died in 1949, almost twenty years before, only four years after the person singing was born, but he's here now, and he'll answer you if you know how to ask. And for a moment you do. "Would you, kiss my eyes"—what a surrender of body and soul are in those lines! It's an opening into what Lester Bangs called the "mystical awe that cut right through the heart of the work." It's an acceptance both of death and of anything else that might happen, like the magical appearance of a long-dead avatar to tell you that, yes, you are his true heir, you are the child he never had. And magic, as the British philosopher R. G. Collingwood wrote in 1937,

is a representation where the emotion evoked is an emotion evoked on account of its function in practical life . . . Magical activity is a kind of dynamo supplying the mechanism of practical life with the emotional current that drives it. Hence magic is a necessity for every sort and condition of men. A society which thinks, as ours thinks, that it has outlived the need for magic, is either mistaken in that opinion, or else it is a dying society, perishing for lack of interest in its own maintenance.

Which is a way of saying, with unusual repetitions kin to those that in Morrison's music always signify freedom, a love of words, and a lack of fear for what they might say ("the emotion evoked is an emotion evoked"), that to be born again might be understood as magic, magic as everyday life: what you do to preserve the emotional current that drives everyday life. And that current may be, in the art historian T. J. Clark's phrase, the sight of death—a sight that, when one is as attuned to contingency as the singer on *Astral Weeks* is, you see everywhere.

When Lewis Merenstein says the album "had to happen because it had to happen," that "if I would've gone somewhere else," not to Boston that day, the album "wouldn't have come out the way it did," or even taken any shape at all, he is situating the album as an event: a unique and timeless act or occurrence, like Bob Beamon's jump, something that could not have been predicted and could never be repeated. But that is only half of it. In "Astral Weeks," "Sweet Thing," "Cyprus Avenue," "Madame George," "Ballerina," and "Slim Slow Slider," there are everywhere in the music itself tiny events that are just as contingent; that single *hoyyyyyyyy* may be only the most immediately thrilling. These events take place in the breaks and holes in the music. They change what could have been a spot of dead air into a moment of anticipation. They turn the singer's claims into truth, the singer testing that truth with repetitions of a phrase until, now an incantation, not description, the phrase may have sloughed off all ordinary meaning and acquired one without intent or desire. It's the nearly countless "goodbye"s at the end of "Madame George" no longer necessarily signifying "fare thee well" or "I must take my leave" or "I'll never see you again" but "I'm returning," "I could never leave," "I will never forget you."

It's this sense of event within a song, a verse, a line, or even what might occur in the space between one word and another, that raises the cast of drama that hovers over the whole of the album. "I based the first fifteen minutes of *Taxi Driver* on *Astral Weeks*," Martin Scorsese said in 1978, just after the first major screening of his film *The Last Waltz*, sitting on the floor in his living room in the Hollywood hills, playing the album, hearing "Madame George" come up. "That's the song," he said—as in the moment Bernard Herrmann's theme for *Taxi Driver* played from inside of "Madame George," as "I Cover the Waterfront" played inside of that, and you could follow Travis Bickle, driving his hack from 6 P.M. to 6 A.M. every night, talking to himself, "All the animals come out at night, whores, skunk pussies, buggers, queens, fairies, dopers, junkies, sick, venal," as he drives under the spray of a broken hydrant and wishes for a rain that would wash all the sin off the streets, as he tries to talk up the ticket seller in a porn theater, as he sees his dream girl, describing her in his diary in words that could have come from "Sweet Thing": "She was wearing a white dress / She appeared like an angel / Out of this filthy mess."* It's all foreshadowing, as on *Astral Weeks* almost everything is memory, but the sense of tension is the same. Accompanying every shout of exaltation on *Astral Weeks*, every breath of comfort, there is a murmur of jeopardy and danger that makes you afraid for the people in the songs—afraid for Madame George, afraid for the singer who leaves her behind as if she's already dead, afraid that the singer so transformed by his self-raised specter of rebirth may not make it as far as, on the first track on *Astral Weeks*, its title song, he actually does. It's this that over the years has led so many people to take the album as a kind of talisman, to recognize

---

* It's *all* in "I Cover the Waterfront," as Morrison once recorded the song with John Lee Hooker—as Hooker, not Morrison, sings the standard as a ghost, back for another look, to make sure nothing has changed.

others by their affection for it, to say "I'm going to my grave with this record, I will never forget it."

"To this day it gives me pain to hear it," Merenstein said in 2009 of the record he produced, then pulling away from what he'd just said: "Pain is the wrong word—I'm so moved by it." But pain is exactly the right word: the pain, the fear, of knowing that to acknowledge that the music exists at all is to acknowledge that, because it might not have, it doesn't.

What lessons can it teach, what last words might it leave on anyone's lips? What does it say, where did it come from? In 2009, as Van Morrison was setting out to re-create *Astral Weeks* on stages around the world, with charts indicating every half-note, every caesura, every skipped beat, so that Jay Berliner and Richard Davis (who finally bowed out) could replay their parts exactly as they had more than forty years before, I was asked these questions, and I realized I didn't care. What happens on *Astral Weeks* beggars those questions. It was forty-six minutes in which possibilities of the medium—of rock 'n' roll, of pop music, of what you might call music that could be played on the radio as if it were both timeless and news—were realized, when you went out to the limits of what this form could do. You went past them: you showed everybody else that the limits they had accepted on invention, expression, honesty, daring, were false. You said it to musicians and you said it to people who weren't musicians: there's more to life than you thought. Life can be lived more deeply—with a greater sense of fear and horror and desire than you ever imagined.

That's what I heard at the time, and that's what I hear now. There is a difference. I no longer altogether trust the sort of explanations that along with other people I used to pursue so passionately—not, of course, philistine, literal explanations, of course not, but imaginative, contextualizing explanations that made both a work and its setting richer for the introduction of the one to the other. I've played *Astral Weeks* more than I've played any other record I own; I wouldn't tell you why even if I knew. In the face of work that became part of my life a long time ago and remains inseparable from it, whether it's *The Great Gatsby* or *Astral Weeks*, what I value most is how inexplicable any great work really is.

Dick Schaap, *The Perfect Jump* (New York: New American Library, 1976).

Hank Shteamer, "In Full: Lewis Merenstein, Producer of *Astral Weeks*," 3 March 2009, *Dark Forces Swing Blind Punches*, http://darkforcesswing.blogspot.com.

Barry Franklin, "Crawdaddy?" 1968, unpublished. Courtesy Barry Franklin.

Brooks Arthur, to Josh Gleason, "Van Morrison: *Astral Weeks* Revisited," *Weekend Edition*, NPR, 28 February 2009.

Jon Landau, "John Wesley Harding," *Crawdaddy!* May 1968, collected in *It's Too Late to Stop Now* (San Francisco: Straight Arrow Press, 1972), 52.

R. J. Collingwood, *The Principles of Art* (1937), quoted in Wilfred Mellers, *A Darker Shade of Pale: A Backdrop to Bob Dylan* (New York: Oxford, 1985), 33.

Lester Bangs, "Astral Weeks" (from *Stranded*, ed. GM, 1979), in Bangs, *Psychotic Reactions and Carburetor Dung*, ed. GM (New York: Knopf, 1987), 21, 20.

Martin Scorsese, to GM; see "Save the Last Waltz for Me," GM, *New West*, 22 May 1978, 95.

PiL (Public Image Ltd.), "Albatross," *Metal Box* (Virgin, 1979). Originally three twelve-inch 45s in a film can; the 1990 reissue was one CD in a four-and-three-quarter-inch tin: a PiL box.

Bob Dylan, "All Along the Watchtower," *John Wesley Harding* (Columbia, 1967).

Neil Young, "All Along the Watchtower," on *Bob Dylan 30th Anniversary Concert Celebration* (Columbia, 1993). A tribute show from Madison Square Garden, with, most notably, Johnny Winter on "Highway 61 Revisited," Roger McGuinn with Tom Petty and the Heartbreakers on "Mr. Tambourine Man," Lou Reed on "Foot of Pride," and Sinéad O'Connor on Bob Marley's "War" (leave it to her to break the rules), not to mention quite a few real stinkers.

Jimi Hendrix, "Star-Spangled Banner," on *Jimi Hendrix—Live at Woodstock* (MCA, 1999). The best account of what happened when Hendrix played the anthem is Jeff Bridges's Bob Dylan–written rant in the film *Masked and Anonymous*, dir. Larry Charles (Sony Pictures Classics, 2003). "I don't know, man. All I did was play it," Hendrix said on the *Dick Cavett Show* not long after Woodstock. "I'm American, so I played it. I used to sing it in school. They made me sing it in school, so it was a flashback." Cavett, as Michael Ventre reported in 2009 for MSNBC, "interrupted the interview to point out to the audience, 'This man was in the 101st Airborne, so when you send your nasty letters in . . . ' Cavett then explained to Hendrix that whenever someone plays an 'unorthodox' version of the anthem, 'You immediately get a guaranteed percentage of hate mail.' Hendrix then respectfully disagreed with Cavett's description. 'I didn't think it was unorthodox,' he said. 'I thought it was beautiful.'"

John Lee Hooker, with Van Morrison, "I Cover the Waterfront," from *Mr. Lucky* (Virgin, 1991), included on the posthumous Hooker collection *The Best of Friends* (Shout! Factory, 2007), along with another Hooker-Morrison number, "Don't Look Back." The two also recorded "I'll Never Get Out of These Blues Alive" for Hooker's album of the same name (Crescendo, 1972), but the affinity was always personal, not musical. The laconic, reflective ethos Hooker brought to his music in his later years never really meshed with Morrison's instincts for the blues; no matter how he might have tried to keep it caged, urgency would almost always win out.

Van Morrison, *Astral Weeks* (Warner Bros.–Seven Arts, 1968).

———*Astral Weeks Live at the Hollywood Bowl* (Listen to the Lion, 2009).

ALMOST INDEPENDENCE DAY. 1972.
LISTEN TO THE LION. 1972.
CALEDONIA SOUL MUSIC. 1970

In 1972, Van Morrison closed each side of what might be his richest album, *St. Dominic's Preview*, with a song over ten minutes long.

One was "Almost Independence Day." Notes from Morrison's acoustic guitar twisted into a harsh minor key, then seemed to raise a flag as a skiff pushed off; a synthesizer made the sound of a tugboat pushing through fog, and kept it constant. As it went on, it seemed as if the song itself more than the singer was gazing out over San Francisco Bay to watch the fireworks; as that happened, the Fourth of July receded, and what was left was an unsettled, unclaimed, unfounded land where the event that settled it, named it, found it, had yet to take place.

The other long song was if anything stronger. "Listen to the Lion" was made as a field for the yarragh, an expanse over which, as a thing in itself, it could go wherever it might want to go, disappearing and reappearing at any time—but more than that "Listen to the Lion" was a song about the yarragh.

Writing about Morrison in 1978, Jonathan Cott quoted Yeats on the ancient Celts, living "in a world where anything might flow and change, and become any other thing . . . The hare that ran by among the dew might have sat up on his haunches when the first man was made, and the poor bunch of rushes under their feet might have been a goddess laughing among the stars; and with but a little magic, a little waving of the hands, a little murmuring of the lips, they too could become a hare or a bunch of rushes, and know immortal love and immortal hatred." With that little murmuring of the lips becoming a torrent of wind off a lake, after what appears to be a conventional song, though a particularly pious one ("I shall search my very soul . . . for the lion"), for one minute after another Morrison cries, moans, pleads, shouts, hollers, whispers, until finally he breaks with language and speaks in tongues, growling and rumbling. The feeling is that whoever it is that is singing has not simply abandoned language, but has returned himself to a time before language, and is now groping toward it. The organs of speech have not yet been fixed in the mouth and the throat, because there is no speech. Speech might come from the chest, the stomach, the bowels—and there, in a transporting minute, is where the singer seems to find it, guttural sounds now swirling and spinning around the singer in bodies of their own. "They too could become a hare"—now Morrison has loosed the lion inside himself.

As he sings, a chorus behind him urges him on, resolutely, as if they understand the mission that the singer, caught in his trance, only senses. "Listen to the lion," they chant, drawing out the last word—but what is strange is that in the chorus, among three male voices, you hear Morrison himself, singing at himself.

As this happens they truly are two different, separate persons. It's more than, say, the conscious mind calling out to the subconscious; as the listener, you hear, you recognize, in a way that is tactile before it is anything else, two different bodies. "Listen to the lion," commands the chorus, but the singer already is the lion. *Awwrgh, arrgh, ooo, ah, ooo, mmm, ungh, ooo, ungh, arrgh, ah, ah,* off his feet in the dance—and then, not in exhaustion but with the clarity of a sudden change in the light, the singer removes his animal head to lead a fleet of ships. "And we sailed," he repeats five times, "away from Denmark, way up to Caledonia."

Caledonia is not just a misspelling of "Caldonia," a number-one race music hit for Louis Jordan and His Tympani Five in 1945 and a blues standard ever after—even if, purposefully misspelling the name, Morrison recorded a happily delirious version of the tune and put it out as a single in 1974, with his band credited as the Caledonia Soul Express: "CALDONIA! CALDONIA!" he shouted, as so many had before him, "*WHAT MAKES YOUR BIG HEAD SO HARD!*" No, Morrison will explain if you ask, as he explained to Jonathan Cott, "Caledonia used to be Scotland. This funny thing happened a long time ago—a lot of people from Northern Ireland went over to Scotland to settle, and vice versa. They changed spaces . . . So a lot of people from Northern Ireland are of Scottish descent. And my name suggests that I am."* But, Morrison would sometimes say, there was more to it than that. In the early seventies, as he tried to find a name for what he did, settling for a time on "Caledonia soul music," he came upon the notion that finally the blues came not from Africa but from Scotland. The true source of the blues was in the border ballads and folk songs, from "The Cuckoo" to "Barbara Allen," from "She Moves through the Fair" to "Nottamun Town," that, carried by settlers from Britain to the Appalachians, made up the oldest, deepest, and most persistent American music there is—"Real American Music," as Emma Bell Miles, an educated, middle-class city lady turned mountain woman, wrote in 1904 in *Harper's*. Thus, Morrison might whisper, in a song or in an interview, he was always an American, just as, his ancestors sailing from Scandinavia to Scotland, he

---

* "Well, actually it's Ulster Scots," Morrison said as he retraced the story in 2009 in a conversation with Dave Marsh. "We're taught in school, and also places in Europe—I don't know if they teach it in America— the Scots were actually from Northern Ireland, originally. When they went to Scotland, they called them Scots. It's the same people. And the same people also later went back to Ulster. They were going back and forth all the time. And at one point, the kingdom of Delradia was Northern Ireland and the western part of Scotland—which was a kingdom unto itself. They're so close, Northern Ireland and Scotland—it's so close, you can see it on a clear day."

was fated to become Irish. That here came from there, that there are no separations, that all parts of himself and his music are one. Picking up the notion from Morrison, Mark Knopfler might have caught it best by throwing it away. There's a Scottish piper and highland drums in his 2000 "What It Is," a heartbreakingly hard-boiled history lesson—when he bends the line "The ghost of Dirty Dick is still in search of Little Nell" against a thief-in-the-night fiddle part, it breaks my heart, anyway—and buried in Knopfler's muttering is "the Caledonian blues." When in 1970, at the heart of *Moondance*, the album that brought Morrison an audience that would stay with him, he let the words "Ere the bonnie boat was won / As we sailed into the mystic" float the music, this might have been what he meant.

The most remarkable aspect of this crackpot theory is that it might be true. Certainly that is how the Virginia novelist Sharyn McCrumb sees it. "The first Appalachian journey," she writes, citing the geologist Kevin Dann's 1988 study *Traces on the Appalachians: A History of Serpentine in the Americas*, "was the one made by the mountains themselves."

The proof of this can be found in a vein of a green mineral called serpentine which forms its own subterranean "Appalachian Trail" along America's eastern mountains, stretching from north Georgia to the hills of Nova Scotia, where it seems to stop. This same vein of serpentine can be found in the mountains of western Ireland, where it again stretches into Cornwall, Wales, Scotland, and the Orkneys, finally ending in the Arctic Circle. More than two hundred and fifty million years ago the mountains of Appalachia and the mountains of Great Britain fit together like a jigsaw puzzle. Continental drift pulled them apart, at the same time it formed the Atlantic Ocean.

The mountains' family connection to Britain reinforced what I had felt about the migration patterns of the early settlers. People forced to leave a land they loved come to America. Hating the flat, crowded eastern seaboard, they head westward on the Wilderness Road until they reach the wall of mountains. They follow the valleys south-southwest down through Pennsylvania, and finally find a place where the ridges rise, where you can see vistas of mountains across the valley. The Scots, the Irish, the Welsh, the Cornishmen— all those who had lives along the other end of the serpentine chain— to them this place must have looked right. Must have felt right. Like home. *And they were right back in the same mountains they had left behind in Britain.*

"Caledonia Soul Music," an eighteen-minute piece recorded in 1970, passed on to the FM station KSAN in San Francisco, played often, and never released, can contain all of that without distortion. With almost no words, it is all suggestion, and the music is so bottomless that any words one might bring to it from somewhere else can seem true, just as the right melody, the right voice, can make banal lyrics seem unbearably profound. It's the most complete and in a way the most modest statement of Morrison's music: as if there were, somewhere, a form to which all of his best work aspired, a form that could never be realized, except that this time it was.

Here Morrison is a bandleader, not a singer. Really his role is as a conductor, but he appears more as a pathfinder, issuing directions under his breath, his mission to lead everyone out of the forest and into the light, except that sometimes the light in the forest is too much to turn away from, and so as a pathfinder he tries to get the band lost. Thus after stolidly announcing the title as acoustic guitar, bass, and piano slowly open the theme, a mandolin behind them hinting at a story that for the time being will be untold, Morrison lets his lips murmur, and you can think he's building up to words to sing. He isn't. There's a sigh: *Yeah*. They have all night.

"Only rarely onstage do bands achieve reality," David Thomas, the leader of Pere Ubu, the Cleveland band that in 1975 set out to find what, it seemed to them, no one else was looking for, once said. "Mostly it's in rehearsals, in lost moments." As with the Beatles in 1969, chasing all over the room for songs that were running from them like mice as they tried to make the album that would appear as *Let It Be*, seizing for a moment on Buddy Holly—after all, hadn't they named themselves for his Crickets? It's a mess, one stumble after another, and then John Lennon finds "Maybe Baby." "We used to do it," he says pathetically, as if there's no chance they could do it now. George Harrison follows, and there's an explosion of longing and loss, and now one song is another, there are no borders, they're rolling in the meadows of melody, no difference at all between "Peggy Sue Got Married" and "Crying, Waiting, Hoping"—and then Lennon moves into "Mailman Bring Me No More Blues" and the rhythm is fixed, the others lock in behind him, the progression is firm, the words are clear, and all the life is gone. It's like Dana Wynter turning her face to Kevin

McCarthy at the end of *Invasion of the Body Snatchers* just after she's gone over to the other side.

The reality that the Beatles found for a few unshaped, indelible seconds is what Morrison sustains for eighteen minutes. As he says softly every time the piece seems about to run away from itself, "Take it . . . take it slow," he could be shaking hands with Morton Feldman, the composer complaining that no matter how quietly anyone tried to play his music it was still "too fuckin' loud and too fuckin' fast." Here Morrison is at once composer and audience. As the composer he knows what he wants, but as the audience he knows that when the composer knows where he or she wants to go but the musicians don't, anything can happen, and what might happen can go beyond anyone's intentions. So at the center of his circle of musicians, Morrison waits. At times the band is as bent on finality as the Rolling Stones in their 1966 "Going Home," an ordinary three-minute song that turned into eleven minutes that were never repeated; then Morrison takes them to the point where the idea of an ending makes no sense. "Get some horn," Morrison might say, making the three words into a song in itself, and then from a saxophone comes a sound so warm you regret the fact that it will go away even as you grasp for it.

"You got it," Morrison says. Everywhere, pieces of music are hiding within the foreground sound, stepping out at any time. The drift of the music, a sort of nineteenth-century campfire lullaby, a crew looking for the headwaters of the Ohio but for a night allowing the music to let them believe they've already found it, is so complete that when in a flat, dumbly unmusical voice Morrison announces that "John will play a taste of mandolin" (*The kitchen will close in ten minutes*) it sounds like a joke on the credulousness of the musicians themselves: *Can you believe it? They thought I was serious!* But John Platania takes up the cue, quietly ringing out a calm, head-down progression over drums, bass, a bare piano, a spectral saxophone, as Morrison mutters and hums—and then, perhaps two minutes in, he hits what is almost a discord and the notes lift in volume. "*Ahhhhh!*" Morrison responds, involuntarily, as pure reflex, feeling the music in his stomach, the yarragh as pure pleasure.

There's a way everything he did before this moment was to reach the point where as a musician who is also a listener, he would find that sound, and everything he has done since an attempt to find it again.

Jonathan Cott, "Van Morrison: The *Rolling Stone* Interview," *Rolling Stone*, 30 November 1978, 51, 54.

Sharyn McCrumb, "A Novelist Looks at the Land," *Appalachian Voice*, Late Winter 2005.

"Only rarely do bands": David Thomas to GM, 17 February 1998.

Mark Knopfler, "What It Is," on *Sailing to Philadelphia* (WEA/ Reprise, 2000).

Beatles, "Maybe Baby," et al. Devin McKinney: "State of the art bootleg versions are on Disc 4 of the January 29 [1969] in-stallment of A/B Road, the 83-disc collection of Get Back sessions from Purple Chick (2004)." So there.

Van Morrison, "Almost Independence Day" and "Listen to the Lion," on *St. Dominic's Preview* (Warner Bros., 1972).

————with the Caledonia Soul Express, "Caledonia" (Warner Bros., 1974), included on *Catalog Strays 1965–2000* (Wild Card bootleg).

————"Caledonia Soul Music," included on *No Stone Unturned* (Head bootleg).

MOONSHINE WHISKEY. 1971

It's the way he affirms "I'm gonna put on my hot pants" as
if he's trying to twist himself into them. But were they pink?

Van Morrison, "Moonshine Whiskey," on *Tupelo Honey* (Warner
Bros., 1971).

JUST LIKE A WOMAN. 1971

It's an affront, this performance—to the song if not the songwriter. And where does someone get the nerve to take on a song like this?

In 1966, on Bob Dylan's *Blonde on Blonde*, the arrangement was a web, a cocoon for the singer. The more he filled in the story, the hazier it became. The touch was soft, the music sweet. By the end, it didn't matter if knowledge won out over regret. The final "I / Just can't fit" was a sad wave goodbye. It was a great make-out song.

By 1971, when Van Morrison and his Caledonia Soul Orchestra went into Wally Heider's Pacific High Studios in San Francisco to play a show for a live broadcast on KSAN, the Bay Area's leading independent contemporary music station, he was a hometown star. The year before, having flown in for a show from his home in Woodstock, he'd spent a day driving from San Francisco to Marin County to

Berkeley and back to San Francisco; the radio was on and he was all over it. Just as "Gloria" dominated the AM airwaves in the Bay Area in 1965—the next year the local Top 40 station KFRC held a poll to determine the three hundred greatest records of all time (the previous fifteen years), and "Gloria" was in the top ten along with the Rolling Stones' "(I Can't Get No) Satisfaction," the Righteous Brothers' "You've Lost That Lovin' Feeling," the Byrds' "Mr. Tambourine Man," Bob Dylan's "Like a Rolling Stone," and two versions of "Louie Louie"—by 1970 Morrison, an indistinct name almost everywhere else, probably got more airplay on KSAN than anyone else. "Madame George." "Brown-Eyed Girl." "T. B. Sheets." "Here Comes the Night." Practically everything from the 1970 *Moondance*, except for the TV-commercial jazz of the title song: "Come Running," "Caravan," "Crazy Love," "Into the Mystic," "Brand New Day," "Glad Tidings." All in an afternoon. You could almost see the lightbulb going on over Morrison's head.

In 1968, Morrison married a Bay Area native who called herself Janet Planet and moved with her from Cambridge to Woodstock—as she would say later, to meet Bob Dylan. Morrison, she said, considered him his only peer. Now Morrison had a home in Marin County. Nationally his albums were charting in the high twenties or low thirties; here he was number one. He could do no wrong.

That night in San Francisco, with an audience in the studio, he sang Woody Guthrie's "Dead or Alive." He sang "Hound Dog" and Sam Cooke's "Bring It On Home to Me" and Fats Domino's "Blue Monday" along with songs from

Moondance and the new *Tupelo Honey*. He sang "Friday's Child," an all but unknown song he'd recorded with Them. All in all it was a happy night, which made the perversity of Morrison's "Just Like a Woman" that much more stark.

With Dylan's original the music is like a wheel. With every break between chorus and verse the song returns to its beginning, and a feeling of calm settles over the traumas the people in the song have already left behind. It's not just a great make-out song: at the end, when the singer imagines himself and his old lover meeting again, at some party where nobody knows what they once were to each other, it's a seduction song. "You break just like a little girl." Oh! No one understands me like you do!

All of that is stripped away when Morrison starts in on the tune. He takes the first lines flatly, simply, as if he has too much respect for the words to sing them. The backing— guitar, piano, light drums—is perfunctory, until it's stiff, its stiffness soon enough turning hackneyed, with Morrison using the instruments as one to smash down after each word of the chorus:

And she! *wham* Makes! *wham* Love! *wham*

There are melodramatic touches, as in almost any TV drama or bad movie where any important phrase is paused and repeated—*No matter what happens, I'll be there for you—I'll be there for you*, except that here it's "Queen Mary, she's, she's my friend," or "It was your, your world"—all but semaphore flags to alert the audience that something terribly important is being said, to drive home the actor's or the singer's sincerity, to the point that any phrase that might smell of portentousness is guaranteed to perfume the room.

Is it all a setup, a man casing a joint in respectable clothes because tomorrow he's going to rob it blind? That's a question the performance refuses to answer; you have to answer it yourself. As Morrison moves into the second verse

> It was raining from the first
> And I was dying of thirst

he seems even more stolid than before. He could be giving a speech. The band is still merely following along, the piano perhaps slightly brighter than before. But then the pianist adds a triplet, and the music exerts the smallest pull on the singer. You might not even notice—but unconsciously, your memory registers the moment. There's a shift—

> And your long-time curse hurts but what
>   is worse
> Is this pain in here

—and there's a lilt in the last phase, an opening to

> I can't remain in here

and as you feel Morrison draw a breath you feel the band rush forward to draw it for him—

> I can't stay in here

—the "stay" shredding in his mouth as the words are blown out of their own song by a scream that is somehow more controlled, more melodic, than anything before, the melody now armed with passion behind it or the fright it creates

AIN'T IT CLEAR

and you feel that nothing could rise higher than this fire until the next word does, and the next word is "I," five times, not repeated but each exploding syllable modulated into the next until it is all one unholy word, a plea the singer is addressing to himself. What just happened? Is there anybody left alive?

And then, in the most perverse gesture of all, Morrison produces the next lines, again flatly, as if he could care less. He ornaments a phrase with that TV-script repetition that mocks you for buying the phony emotion behind the delivery in the first place

I believe I believe I believe I believe I believe
it's time for us to

and so floridly that when he finishes with a curt

Quit.

there really is a period after the word.

And then he does it all again. You want to say you won't be fooled this time, but you are. After the song is blown apart for the second time, you want him to say he meant every ache, every cut, but he doesn't.

He does get out of the song in a way that humanizes what he's done, that puts the singer in the song, for the first time one of its characters, not its assassin: "You were weird, and I was weird, too." You play the song again, trying to make it happen as your own heart has played it.

Bob Dylan, "Just Like a Woman," on *Blonde on Blonde* (Columbia, 1966).

Van Morrison, "Just Like a Woman," on *The Inner Mystic: Recorded Live at Pacific High Studios*, California, September 1971, as broadcast on KSAN-FM, San Francisco (Oh Boy/Odyssey bootleg).

Janet Planet, see Michael Gray, *Bob Dylan Encyclopedia* (New York: Continuum, 2006), 465.

THE LAST LAUGH, ON MARK KNOPFLER, *SAILING TO PHILADELPHIA*. 2000

Ever since Dire Straits' "Sultans of Swing," his first record and a worldwide hit, Mark Knopfler has had a touch. Usually it's the ability to find a doomy, fatalistic melody and let it send a man who gives off the feeling of someone who never stops looking over his shoulder down the street. When it works—on "Romeo and Juliet" and "Wild West End" on Dire Straits' 1980 *Making Movies*, or the single "What It Is," from *Sailing to Philadelphia*—you could be walking in the footsteps of Michael Caine's Jack Carter.

Anyone who bought *Sailing for Philadelphia* hoping for more of what he or she was hearing on the radio was not going to be happy. It was a famous-names showcase, and the first thing that caught your ear was James Taylor on the title song, in his wounded-puppy "You've Got a Friend" mode. Elsewhere there were the Christian pop singers Chris

Rodriquez and Tim Davis, the Americana duo Gillian Welch and David Rawlings, and Glenn Tilbrook and Chris Difford of the once-wonderful British pop group Squeeze.

The first four songs on the album were so bland you could forget you were listening to it. The first verse of "The Last Laugh," crooned by Knopfler, was no different. And then, one minute into the song, there was Van Morrison.

A single word—the "learned" in "Games you thought you'd learned"—is enough to take you off the record, into a country whose only maps are in Morrison's pockets. This is a place made of regret, where the deepest impulse is to return to the scene of the crime, so everything can be made right. If you can't do that, can't you sing a song that the person you wounded might hear, and wouldn't that be almost as good? But what if the wrong was done to you, by someone who likely hasn't thought of you since? If that person heard you, coming out of a radio they didn't turn off because they like Mark Knopfler, would anything happen in their heart?

Knopfler's song itself is nothing—but all of these questions are put into the air as Morrison draws them from his chest. It's not that so much is being expressed; it's that the fullness of Morrison's voice as he steps up to the song immediately erases the limits that Knopfler himself has already established as to what could be expressed. Now the possibility that anything could be said hangs in the air. It's not a singer's trick; it doesn't always happen when Morrison steps through someone else's door. On the Chieftains' 1995 *The Long Black Veil*—featuring Mick Jagger on the title song with a voice that a resident of a certain mountain county in Virginia claims can be traced to just that place, Sinéad O'Connor on "The Foggy Dew" and "She Moved Through the Fair," Marianne Faithfull on the ancient "Love Is Teasin'," Tom Jones on "The Tennessee Waltz," and for that matter Mark Knopfler on "Lily of the West"— Morrison has nothing to offer "Have I Told You Lately That I Love You" other than to reveal how little the song might tell a singer. In Mike Figgis's 2003 film *Red, White & Blues*, about the British blues world, Morrison raises his guitar and launches into "Rambler's Blues." Formally he's masterful; he's also scholastic, more writing about the song than singing it, and his writing misses the song. Tom Jones hovers in the background; after a minute or so you wish he'd open his mouth and take the song away.

There's no saying why in "The Last Laugh" Morrison finds a story to tell. Maybe he heard someone had to save the song, even if he hadn't yet heard if it was worth it. Maybe it was the line "You've neither lost or won" or simply "Out on the highway," which opens into that whole country, and suddenly the whole song is bigger, fuller, wanting more from Knopfler, as he moves into a guitar solo, than he can give, and more from the listener.

One of those things: you put a man next to a microphone, hand him a sheet of words, and soul comes out.

Mark Knopfler, "The Last Laugh," *Sailing to Philadelphia* (Warner Bros., 2000).

The Chieftains, *The Long Black Veil* (BMG, 1995).

Van Morrison, "Rambler's Blues," in Mike Figgis, *Martin Scorsese Presents the Blues: Red, White & Blues* (Hip-O, 2003).

PART THREE

A BELIEF IN THE BLUES AS A KIND OF CURSE ONE PUTS ON ONESELF

COMMON ONE. 1980.
BEAUTIFUL VISION. 1982.
INARTICULATE SPEECH OF THE HEART. 1983.
LIVE AT THE GRAND OPERA HOUSE BELFAST. 1984.
A SENSE OF WONDER. 1984.
NO GURU, NO METHOD, NO TEACHER. 1986.
POETIC CHAMPIONS COMPOSE. 1987.
IRISH HEARTBEAT, WITH THE CHIEFTAINS. 1988.
AVALON SUNSET. 1989.
ENLIGHTENMENT. 1990.
HYMNS TO THE SILENCE. 1991.
TOO LONG IN EXILE. 1993.
A NIGHT IN SAN FRANCISCO. 1994.
DAYS LIKE THIS. 1995.
HOW LONG HAS THIS BEEN GOING ON. 1996
TELL ME SOMETHING. 1996

How do you write off more than fifteen albums and more than fifteen years of the work of a great artist? You might do the same with Bob Dylan's records from *Street Legal* in 1978 right up to the bend in the road of *Good As I Been to You* in 1992—or I might, anyway, remembering how everything from *Slow Train Coming* to *Infidels* to *Empire Burlesque* to *Knocked Out Loaded* to *Down in the Groove* to *Oh Mercy* to *Under the Red Sky* was marked by a *Rolling Stone* review celebrating it as *yes, finally, not like the last one, this is the real comeback!* and with the actual turn toward something crawlingly alive missed for the lack of a signpost. But that was a singer who for a long time had nothing to sing about. Something different was happening with Van Morrison.

"What defines great singing in the rock and soul era," Jonathan Lethem wrote in 2008, "is some underlying tension in the space between singer and song. A bridge is being built across that void, and it's a bridge we're never sure the singer's going to manage to cross. The gulf may reside between vocal texture and the actual meaning of the words, or between the singer and the band, the musical genre, the style of production, what have you . . . " But what if there is no tension—not because the singer has momentarily lost it, but because his goal has been to transcend it, and he's succeeded?

In 1975 I found myself passing the road leading to Van Morrison's Marin County house; it was posted with a sign reading "Van Morrison Self-Improvement Camp." He was working on it at the time. His career remained a kind of war, with producers, managers, himself. His music was a Möbius strip: no new work had ever made his past work inaccessible; none of his best work had caused anything else to sound dated or immature. His mistakes didn't subvert the shape of his story, because scars and wounds were part of it. He might stand still on stage, but you never knew where you, as part of the audience, stood with him, or vice versa. His relationship to the audience seemed somehow accidental, or worse. There was a show in Berkeley in 1973 that began with cutting versions of Morrison's own "St. Dominic's Preview," Sonny Boy Williamson's "Help Me," and Muddy Waters's "I Just Want to Make Love to You," and then careened out of control. Morrison had been standing in a dim blue light—not bright enough to see his face, but bright enough to see he had one. He broke off the Waters song and ordered "the spotlight" out. He didn't have his shades, he said. He wasn't in L.A., whatever that meant. He continued in complete darkness. It seemed appropriate—mercurial weirdness was part of his appeal. But out of the dark came a throwaway version of "Listen to the Lion," a flat "Caravan," and then the announcement of the last song: "Misty." "As I wander through this garbage world alone," Morrison sang, leaving the garbage world—the audience—alone.

God knows it was a memorable show. There was nothing obvious about it. Lethem's bridge came into view, suspense over whether Morrison might cross it grew, he didn't cross it, and that failure stuck more than the triumphs of countless other good performers, who leave you feeling you've seen something unforgettable, something you can hardly remember a week later. Morrison's resistance to an audience in those years was palpable, so concrete you could feel it pressing on your chest, as if to say, *Where is it written*

that just because I want to come out on stage with the musi-
cians I trust and take my songs where they've never been be-
fore there has to be someone there to watch?

At a show in San Francisco in 1978, Morrison encored
with "Caravan." He opened up space in the song, as if daring the crowd to anticipate his timing. He'd done this sort
of thing for years, perhaps most shockingly in a passage
captured on "*... It's Too Late to Stop Now...*," his first live
album, recorded in 1973 in a nightclub in Los Angeles and
a theater in London. The last number—on a double album
that unfolded like a single show—was "Cyprus Avenue,"
from *Astral Weeks*. Morrison used a stop-time beat, allowing for long pauses between lines, spaces where he could
try anything, crossroads where he could take the song in
any direction. Inside the story of the song, the singer
watched all the fourteen-year-old girls parading down the
street on their way home from school: "And the leaves fall
one by one by one by one by one by one by one by one—on
the hometown fool." He looks at one of the girls, the one
he's waited for. He thinks about what he wants to do to her.
He makes no move to cross the street, to approach her, to
speak to her, but he can't help thinking about speaking to
her, and as soon as he does think about it, he freezes. "And
my tongue gets tied" is what he sang when he recorded the
song. But that's too easy. Now it's "And my tongue gets t—,
t—"—and the act is so convincing, the break in the song so
violent, the drawbridge opening so that the only way to
cross it is to back up, floor the accelerator, and pray, that
the whole show is sucked into the suspended moment. It's

as if there's no way out—in the instant, you might be plunged back into memories of the times you sat nervously with a stuttering friend, and how you ached with everything you had for him to get the word he was trying to say out of his mouth, to the point where you could see yourself reaching your hand down his throat and grabbing it. Onstage, someone in the band makes a cheek-popping sound, right on the beat. There's nervous laughter in the crowd. A saxophone seems to walk around the stage, and you can imagine the player circling the singer, pointing at him, as if to ensure that no one misses his humiliation, which he can't escape. "It's too late to stop now!" are the triumphant last words of the show, but right now the singer can't stop and he'd give anything if he could. "Every time I try to speak," he wants to say, but it comes out "Evry tam, tr—, tr—, sp—" The saxophone stutters, the piano hits random notes, "Every," he tries again. It comes out "errry," and then, as it happens in real life, the curse is lifted: "And my insides shake," clear and smooth, and then a rush, as if to outrun the stutter that only pauses to take a breath: "Justlikealeaf-onatree." The whole crisis lasts barely more than twenty seconds, but while it's happening it feels like a trap you'll never get out of.

At the show in San Francisco five years later, in the midst of "Caravan," the stops in the music, the seemingly atonal, irrational bursts and jerks, were as dramatic and disconcerting as they were in that "Cyprus Avenue"; instead of titters, shouts, or even heckling, the crowd responded with unison clapping, as if to stop the music altogether, or force it back into a regular time. For the first time that night, save for an introduction of the band, Morrison spoke to the crowd. "Just shut up," he said. "Just shut up. We do the work here, not you."

That was the highlight of the show. In some ways, looking forward, now, to the years that would follow, it was predictive, an acting out of things to come, because otherwise there was no tension in the show at all. It was formal. Everything was pitched to a middle range: desire and pleasure, never joy or rage. The band held strictly to arrangements, giving Morrison nothing to sing against. The people in the audience were pushing harder than the people on the stage.

Outside of that strange "Caravan," what Morrison was offering, as he turned songs over to background singers, pressed each number into a single dimension, and sang at his songs rather than from inside of them, was one true side of himself as a performer: the romantic of "Tupelo Honey," the person who makes music of affection, sensuality, and acceptance. He wants peace of mind and ordered satisfaction most of all, and sings as if he already has them. But the singer who by 1978 had already caused some people to commit themselves to his music as if it was their quest as well as his had won them because of his distrust of conventional satisfactions and his inability to rest with any sort of peace. This was the person behind "Listen to the Lion" and "Mystic Eyes." What he wants most is freedom, and what he has to say is that getting hold of freedom is perhaps not as hard as living up to it, standing up to it. When both sides of Morrison's music come together, the result can be a sort of mystical deliverance. The listener is spared not a single fear, but he or she is somehow insulated from all fears—as is the performer. This is what happens on *Astral Weeks*, in "Almost Independence Day," in the wild shrieks of the steel guitar on "St. Dominic's Preview," or the insistent fetishism of windowsill, letter box, door, and backstreet jellyroll—*No, you don't take off the left shoe first, you take off the* right *shoe!*—in "And the Healing Has Begun." But when only one side of the conflict is presented, one is only too aware of what is being held back—and what is held back will find its way out one way or the other, as it did this night, when Van the orderly romantic told his audience to shut up.

Perhaps the real harbinger of what was to come came with "Help Me." "I've transcended myself," Morrison shouted at one point; here he was back in the pit, switching back and forth between his harmonica and the words of the song, long, harsh, overblown, pure sleazy 1967 Fillmore Auditorium white blues but the feeling of blood on the floor just the same, like Dennis Hopper reciting Roy Orbison's rewrite of the song, "In Dreams," in *Blue Velvet* ("In dreams—I *walk* with you—In dreams—I talk—to *you*"): "When you walk, walk with me—when you talk, talk with me! You gotta help me—I can't do it all by myself!" Morrison wasn't asking the crowd for encouragement, as most singers would do with this song—just as Dennis Hopper's Frank couldn't have cared less what Kyle MacLachan's Jeffrey made of what he was spewing in his face. Morrison's plea was aimed at someone, or something, much harder to reach.

Over the next fifteen years, that plea would be almost constant—a hole in the nearly seamless fabric opening up with the fatalism of "Raglan Road" on *Irish Heartbeat*, all sides of Morrison's music coming together as if in the ultimate and yet transcendently raceless minstrel show of *A Night in San Francisco*, John Lee Hooker, Georgie Fame, the bluesmen Junior Wells and Jimmy Witherspoon, the saxophonist Candy Dulfer, and Morrison's own daughter Shana Morrison along for the ride. The romantic would be replaced by the seeker, and the seeker would replace the anti-romantic's refusal of an audience with an insistence that no one be permitted to miss the point. You couldn't tell religion from therapy. "Were you healed tonight?" someone shouts to the crowd as the last number on *A Night in San Francisco* railed to a close—it was "Gloria" pulled out of Johnny Kidd and the Pirates' 1960 "Shakin' All Over," perhaps the first true British rock 'n' roll hit, as if by cesarean section.

As a soul man Morrison had been a lyric poet; he could suggest Yeats. In 1980, on *Common One*, he began to insist on the connection, which meant the songs didn't remotely suggest it. With two of the six numbers passing by at more than fifteen minutes—by far the longest pieces he'd ever released—Morrison had time to claim his roots; he pretty much had time to research them, write up his findings, publish them in a book, and watch it go out of print. Instead he name dropped. "Yeats and Lady Gregory corresponded, corresponded, corresponded"—his familiar obsessive repetition no longer changing the shape of the words, making them speak in new tongues, but telling you Yeats and Lady Gregory wrote a lot of letters. "James Joyce wrote streams of consciousness books." "Did you ever hear about Wordsworth and Coleridge? Did you ever hear about William Blake?"

Since as a lyric poet, or even a lyric poetaster, Morrison was a soul man, this shouldn't have mattered. In 1974, on the hypnotizing "You Don't Pull No Punches, But You Don't Push the River," Morrison was searching for the Veedon Fleece—what he named the album the song came from—and no one has ever figured out what that was.* The Veedon Fleece seemed to float above the churning music, which soon enough—a lift from an acoustic guitar, a piano thinking it over even as the boat is untied, drums on the offbeat, a flute as second mind, strings as a single rhythm instrument—was that river itself. There was a feeling caught in *Once Upon a Time in the West*, not even the movie, merely the title; suspense rose like a cloud. "The real soul people, the real soul people," Morrison chanted, pointing toward "the west coast," though he didn't say of what; as he summoned William Blake and the Eternals they were a band, just as the Sisters of Mercy he called for would become one, and together they sought the Veedon Fleece, but now the bridge was underwater, every shape shifting as you

---

* In 1974, just as he was about to release the record, Morrison went on KSAN in San Francisco to promote it. "The album's called *Veedon Fleece*," he said. "V-E-E-D-O-N F-L-E-E-C-E. And it doesn't, it means, ah"—and at just that instant there was a huge burst of static. He might have been saying "it means what it says," but I wouldn't bet on it.

tried to see your way to the bottom. The nearly nine minutes of the song went by like wind.

On *Common One*, as on so many of the albums to follow, the singing was so characterless and the sax-and-trumpet ensemble playing so faceless that the mention of a famous name became an event, something to hang on to—as it would be for so long for someone with nothing to say and an infinite commitment to getting it across. The tedium was almost heroic in its refusal to quit.

Near the end of "You Don't Pull No Punches, But You Don't Push the River," the music loosens to the point that it begins to break up, its elements separating. The song isn't falling apart—each part is moving off as a song in itself. You don't know where the song is. Strings shake, giving off the long horn of a storm warning, a yarragh if anything is. But for all Morrison returned to this river between 1980 and 1996 it could have had corpses floating on it. Even from a bridge you wouldn't want to look.

Jonathan Lethem, "The Fly in the Ointment," collected in *Best Music Writing 2009*, ed. GM (New York: Da Capo, 2009), 186–187.

Van Morrison, "Cyprus Avenue," on *". . . It's Too Late to Stop Now . . ."* (Warner Bros., 1974).

———"You Don't Pull No Punches, But You Don't Push the River," on *Veedon Fleece* (Warner Bros., 1974).

———*Common One* (Warner Bros., 1980).

———*Beautiful Vision* (Warner Bros., 1982).

———*Inarticulate Speech of the Heart* (Warner Bros., 1983).

———*Live at the Grand Opera House Belfast* (Mercury, 1984).

————*A Sense of Wonder* (Mercury, 1984).

————*No Guru, No Method, No Teacher* (Mercury, 1986).

————*Poetic Champions Compose* (Mercury, 1987).

————and the Chieftains, *Irish Heartbeat* (Mercury, 1988).

————*Avalon Sunset* (Polydor, 1989).

————*Enlightenment* (Mercury, 1990).

————*Hymns to the Silence* (Polydor, 1991).

————*Too Long in Exile* (Polydor, 1993).

————*A Night in San Francisco* (Polydor, 1994).

————*Days Like This* (Polydor, 1995).

————with Georgie Fame & friends, *How Long Has This Been Going On* (Verve, 1996).

————*Tell Me Something: The Songs of Mose Allison* (Verve, 1996).

LINDEN ARLEN STOLE THE HIGHLIGHTS. 1974

"**Do you** hear that? That's a prayer," Jonathan Cott said to me as we listened to the second cut on Van Morrison's 1974 *Veedon Fleece*. The first song, "Fair Play for You," a harmlessly slow reverie, was no preparation.

What Cott was talking about was the piano piece that opens "Linden Arlen Stole the Highlights." It seemed to begin and end the song—to be utterly complete in itself—before Morrison sang his first word. I'm not sure what I heard that day—I remember saying *Yes, yes*, as if Cott had unlocked the song, and so fully it didn't matter whatever "Linden Arlen Stole the Highlights" meant. What I hear now is a long series of earned wishes, the plea—if it's a prayer, it's the Platters'—of someone who knows what he or she wants, knows what he or she deserves, has little or no expectation of getting any of it, and who is absolutely at peace with such a life, or such an ending. The knowledge is enough. I don't hear a door anymore; I hear a pool that you dive into simply by listening.

There's no need to come up. I didn't catch the words that day, or for years to come. It didn't occur to me that the song needed them—or maybe it was that even as Morrison sang the words, the song itself forgot them.

As Morrison slides back and forth along the planes of the melody, as if he were a drop of mercury and someone were tilting a hand mirror now up, now down, he slides past the literal story he's telling—a crime story, as it turns out—into a tale of thought, dream, desire, where the claims of each shift in primacy. Passion rises and his voice fills up, and you are in the moment, but when Morrison lets his voice fade, as if he can hardly bear to listen to himself, because the thought he's trying to bring into view is so elusive the act of listening will break it, there is the feeling of someone looking back at himself from a future that has itself already passed. This is a greater kind of slowness. Whatever movement the music makes, it also pulls against itself: *not yet.*

It was hundreds of listenings to this song later, decades after listening to it with Cott, that, driving in a car, the radio on, I heard the story the song was carrying—I can't say, *about.* With a speaker a few inches from your face, words come across like traffic reports: out of the Druidic forest of the music comes a killer. Other killers track him from Ireland to a bar in San Francisco. He faces them down and kills them all. Dirty Harry straight off the boat.

The pool is always there, though. What happens in those first seconds with the piano, then in the way Morrison high-steps across an arc in the melody that has only just appeared to carry the listener across the first line, "Linden Arlen stole the highlights"—if that was his crime, what kind of crime is that? When you kill someone, do you not simply put out their lights but take them?—returns the song at any time from its words to its music, the words remaining only as a signifier that a particular person is singing the song.

It's the quieting of the music that's uncanny. With Robert Johnson's "Stones in My Passway"—the kind of deep blues, constructed with an art so realized it conceals itself, that's one source of "Linden Arlen Stole the Highlights"— there's nothing you can do to quiet it. The more you turn the volume down, the more the irreducible loudness of the song, its nightmare desolation and fright, creeps forward. But with "Linden Arlen Stole the Highlights," the louder you try to make it, the more it recedes, until it reaches as far as it will go toward silence, making you lean into it.

When the Miracles' "The Love I Saw in You Was Just a Mirage" appeared in 1967, it radiated a sublimity that made everything that surrounded it on the radio sound faintly obscene. This song can do the same to whatever you happened to be doing with your life before you heard it, for the first time or the thousandth. Whether that is art ennobling life or corrupting it I don't know.

Robert Johnson, "Stones in My Passway" (1937), collected on *Robert Johnson—The Complete Recordings* (Columbia, 1990).

Smokey Robinson and the Miracles, "The Love I Saw in You Was Just a Mirage" (Tamla, 1967).

Van Morrison, "Linden Arlen Stole the Highlights," on *Veedon Fleece* (Warner Bros., 1974).

BREAKFAST ON PLUTO. 2005

In Neil Jordan's 2005 film *Breakfast on Pluto*, the young transvestite Kitten, who was raised with the name Patrick Braden, has left her hometown in Ireland to find the mother who abandoned her at birth: "She went to London, the biggest city in the world," Kitten says to anyone she meets, "and it swallowed her up." But now Kitten has discovered where her mother lives. Flamboyant, shrieking, weepy, yet with the self-possession of someone with an infinite sense of irony, she sits in the dressing room of the Soho peep show where she works, surrounded by women from the club. She's wearing a short blond curly wig and a demure suit, applying light makeup, speaking in a quiet, careful voice; a folded newspaper propped up against the mirror, with a laughing photo of Margaret Thatcher and the head-line "VICTORY," tells us the year is 1979. Then we see the movement of an escalator, with people emerging from a tube station, and as Kitten's face comes into view Van Morrison's "Madame George," from eleven years before the historical moment of the film, creeps almost imperceptibly onto the soundtrack. It sounded like an invocation loosed from time when it first appeared, and it does now.

Breakfast on Pluto floats on a sea of music—a sea wide enough to make plain both the world in which Van Morrison has since the mid-1960s done his work, and how different and deep that work has been. A product of the ear as much as the eye, the film opens with "Sugar Baby Love," a 1974 hit by the made-up group the Rubettes—a delirious producer's fantasy of the Diamonds' 1957 doo-wop parody "Little Darlin," which was so good it turned into the real thing, as this does. "Bop she-waddy, *bop* she-waddy," goes the chorus behind the falsetto lead, which dives down on Kitten as she pushes a stroller on a London street while a construction worker hoots at her, as she invites him "and all the boys" back to her place as his face falls, as she begins to tell the baby in the pram the story of her life—and the movie ends the same way, with Kitten pushing the same stroller, the same baby, which by now we know is the child of her best friend, Charlie, and Charlie's murdered boyfriend, Irwin, the song simultaneously homing in on Kitten like something out of *The Birds* and lifting her feet off the ground. It's the most glorious, irresistible sound imaginable.

Yes, Cillian Murphy's Kitten tells the baby, my mother left me on the doorstep of my father, the local priest, for whom she kept house. Yes, I grew up with a foster family, but when I put on my foster mother's dresses and lipstick, and when I wrote stories in school about my father Father Liam and my mother Eily Bergin and where could I get a sex change, I got in trouble, and I ran away. To join the circus, of course! And then I went to London—

In the circus, or rather with the band Billy Hatchett and the Mohawks, there's Gavin Friday's madman lead singer with his outrageously camped-up version of Johnny Preston's 1960 Indian epic "Running Bear" ("Loved little White Dove," the Big Bopper wrote before stepping onto the plane that would take him, Buddy Holly, and Ritchie Valens to the Happy Hunting Ground), then Kitten onstage as a squaw to Hatchett's chief for Sweet's 1973 "Wig Wam Bam," then Hatchett railing from the stage over "Thirteen dead in Derry" and the evil of British rule and Protestant barbarism in Northern Ireland. There's one of Kitten's favorite songs, Bobby Goldsboro's 1968 "Honey," playing on the radio, entering a scene like weather; there's a generic version of Cole Porter's "Why Am I So Gone (About That Gal?)." As Kitten arrives in London to search for her mother the film offers her Harry Nilsson's 1971 "The Moonbeam Song"; sleeping in doorways, waiting in government offices, wandering the streets with her cardboard suitcase, she's picked up by a man in a car, and it's Bryan Ferry, with sallow, oily skin and a moustache like dirt, who plays Kitten Morris Albert's sallow, oily 1975 "Feelings" on his cassette machine before shoving her head into his lap. She's taken under the wing of a magician ("She came to London, the biggest city in the world," she tells him almost before she tells him her name, "and it swallowed her up"); for his act he hypnotizes Kitten to Dusty Springfield's shimmering 1969 "The Windmills of Your Mind." "I think I see your mother over there," the magician crows, sending Kitten hurtling across nightclub floors to embrace laughing men with the insensate cry of "Mummy!" and then again, "No, over there—" In England to abort the baby she's carrying, Charlie tracks down Kitten and drags her away from the magician, appalled at his cruelty; as they dance in a nightclub, a soldier hits on Kitten. You'll be Bobby, she tells him, as "Honey" plays again; the club is blown up by an IRA bomb and as an Irish survivor, a man disguised as a woman, Kitten is arrested and tortured to the sounds of Buffalo Springfield's 1967 "For What It's Worth." Released, she stares into a store window full of TV sets all playing the theme to the 1955 *Love Is a Many-Splendored Thing*, and the song swallows her as London does. One of the cops who beat her finds her turning tricks on the street, and takes her to the peep show emporium for honest work. A client demands she sing Patti Page's 1953 "How Much Is That Doggie in the Window?"—the one song, it will turn out, that everyone in the film knows, as Kitten and Charlie and eventually Father Liam struggle continually over whether it's "the one with the waggedy tail" or, as the client first screams at Kitten, "'Waggley!'" When Father Liam—played by Liam Neeson, who years before had recorded a version of Van Morrison's spoken-word piece "Coney Island"—appears in her booth, to tell her who her mother is and where she lives, "The Windmills of Your Mind" rises up once more. But it's all prelude.

"I want English," she says as she makes up in her back-stage mirror, using Margaret Thatcher's picture in the paper as her model. "I want conservative. I want East Finchley"—Thatcher's constituency. "I want powerful—do you think it works?" She looks hard at herself. "I think I look better than she does," she says. She is about to step out of her picaresque adventures into tragedy, into a real life she has no idea how to make real.

When Van Morrison recorded "Madame George" in 1968, it opened with thirteen seconds of the lightest strum on an acoustic guitar, the quietest fanfare, the most modest and thus the most fatal foreshadowing, as the theme is stated twice: a sense that the story is over before it begins. In the way the film has taken the song into itself, it is over. "Madame George" tells the tale of a Belfast drag queen who with the promise of the forbidden, of drink and cigarettes, drugs and music, sex and fantasy, gathers young boys around herself to stave off a killing burden of loneliness and difference; the song has been placed in the film for those who already know it, for those who will bring the whole of it instantly to bear on who Kitten is and what she is about to do. Its rightness in this moment is so absolute the frisson of the song's appearance creates a kind of swoon. It is so right you can imagine that, at bottom, it is the song that wrote the film, adapted by Neil Jordan and Patrick McCabe from McCabe's novel, which, not having a soundtrack, did not include "Madame George": that the film was made to reach the moment when "Madame George" could play the film rather than the other way around, the song sucking the film into itself, to reveal the pathos of its heroine's quest as nothing else could.

As the first faces come up on the tube-stop escalator, you hear this first body of the song before Kitten's face appears in turn. There is a dream-like synchronicity in the way that Kitten's suit—soft black dots on a white-gray background, black pumps, a small black hat, and strong black vertical stripes on the skirt—matches the silver panels and black borders of the escalator, the panels moving as if of their own will as she, still on the steps, seems pushed by another's hand. Everything moves slowly, inexorably, inevitably.

Like a broom sweeping, a single note from Richard Davis's double bass, the note bending like a finger, beckoning, opens the door of the song—before, the song was poised on the front steps, not ready to enter, not ready to leave. "Down Cyprus Avenue," Morrison sings—but that's not what you hear, and that's not what the scene was made to capture. All the gravity of the moment is in the first word, *down*, itself bent like Davis's first note, into a *dow-nnn*, the tail of the syllable rising; not exactly a word at all, but an exclamation somewhere between a reverie and a curse, a sound that despite the instant it takes to sing or hear contains as much time as you might want to let it echo. The word isn't stretched out but lifted, curled, suspended in the air, something the singer himself can throw out in front of himself and watch.

The song remains on the soundtrack for forty seconds, as Kitten reaches her mother's street and begins to look for her address, the tempo not changing but doubled notes from Davis pressing a single five-line verse in which the listener barely glimpses the figure behind the curtain of the song. As Kitten begins to talk to a pleasant boy of about ten—her half-brother, named Patrick as she was—the music drops down and continues almost silently under the dialogue. The drummer Connie Kay has come in, playing a martial roll with brushes for six seconds, but you can't hear him. Pretending to be an agent for British Telecom, conducting a survey, Kitten begins to ask the boy questions about telephones in his house. "Shouldn't you be asking my mother?" he says.

She's frightened; she's not ready for this, but the boy brings her into his house, and after thirty seconds in the deep background of the film the music lifts sharply up again. From behind, in counterpoint to Kitten's rise on the escalator, we see the back of Kitten's mother's head as she descends the stairs of her house to the foyer, and as you hear Morrison sing "That's when you fall," Kitten sees her mother and crumples to the floor. "That's when you fall," Morrison repeats, but from a distance, as his slightly distorted, echoed voice vanishes into the soundtrack equivalent of a dream dissolve, and as the screen goes black the music goes silent. The match of Morrison's words to the action on the screen would be a cheesy literalism but for the way that, here, the feeling is not that the song is singing the movie, but that the movie is singing the song.

The whole story, the whole quest—Kitten's quest, and Van Morrison's—is in that first word, that single *down*. It's not a studio effect. As Morrison sings certain words, as he finds them, as they find him— "In some ways," he said in 2009, "I'm picking them up from under the surface"—they contain their own echoes, and they echo in other voices. There is Sinéad O'Connor in 1990, twenty-two years after *Astral Weeks* changed the landscape in which she grew up. Now at twenty-four, a year older than Morrison was when he made his album, she is herself crossing from Ireland to London to pronounce, in her soft, thoughtful, steely way, that "England's not the mythical land of Madame George and roses / It's the home of police who kill black boys on mopeds." In the silent places in *Breakfast on Pluto*, Kitten's repeated incantation, "London, the biggest city in the world, and it swallowed her up," combines with the sense of utter devastation and loss that is the engine of "Madame George" to call up Thomas De Quincey in 1803, walking "up and down Oxford-street" with the teenage prostitute Ann, herself then swallowed up by London. In the way that Kitten never reveals herself to her mother, only gazes at her, seated in her mother's living room after her faint and talking about telephones, from two feet away maintaining the distance of her whole life, De Quincey's Ann can hover in the dim shadows of the film, to remind you of how close Kitten comes to refusing her brother's entreaty and walking away, back to her life on the streets of the city, sooner or later turning up dead, never to see her mother, as De Quincey never saw Ann again: "If she lived, doubtless we must have been sometimes in search of each other, at the very same moment, through the mighty labyrinths of London; perhaps even within a few feet of each other—a barrier no wider than a London street, often amounting in the end to a separation for eternity!"

As Morrison sings the first word of "Madame George," all of that can be contained in his *down*, and all of that can be released. It is at the heart of Morrison's presence as a singer that when he lights on certain sounds, certain small moments inside a song—hesitations, silences, shifts in pressure, sudden entrances, slamming doors—can then suggest whole territories, completed stories, indistinct ceremonies, far outside of anything that can be literally traced in the compositions that carry them. Those moments can travel, as the pacing of "Madame George" makes its Cyprus Avenue, a four-block stretch of Belfast, into a thoroughfare as endless as De Quincey's Oxford Street. They can transfer themselves; they can be transferred; they can transfer situations they might inhabit, as "Madame George" briefly inhabits a film about a young Irish transvestite, into realms outside their own literal space—as with, in the long fade of Morrison's *down*, Kitten's rising on the escalator suggests someone rising from the dead, that moment itself rewriting the song, even if Neil Jordan could only afford a little more than a minute of it.

Thomas De Quincy, *Confessions of an English Opium Eater* (1821; New York: Penguin, 1981), 64.

Breakfast on Pluto, dir. Neil Jordan (2005, Sony Pictures Classics). With Cillian Murphy as Kitten, Eva Berthstle as his mother, Eily Bergin, Liam Neeson as Father Liam, Ruth Negga as Charlie, Laurence Kinlan as Irwin, Gavin Friday as

Billy Hatchett, Stephen Rea as Bertle the magician, Bryan Ferry as Mr. Silky String, and Sid Young as Patrick in London.

Rubettes, "Sister Baby Love" (1974), on *Breakfast on Pluto—Original Soundtrack* (Milan, 2006). Also includes Harry Nilsson's "Me and My Arrow" and "You're Breakin' My Heart," Joe Dolan's "You're Such a Good Looking Woman," Bobby Goldsboro's "Honey," "(How Much Is) That Doggy in the Window?" by Patti Page, "Caravan" by Santo and Johnny, "Feelings" by Morris Albert, "The Windows of Your Mind" by Dusty Springfield, "Wig Wam Bam" by Gavin Friday, "Sand" by Friday and Cillian Murphy, T-Rex's "Children of the Revolution," and nothing by Van Morrison.

Liam Neeson, "Coney Island," on *No Prima Donna: The Songs of Van Morrison* (Polydor, 1994).

Sinéad O'Connor, "Black Boys on Mopeds," on *I Do Not Want What I Haven't Got* (Capitol, 1990).

THE HEALING GAME. 1997

The black-and-white photo that appears on the face of *The Healing Game*—and on the disc itself, and on the back of the CD box, insisting that you look at it again and again, that you think about it—shows a short, very stocky middle-aged white man on the street, and a taller black man behind him. Both are well-dressed, in dark clothes, with dark hats. The short man, Van Morrison, is wearing blackout glasses and an expensive white shirt buttoned to the neck; the taller man, the saxophonist and one-time James Brown band director Pee Wee Ellis, who wears a white shirt and a striped tie, gazes over Morrison's left shoulder, as if on the lookout for trouble. It is, you can imagine without trying, a mob boss and his number one on their way to settle a score. The expression on Morrison's face, all stone, is appallingly determined and cold.

If this is the mood you carry with you as the music starts, straight away the music tells you you're right: the first lines of "When That Rough God Goes Riding," the first song, describe "mud-splattered victims . . . all along the ancient highway," and you catch the echoes of a vendetta as old as the highway, some internecine tribal conflict that will never be settled. If as the Sex Pistols rammed it home in 1976 in "Anarchy in the UK" Morrison's verses call forth the conflict in Northern Ireland between the UDA and the IRA—and London's war against Catholic Belfast, the war that began with Cromwell and continued, as Morrison sang in 1997, under Tony Blair—the war John Lennon sang about under Edward Heath, the war Gang of Four sang about under James Callaghan—the chorus is mythic, outside of any historical time.

As soon as the scene is set everything changes, even if the story being told holds to its violence. With the first verse done, Morrison, his voice thick and heavy, glides like an athlete into the chorus, and a tremendous feeling of warmth, of being in the right place at the right time, takes hold. It carries the listener into a musical home so perfect and complete he or she might have forgotten that music could call up such a place, and then populate it with people, acts, wishes, fears. The deep burr of Morrison's voice buries the words, which cease to matter; you might not hear them until the tenth time you play the album, or long after that. "It's when that rough god goes riding," he sings, drawing the words both from Yeats and down in his chest, and you might never know it's the angel of death that has you in its embrace. "I am this serpent filled with venom," Morrison sings later in "Waiting Game"—but here his voice, like Vito Corleone's voice as Robert De Niro plays him, is so filled with quiet, earned authority that you trust it, you ask it to keep speaking to you, to offer you its comfort, even as the man behind it pushes a pillow into your face. The very slowness of the introduction to the song—at first, only piano, the lightest percussion, and Morrison's slurred harmonica, then the way he waits behind syllables even as he voices them—validates everything to follow: validates it musically, emotionally, morally. These first passages create a setting that allows the singer to contemplate the world around himself, and, perhaps for the first time in Morrison's music, to judge it. "I am the god of love and the god of hate," he sings—that is validated. As Morrison all but swallows the words, then lets them shudder in his mouth, it doesn't feel like a grand claim; it feels like what it means to be in the world.

Nearly all of the songs on *The Healing Game* stay on this plane. The melodies build on themselves until they communicate like rhythms; the rhythms, slow and weighted, create a feeling of a definite pace being kept, a pace of readiness. As with Gene Austin's unsettled, visionary 1928 "The Lonesome Road"—filled with specters from the oldest Appalachian ballads, and a backwoods, farmer's kin to "Old Man River," which appeared in the original theatrical production of *Show Boat* the year before*—it's the pace of someone who's seen almost everything, but who knows there might be someone

---

* When the movie version came out in 1929, the producers took no chances: Austin's song was right there too, with Jules Bledsoe's dubbed vocal coming out of Stepin Fetchit's mouth. Morrison recorded a colorless version in 1993.

waiting around the next turn. The volume is never raised. There's no shouting. There's a long walk ahead.

The tunes open up like stories you know in your heart but haven't thought of for years. This is soul music, with the passion of Frankie Laine's "That's My Desire" in 1947, the sadness rolling over a rock 'n' roll beat in Lloyd Price's "Lawdy Miss Clawdy" in 1952, the sympathy of Bobby Bland's "I'll Take Care of You" in 1959, the certainty of Irma Thomas's "Ruler of My Heart" in 1963, the sweep of Aretha Franklin's "Ain't No Way" in 1968, the refusal to walk a step faster or a step slower of Sinéad O'Connor's "Nothing Compares 2 U" in 1990—but without glamour, or even a hint of performance, of gestures extended or notes held for effect. The street this music moves on never disappears.

With "Waiting Game" and the title song, which comes last, *The Healing Game* kept company with Neil Jordan's 1992 film *The Crying Game*, that whole drama of Irish resistance, sexual uncertainty, murderous fate. It was Morrison's best work in more than twenty years. Go back to 1979, for *Into the Music*, a buoyant, serious, playful, blazingly ambitious testament—against *The Healing Game* it sounds thin, poppy, ephemeral, though it isn't remotely so when it's allowed to claim its own air. Morrison's records of the previous seventeen years fade into irrelevance against what he has to offer here. They don't even make sense.

The deep grounding of *The Healing Game* makes me think of the original Fleetwood Mac, the finest flowering of British blues, formed by Peter Green in 1967. As a blues guitarist, Green, who had earlier replaced Eric Clapton in John Mayall's Blues Breakers, had by 1970 been and gone from places—places in the heart, places in the blues—Clapton would never get to. Compared to Them, Fleetwood Mac was a purist band, in quest of the spirit of the Mississippi blues of the 1920s and '30s—though while Them was purist in its own way, in its refusal of the slightest suggestion of levity or even peace of mind, Fleetwood Mac made room for the most raucous rockabilly humor and mercilessly funny parodies of the British blues scene. It was a band of many parts—but while he remained Green was always its center. He played an occult blues, a fantasy blues, where in his most lucid songs and performances—in "Man of the World," "Long Grey Mare," "Albatross," "Trying So Hard to Forget," "Love That Burns," his guitar playing alone on "Something Inside of Me"—every element was slowed down and emotions appeared only to decay.

As a singer, he sang in his own voice. There was never any doubt that he was white and English—and, maybe, little doubt that he was Jewish. The remorse in his voice, you could think, wasn't for the love he'd lost or the life that failed him—the predicament that, sometime around the end of the nineteenth century, the blues was invented to affirm. It was a sorrow over his conviction that as a white Englishman the blues would always be out of his reach. It was that conviction, though, that sense of displacement, that made his blues ring so true: a conviction that in Green's highest moments gave the lie to itself. Over all the years I've listened to his "Love That Burns," trying to keep up with the tragedy it enacts, waiting for the closing guitar part that comes when words have taken the singer as far as they can, but not far enough, forcing him to leave words behind and plead with his bare hands, I don't think I've ever been able to play it twice in a row. It is just too strong.

Morrison came from a similar place, with the same belief in the blues as a kind of curse one puts on oneself, but for a long desert in his career he fled from it, his voice hollowing out along with the placid, reassuring world his music described. Sometimes he fell back before his masters and performed merely as a product of his influences, coming to life the most when he sang with John Lee Hooker; he reached his dead end, with album after album, when he seemed most of all influenced by himself. His music was all self-reference, until solipsism ruled and awarded its crown: the solipsist is always king of his own kingdom, and who willingly gives up a crown? All of that is left behind on *The Healing Game*; as a singer of confidence and pride, Morrison sometimes goes almost as far into the dark as Green did.

Morrison dominates each song on *The Healing Game*— but the word song seems much too small. Like the rough god he sings about, Morrison is astride each incident in the music, each pause in a greater story, but often the most revealing moments—the moments that reveal the shape of a world, a point of view, an argument about life—are at the margins. It might be Pee Wee Ellis's twisting saxophone, or the backing vocals of Katie Kissoon, or the side-singing of Georgie Fame, but each of them brings a certain realism to the setting. Morrison is the philosopher, the man of knowledge and experience; the others are the street he walks on. Ellis's work is too individualistic to rest as mere accompaniment—from the first minutes of *The Healing Game*, his baritone sax and Leo Green's tenor are part of a loose, casual interplay with

Morrison and the other singers, a conversation of asides and pointed fingers. He can make you forget you're listening to a self-evident, self-presenting master, and Morrison, often mumbling, sometimes stepping back from his own lines, as if to question himself, gives Ellis his room. Kissoon and Fame are slight singers, ordinary in every respect; they sing and talk like passers-by, like stand-ins for listeners. In the furious "Burning Ground," which is about getting rid of a body, it's clear who'll be doing the dirty work—Morrison wouldn't give up the pleasure to anyone else. Sounding as gleeful as the Kray Twins—the London gangsters who, with a plan to blackmail Brian Epstein over his homosexuality, supposedly once tried to take over management of the Beatles—Morrison orchestrates the action and gets the kicks. The listener gets to watch.

"I'm not going to fake it, like Johnny Ray," Morrison declaims in the middle of the otherwise unbroken, insistently measured "Sometimes We Cry." It's a cruel dismissal of a once-groundbreaking singer who died miserable and forgotten, just seven years before Morrison put another nail in his coffin—but there's such strength in Morrison's tone it can make you wonder what the cruelty is about.

It was in the early 1950s that Ray, with an emotionalism that was shocking in its nakedness, set the stage for the rock 'n' roll performers, black and white, Bobby Bland no less than Elvis, James Brown no less than David Bowie, who would follow him. "Sometimes We Cry" isn't casually titled—Ray's "Cry" was number one in 1951 for eleven weeks; the flipside, also a huge hit, was "The Little White Cloud That Cried." He was white, frail, with the energy of a dying man reaching out to grab your neck. "He'd hunch into himself," Nik Cohn wrote in 1969 in *Pop from the Beginning*,

choke on his words, gasp, stagger, beat his fist against his breast, squirm, fall forward on to his knees and, finally, burst into tears. He'd gag, tremble, half strangle himself. He'd pull out every last outrageous ham trick in the book and he would be comic, embarrassing, painful, but still it worked because, under the crap, he was in real agony, he was burning, and it was traumatic to watch him. He'd spew himself up in front of you and you'd freeze, you'd sweat, you'd be hurt yourself. You'd want to look away and you couldn't.

Even if it began as a show, the tears coming every night like Pete Townshend smashing his guitar, soon enough the desperation Ray sparked in his audience blew back at him, and some nights, in the face of the crowd, he would truly break down. Then his moment passed. His career collapsed with arrests in men's rooms and attempts to go straight, both musically and as a public figure. His obloquy wasn't far from that of Peter Green, who at the height of Fleetwood Mac's popularity walked away from the band into religious insanity, electroshock, institutionalization, years living on the streets or in the woods, returning finally with his guitar, his voice, and no spirit, no insight into the music he played, a once-handsome man covered in fat and matted hair. So how did Johnny Ray fake it? What was it that he held back? Was it that, exposed to everyone for who he really was, he tried to pretend he was just like everybody else—a pathetic surrender that was itself no less fake than his performance? Johnny Ray had an act, Morrison seemed to be saying, and

I don't. He tried to pretend that he was just like everybody else; I never have and never will.

In the interstices of *The Healing Game*, in the spaces between the words as Morrison sings them and the notes as he hits them, you can believe it. The depth and mastery of the music Morrison left on that album is such that, for me anyway, it calls up only one real familiar.

Mattie May Thomas was a prisoner at the state penitentiary in Parchman, Mississippi, when on 1 June 1939 the folklorist Herbert Halpert arrived to make recordings. Thomas and other women were gathered in a sewing room. "A made-up song, just about being in prison, alone," Thomas said to introduce what she, or Halpert, titled "Workhouse Blues." Was it made up? All the lines were commonplace, taken from the vast pool of floating verses from which people made their own songs. Thomas began around the time the blues took shape—"In the empty belly, black man, in the year nineteen hundred and nine, I was a little young hobo, all up and down the line"—and then leaped back to the brags, taunts, and japes that were circulating in Davy Crockett's day, a lot of them out of his mouth, or put in it:

> I wrassled with the lions, black man, with the lions on
>   the mountains high
> I pulled they hair out, black man, hair out strand by
>   strand
> Leaping spiders, lord, began to bite my poor heart
> But let me tell you, baby, they crawled away and died
> I wrassled with the hounds, black man, hounds of hell
>   all day

I squeeze them so tight, until they faded away
I swim the blue sea, with the mountains on my back
I mean I conquered all the lions and I even turned they
    power back

Whoever Mattie May Thomas was, she was not a folk singer, in any meaning of the term.* Coming out of white frontier settlements, the words were men's words; simply by claiming what is not supposed to be hers, she takes title. That is the folk process. But the voice is not. It's plainly a professional voice, a nightclub singer's, "the devil coming out of

---

* Along with "Dangerous Blues," "Big Mac from Macamere," and "No Mo' Freedom," Mattie May Thomas's "Workhouse Blues" appeared in 2005 on *American Primitive II—Pre-War Revenants*, a collection of 1920s and '30s recordings by performers about whom almost nothing was known. A few years later, as entranced by Thomas as I'd been when I first heard her, it occurred to me that the general release of her songs might have sparked someone—a relative, a neighbor, a friend of a 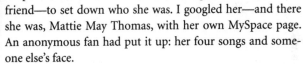 friend—to set down who she was. I googled her—and there she was, Mattie May Thomas, with her own MySpace page. An anonymous fan had put it up: her four songs and someone else's face.
The fan turned out to be the Greek techno artist who records as Biomass, who later posted videos of his reworkings of Thomas's music. Each takes a Thomas performance and cuts it up, loops it, shuffles words and phrases, repeats them in stuttering echo, adds clicks and hum and whine, and sets it against footage of conflict: a tank speeding through the Iraqi desert; heavily armed police driving back Italian protesters; what might be film from the Vietnam War. Most striking is a piece that opens with split-second flashes of people running separated by much longer segments of black screen. As it goes on, the moments of action imperceptibly lengthen, until you begin to realize you're watching the riots in Paris during May 1968. The glimpses of people and streets accumulate, building a tension to the point of explosion, all to

your own mouth":* clear, strong, claiming its own demons, using folkloric words to affirm that the frights and triumphs they describe happened to her and no one else. Like Morrison, Thomas presses words like bricks, then flies over verses toward some unreachable shore of release.

Emotional release, for both, but for Thomas standing for true release, from prison, and that release symbolizing the shared slaves' dream, shared as fable and prophecy, of flying back to Africa. For Morrison, his own dreams of a Viking's voyage from Denmark to Caledonia and then a magic transport from the old world to the new and back again with ancient songs for a skyway. But if both voices are unique and capable of transcendence, Thomas not at all and Morrison at his fair best never jettison the ordinary, the inescapable, the

---

Thomas as if she's looking back on the event, not forward to it, not on some other plane of being, her voice carrying "No mo' freedom" as students throw stones, rush forward, burn cars, are beaten, and even when as a comment on the ameliorating powers of modern capitalism they are replaced by three black women in a nightclub, dressed in furry bikinis and doing the limbo—one of the women giving Thomas the face she now bears.

As I write, you page down to Thomas's 134 MySpace friends, including Nina Simone, Pablo Neruda, Miles Davis, Patti Smith, Sun Ra, Jack Kerouac, Alicia Keys, Janis Joplin, Suicide, James Brown, and Guy Debord, whose 1973 film *La Société du Spectacle* is the clear inspiration for Biomass's "No Mo' Freedom" video. It's something to contemplate: What if these people, almost all of them dead, really had heard Mattie May Thomas? What if those living still haven't? How lucky they are to have that ahead of them.

* A mother's curse on her blues-singing daughter, from Gayl Jones's *Corregidora* (New York: Bantam, 1976).

squalid, the real. For both, it's all in the refusal to be rushed. Ordinary life, after all, guarantees only death and oblivion. Morrison has faced oblivion; though she is almost certainly dead, somehow Mattie May Thomas escaped it, and Morrison may not. In their tone they both say the same thing. Death has waited all these years; it can wait another day.

Nik Cohn, *Awopbopaloobop Alopbamboom*, revised edition of *Pop from the Beginning* (1969; New York: Grove, 1973), 13–14.

"Crime Leaders Kray Twins Schemed to Take Over as the Beatles' Managers," *Entertainment Daily*, 21 June 2009.

Sex Pistols, "Anarchy in the UK" (EMI, 1976).

John Lennon, John & Yoko/Plastic Ono Band, "Sunday Bloody Sunday" and "The Luck of the Irish," on *Some Time in New York City* (Apple, 1972).

Gang of Four, "Armalite Rifle" (Fast, 1978).

Gene Austin, "The Lonesome Road" (1928) collected on *Gene Austin—The Voice of the Southland* (ASV, 1996). Gene Austin's number one hits between 1925 and 1929 included songs that for good or ill have stuck in the American memory: "Yes Sir! That's My Baby," "Five Foot Two, Eyes of Blue," "Forgive Me," "My Blue Heaven," "Ramona," and "Carolina Moon." "The Lonesome Road" reached #10; I have never played it for anyone, over eighty or under twenty, who didn't drift off to another place while listening, or who failed to say "What was *that?*" when it was over. Judy Garland and Bobby Darin performed a bright and soulful version on *The Judy Garland Show*, taped and broadcast just eight days after the assassination of President Kennedy; see *The Judy Garland Show That Got Away* (Hip-O DVD, 2002).

Fleetwood Mac, "Albatross," "Long Gray Mare," "Love That Burns," "Trying So Hard to Forget," (1968), and "Man of the World" (1969), collected on *The Original Fleetwood Mac—The Blues Years* (Castle, 1990). Green's work on Fleetwood Mac member Danny Kirwan's "Something Inside of Me" is best heard on Fleetwood Mac's *Shrine '69*, a live recording from Los Angeles (Rykodisc, 1999).

Johnny Ray, *Cry* (Bear Family, 1990). A definitive collection, including "Cry," "The Little White Cloud That Cried" (1951), and Ray's hit cover of the Prisonaires' "Just Walkin' in the Rain" (1955).

Mattie May Thomas, "Workhouse Blues" (1939), on *American Primitive Vol. II—Pre-War Revenants (1897–1939)* (Revenant, 2005). Information on Herbert Halpert in Scott Baretta, "The Parchman Prison Band: From the Cruelest Place on Earth Came Music," Oxford American #58 (2007).

Biomass, *Market* (Quetempo, Greece, 2006). A CD/DVD that includes both audio and video versions of Mattie May Thomas performances, though the piece for "Workhouse Blues" is here all action, no blackout.

Van Morrison, "The Lonesome Road," on *Too Long in Exile* (Polydor, 1993).

———*The Healing Game* (Polydor, 1997).

PART FOUR

THERE WAS NO FALSE FACE THE SONG COULD NOT ERASE

INTO THE MUSIC. 1979

It was Morrison's last album before his long swan dive into the pool of contemplation, and it raises a question that all the moments of freedom musicians have contributed to Morrison's own pursuit of freedom—Richard Davis's bass on *Astral Weeks*, Jef Labes's piano on "Linden Arlen Stole the Highlights," John Platania's mandolin on "Caledonia Soul Music"—only hint at: is the greatest creative freedom in making a field where others can find it?

This album had Van Morrison's name on it, but it belonged to Toni Marcus, credited on violin, viola, stroviola, and mandolin. Today as Talia Toni Marcus she leads her own jam band; she has fourteen MySpace friends. On *Into the Music*, as it moved out across its fifty minutes, it was an open question whether Morrison was granting freedom to her or if she was granting it to him.

It's a strange album for 1979. Like the old *Oldies But Goodies* albums, it has a "Rockin' Side" and a "Dreamy Side," and one of the songs on the Dreamy Side is a song that actually appeared on the Dreamy Side of an *Oldies But Goodies* album. The first two numbers—"Bright Side of the Road" and "Full Force Gale"—are the most immediately arresting; they fade against what follows. Both have quick rhythms and dashing melodies. On "Bright Side of the Road," near the end, Morrison begins to growl the lines, making himself into a bear, and Marcus swoops over him and then digs into the song. She adds a fervor, a seriousness, that Morrison is dancing away from; he picks up on it, and for a second his words are on the verge of breaking up entirely. Then it's back to a clean wrap-up: you want more.

With "Full Force Gale" everything is tougher from the first beat, and Marcus is on top of the music from the start. It takes Morrison time to catch up with the song—it seems to know things he doesn't. There's a light guitar solo, shadowed by Marcus's violin, and then she picks up the pace and for an instant, before Morrison returns, the tune finds a hardness, again a feeling of conviction, that was missing. But there's a way that even as the beat seems harder and urgency greater, the song drags against itself. It's a void in the music that took over entirely when in 1996 Morrison re-recorded the song as if its message were being delivered by a procession of defeated—or not very interested—old men shuffling down the street in heavy overcoats: "Like a full force gale. I was lifted up again. I was lifted up again. By the Lord."

The Rockin' Side is really rocking with "Stepping Out Queen." It's pleasant enough as Morrison sings it, but even he

seems to know how it will double in size when he turns it over
to Marcus; it's there in the sense of announcement when he
simply says, "Alright." The word carries a colon: what opens up
is a labyrinth, and within seconds you can't find your feet. You
can't tell where the music's coming from, whether it's one piece
or four, whether it's a human being playing or a Hindu god
with eight hands. Marcus's violin dives for the song, and her
viola counters the rush with an elegance you want to pause
with. The violin presses its demands, but all along there's been
a screech in the background, and now as it rises little notes like
birds flutter around it, to cage it, failing as the sound goes into
the territory first broken by John Cale's viola in "Heroin"—
which now is also the sound of a woman getting dressed.

Here it's clearly Morrison opening the doors of his songs
to another musician, giving her the spotlight until he has to
take it back. But on the Dreamy Side that changes.

"And the Healing Has Begun" is one of Morrison's signature songs—but at its heart it is his, a book of desires he
can embrace without shame, because he has passed it on to
someone else. It begins with confidence, a lack of fear. With a
bend toward the past that would turn up such riches nearly
thirty years later with "Behind the Ritual," the singer promises that he and the woman he's singing to will go back to the
avenue they once knew and that once knew them. They'll get
out those *Oldies But Goodies* albums; they'll "sing a song
from way back when." This is a man walking down the street
with wings on his feet, who can't wait, who's consumed by
the vision in front of him: her red dress. She's got to wear it.
But then for a long passage the song all but breaks off, and
for what seems like minutes Toni Marcus allows Morrison to

do almost nothing, to get lost in his own song, to wander away from it, certain it will be there when he gets back. For chorus after chorus she's the first voice of the song, pushing it with her violin into a realm of pure freedom, where anything can be said but nothing needs to be. "Alright," Morrison says. "Yeah." "Whoo"—and Marcus presses on, all but sawing her arm off. Morrison comes back stronger, inspired, ready to reclaim the song. "That backstreet rock 'n' roll," he says, "that's where it comes from, man," with *it* morally enormous, everything he or you might ever care about—and the honesty in the way he says it is overwhelming, a truth he finally feels free to let loose in the air. Marcus is merely accompaniment. Then she seems captured by the song, and she shoots out ahead of the singer, and he calls a halt. "Wait a minute, baby—listen, listen, listen, listen"—and he's not talking to her, and he's not talking to the woman who's going to put on the red dress.

There's a woman on the street. He stops her. He starts chatting her up, inveigling himself into her apartment. It's "Gloria" in reverse, and with the insistence of that opening "Gloria" riff—someone running down the street and banging on every door he passes—replaced by a man talking, hesitating, and less to seduce her than to seduce himself. For everything has to be exactly right: she has to move behind the door. "Ah, move on up this, ah, letter box here." He wants to play a Muddy Waters record he's found in her apartment. "Come on in for some of this backstreet jelly roll," he says, as if bowing back to Muddy, and with that the woman disappears. His tone is all low vowels, as if he's talking to himself, as if this is all happening in his head. Marcus has been there all along, simply repeating the theme of the song, and when Morrison again rises up with a celebratory chant, the first woman back again in her red dress, it's the one-night stand back there in the song that stays.

Merely as a story, "It's All in the Game" is in the all-time top ten. It began as a violin piece by one John G. Dawes, born in 1865 in Ohio, a financier and amateur musician who one day in 1911 stumbled on what he called "Melody in A Major": "It's just a tune that I got in my head, so I set it down." A friend got it published; it stayed alive, even as Dawes went on to a career as a civic activist, forming an alliance to fight the growing influence of the Ku Klux Klan in Ohio, Michigan, and the Midwest, in 1925 sharing the Nobel Peace Prize for helping to revive the German economy after the First World War, then serving as vice president of the United States under Calvin Coolidge from 1925 to 1929.

In 1951 a journeyman songwriter named Carl Sigman decided to take a crack at what he knew as "The Dawes Melody"; with words, with a narrower range, he heard a hit. Working with Mac Goldman of Warner Bros. Music, which owned Dawes's composition, Sigman brought in his word sheet the day Dawes died. "Your lyric must have killed him," Goldman said.

> Many a tear has to fall
> But it's all
> In the game
> All in the wonderful game
> That we know
> As love

You have words
With him
And you future's
Looking dim
But these things
You heart can rise
Above

Once in a while he won't call
But it's all
In the game
Soon he'll be there at your side
With a sweet
Bouquet
And he'll kiss
Your lips
And caress your waiting fingertips
And your hearts
Will fly
Away*

The song went first to Tommy Edwards, a nightclub crooner. His recording went to #18—an almost meaningless success. In those days very few records were released with a chance at certified national popularity—most country or rhythm and blues records were excluded in advance. Almost anything

---

* Sigman also wrote a spoken introduction: "Remember this: Where love's concerned, at times you'll think your world has overturned. But if he's yours, and you're his, remember this—"

backed by a major label—Edwards was on RCA—made the top twenty, at least for a week, after which it would be covered by a dozen other people. In those days, there weren't that many songs respectable enough for the likes of Dinah Shore, or even Louis Armstrong, both of whom immediately cut their own "It's All in the Game." Edwards's version was paltry: waltz time, Rimsky-Korzakov strings that seem to come from another room, they have so little to do with the song. Edwards seems to be rehearsing—there's that much heart in his delivery. Within his smooth tone, he doesn't seem to know or care what the song might say, and it dies a third of the way in.

By 1958, Edwards was on the skids. Rock 'n' roll had put his career in the toilet. Singers like Fats Domino and Little Richard and Chuck Berry and a nation's worth of other people who couldn't fit into Edwards's tuxedo and wouldn't deign to were writing their own songs and they owned the charts. So he gave in. He redid "It's All in the Game" with a doo-wop arrangement: a doo-wop backing chorus, more importantly strolling doo-wop piano triplets, a light guitar, strings buried. But it was the vocal that this time made "It's All in the Game" Carl Sigman's biggest hit, Tommy Edwards's biggest hit, a huge number one hit, and in the twists of American history, the one reason John G. Dawes is still spoken of: you argue, he turns his back, you wait, once in a while he won't call, but it's all in the game, that wonderful game we call love, and then he's back, with a smile, flowers, in Sigman's best and most unlikely line, "to caress your waiting fingertips"—and Edwards offers the tale in sadness, regret, as if he's been through this many times and it's too late for him but he's going to pass on what knowledge he's gleaned to you.

It became a standard, done over the years by Bobby Bland, Jackie DeShannon, Elton John—and in 1964, in England, by Cliff Richard. When Van Morrison takes it up, he's right back in the middle of "And the Healing Has Begun." It's barely a performance; it seems to resist taking any shape at all.

"Uhhh—yeah—*yeah*"—he's feeling his way around the song. "Alright." "Whoo. Yeah." He's arguing with the lyric, looking for something that moves him—and "Your future's looking dim," the song's cheapest line, doesn't. But then he finds a place for himself: "Once in a while he won't call—but I heard you." He breaks the song down, into spaces where he can touch what the man in the song is touching: "Just like that." But when Morrison says, "And your heart will—*yeah*—fly away," the last two words are so small, like fireflies, that in their lightness the song takes on an emotional weight it's never had before, in all of its long life. And there's a seductive curl he puts on those two words. The yarragh was just a sound back on that first number, in the growls of "Bright Side of the Road," but now, with Morrison deepening the old song, it's a whisper, and a spell. As with everyone who came before him, Morrison is the witness, the guide, the narrator, but like nobody else he steps into the song as its ghost lover.

Tommy Edwards, "It's All in the Game" (RCA Victor, 1951, 1958). 1958 version included on *Oldies But Goodies, Vol. 7* (Original

Sound, 1963), along with (Rockin' Side) "Tequila" by the Champs, "New Orleans" by Gary (U.S.) Bonds, "Runaround Sue" by Dion, "I Know" by Barbara George, "Handy Man" by Jimmy Jones, "Bumble Boogie" by B. Bumble and the Stingers, and (Dreamy Side) "I Love How You Love Me" by the Paris Sisters, "Donna" by Ritchie Valens, "Teen Angel" by Mark Dinning, the Chimes' "Once in a While," and Jerry Butler's "He Will Break Your Heart." The 1951 version is not included on any Tommy Edwards collections but can be found on YouTube; see below.

Carl Sigman Songs (MajorSongs, 2003). Produced by the unmatchable Gregg Geller, a three-disc collection of recordings of Sigman's compositions, including numbers by, among many others, Count Basie with Helen Humes, Benny Goodman with Helen Forrest, Mildred Bailey, Louis Armstrong, Billie Holiday, Louis Prima, Frank Sinatra (including "Ebb Tide"), Dean Martin, Ella Fitzgerald, the Angels, Cilla Black, Shirley Bassey, Peggy Lee ("Shangri La"), Aretha Franklin, Esther Phillips, Ben E. King, the Righteous Brothers ("Ebb Tide" again, and a hit again), Sonny and Cher, Darlene Love ("It's a Marshmallow World," produced by Phil Spector for the 1963 *A Christmas Gift for You*), Tom Jones, Sarah Vaughan, Jerry Lee Lewis, Joni Mitchell, and the Specials, with "It's All in the Game" by Tommy Edwards (both versions), Morrison, the Four Tops, and Merle Haggard.

Van Morrison, "Full Force Gale" (1996), included on *Catalog Strays 1965–2000* (Wild Card bootleg).

———*Into the Music* (Warner Bros., 1979).

FRIDAY'S CHILD. 1971

In 1994, for a Van Morrison tribute album that Morrison himself co-produced, the fine British soul singer Lisa Stansfield took up "Friday's Child," a song Morrison cut with Them in its last days, a recording that went unreleased at the time. It was a brave choice; the song defeated her. She hit all the right notes and made none of them stick. Backing singers repeated Stansfield's "Don't stop" in staccato, "Don't! Stop!" as if for emphasis, but all they did was stop the music; when they repeated "Friday's child, Friday's child," their plug-in tone made whatever Stansfield had done that seemed real feel fake. The soul tricks Stansfield used—pauses meant to spark a sense of suspense that collapsed instantly into melo-drama, moans, high murmurs to herself, as if to indicate an emotion too rich to communicate directly—came across as tricks. Nevertheless, there was something instructive, even interesting, about what Stansfield had done with the song:

you could catch the words. "Monday's child is fair of face / Tuesday's child is full of grace / Wednesday's child is full of woe / Thursday's child has far to go / Friday's child is loving and giving"—in this song, heedlessly. Stansfield told the song's story: a cautionary tale for someone who burns up the ground behind himself or herself, sleeps with anyone who gives them the eye, stays up all night drinking and doping, and trusts everyone who takes everything he can steal.

When Morrison sang it the song was its own wind; as its own wind it blew its own words away. With Them, Morrison was tentative; still, after a verse, the wind began to rise, and a passion far too great for any words to contain was on the horizon. It never got any closer, but it made you lean toward it emotionally, wanting to know what it knew, even if the words "You got something, they all want to know" ("You got something, they don't want to know," in Stansfield's one fascinating moment) had already gone right past you. "You can't stop now," Morrison sang in 1966, for the first time unfurling a flag he would wave for years to come at the end of his shows, but it had nothing to fight against.

At Pacific High Studios in San Francisco five years later a performance is about to erupt that will make "Just Like a Woman" into a warm-up, even if, this night, "Friday's Child" came first. There's a fanfare on the piano, then a military drum roll before Morrison takes hold of the song. Because the song is yet to really begin you do hear the first words, but they are so big for a beginning, so full of a quest that could be taking place at any time and could go anywhere, the words sung with such fervor that a whole, huge map of the world might appear before you as you hear them—

> From the north
> To the south
> You walked all the way

—the words don't necessarily register. The verse proceeds, still nothing but piano and drums, but as if they've doubled themselves, the pressure increasing, the warning the song was written to be emerging in the shape of its own body, so that when a guitarist begins to count toward the looming chorus, and then backing singers dig down deep for what it will take to match Morrison's own leaping incantations, they seem to have been there all along. What happens now, as a trombone plays off the bass drum to make a single instrument, a single crumbling wall, is frightening—this is a warning so strong it has rushed right by its subject, that person who was all so ready for the world he or she walked all the way, to take on the world as such. And you know you're in for it.

In *Control*, Anton Corbijn's 2007 film about the late-1970s Manchester band Joy Division, the four young men take the stage for the first time, the actors themselves playing and singing—and when they finished "Transmission" I realized half a minute had gone by and I hadn't taken a breath. What Sam Reilly as the singer Ian Curtis had done with his face even more than his voice was as shocking as anything I'd ever seen on a screen.

That's what happens here. The out-of-nowhere assaults in "Just Like a Woman," those split-second explosions of rancor and desire, will here be the whole song.

The ensemble drops back, again leaving only the piano player and the drummer, but its arrival was so thrilling it remains as a shadow, a threat that could return at any time. A saxophonist has begun to noodle behind Morrison, like someone wandering in from another room, too stoned to notice he's barged into someone else's song. "You got," Morrison shouts, his volume high, a sense of abandon pushing against his control of every word, the tension between abandon and control turning each word into a bomb, with the feeling that the singer is himself frightened by his own words, "to hold on,"

> Hold
>
> Hold
>
> Hold
>
> Hold
>
> Hold
>
> Hold
>
> Hold it—

The second chorus clamps down, the desperation in the title phrase so intense you can't imagine where it is that's left to go. Everyone pulls back—and inexplicably, as if maybe each and every one of them has gone as far as they can (maybe everyone needs a drink, needs a cigarette), they leave the song to the saxophonist.

It might be the worst instrumental break in the history of the form. Meandering, tripping over his own feet, bumping into the amplifiers, hitting sour notes again and again, the saxophonist takes you out of the song, out of the music, out of the building, into the street, and not up to your room with Gloria following to knock on your door as soon as you've closed it, merely back to your car, which has a smashed right window and a ticket on the windscreen.

But a certain gravity has already made itself felt; you can't see it, you can't necessarily feel it even if you try to call it back, but as soon as the band returns it's as if it never left. They begin right where they left off, at the edge of the same cliff; if anything they're closer to the edge. As Morrison presses on, the guitarist begins to chime, quietly, tiny high notes building toward a finale that is already present as an inevitability, a presence that already gainsays whatever might be left to be said.

The chiming gets louder. Morrison begins to pound single words, one sequence after another. "Even even even even even" shoots out like white water, but "Watch it! Watch it! Watch it!" pulls against the momentum of the band—it couldn't be more sudden or complete if Morrison were holding up the flat of his hand. In the drama in which Morrison has trapped you, at first it might seem that he's doing this to forestall the fate of the person to whom the song is addressed: to save her, to save him. But as soon as that thought appears, if it does, it turns on itself. What you're hearing is the singer's rage that it's too late, his bitterness that no one listened, no one heard, that it didn't have to end this way.

They reach the chorus again. It goes on, doubled, tripled, "You can't stop, you can't stop, you can't stop now," the backing singers turning a somersault, "Can't stop now, can't stop now, Friday's child," for a full minute and a half, and it's transporting, but it doesn't matter. The song had already ended, back there in the middle of the curse, the singer pleading with his charge to hold on to what she or he had, knowing he or she had already given it away.

There's applause. Morrison goes right into "Que Sera, Sera"—"I asked my mother, what shall I be"—which turns out to be an introduction to "Hound Dog."

Control, dir. Anton Corbijn (2007; Genius DVD, 2008).

Lisa Stansfield, "Friday's Child," on *No Prima Donna: The Songs of Van Morrison* (Polydor, 1994).

Them, "Friday's Child," collected on *The Story of Them Featuring Van Morrison* (Polydor, 1998).

Van Morrison, "Friday's Child," on *The Inner Mystic: Recorded Live at Pacific High Studios, California, Sept. 1971* (Oh Boy/ Odyssey bootleg of complete Pacific High Studios concert, as broadcast 1971 on KSAN-FM, San Francisco).

MADAME GEORGE. 1968

"**W**ith a record as evocative as *Astral Weeks*," Josh Gleason said to Van Morrison in 2009, for a high-profile NPR piece on the occasion of the release of *Astral Weeks Live at the Hollywood Bowl*, "there's a nagging desire to understand what in your life inspired it—to know where the songs come from, what they mean."

"No, no, no, because, it's not *about* me," Morrison said with a vehemence that didn't sound defensive—as his denials, of anything, so often do. "It's totally fictional. These are *short stories*, in musical form—put together of composites, of conversations I heard, things I saw, and movies, newspapers, books, and *comes out* as stories. That's it," he said, though already his tone had shifted to that of utter wonder that people won't accept this. "There's no more."

It wasn't the first time he'd had to answer the question, which he'd never done in a manner anyone liked. "Did you have anyone in particular in mind?" the folk singer Happy Traum asked Morrison in 1970; it was Morrison's first *Rolling Stone* interview. "Did you know anyone like that?" "Like what?" Morrison said, his guard up in an instant. "What's Madame George look like? What are you trying to say . . . in front. So I know." "It seems to me to be the story of a drag queen," Traum said reasonably. "Oh no," Morrison said. "Whatever gave you that impression? It all depends on what you want, that's all, how you want to go. If you see it as a male or a female or whatever, it's your trip. How do see it? I see it as a . . . a Swiss cheese sandwich." "Everybody gives me a quizzical look, a question mark stare, and they think I know what they're talking about," Morrison said after a moment, stepping back, trying to explain. "'What about like blah blah blah . . .' and they expect me to go 'Yeah!' It's just not that simple."

Eight years later he was again talking to *Rolling Stone*, this time with Jonathan Cott, whose technique as an interviewer has always been to elicit the most direct responses by throwing out the most off-the-wall questions, usually asking his subjects if they agreed with the sentiments expressed by, say, the Hasidic rabbi Dov Baer, "the Mazid of Mezeritch." In this instance Cott stayed closer to home: "A friend of mine thinks Madame George is a perfume—you sing the name as 'Madame Joy,' and then there's that scent of Shalimar." "It seems to me to be the story of a drag queen," Morrison said, as if he were Happy Traum and Cott were Morrison, except that he was laughing, and despite the fact that he had already told someone else that Cott's friend might as well claim the prize: "The original title was 'Madame Joy' but the way I wrote it down was 'Madame George.' Don't ask me why I do this because I just don't know." "The question is," Cott went on, missing a step, "who's singing the song?" "The question might really be," Morrison said, in a friendly manner, but with a gesture toward another plane of meaning that could not have been more pronounced if he'd knocked the writer's notepad out of his hand, "is the song singing you?"

This was nearly three decades before the one-time rock critic Tom Nolan—perhaps following Morrison's suggestion to his biographer John Collis that "Madame George" might have had something to do with his great-aunt Joy, who he, Morrison, thought might have been clairvoyant—argued for the *Wall Street Journal* that Madame George was in truth George "Georgie" Hyde-Lees, the wife of William Butler Yeats, known conventionally as Madame George Yeats, who died in 1968, the year "Madame George" appeared. She was a spiritualist who sparked Yeats's work with automatic writing dictated by the dead, a technique Morrison, who in 1984 recorded Yeats's "Crazy Jane on God" in a cracked voice, has used when blocked, cutting up copies of *People* magazine, rearranging parts of headlines and text, divining a line for a song . . . and never mind that the given name of both Van Morrison and his father is George. If the character cannot be permitted to be made up, if it must be real—to borrow a phrase from another Irishman, well, as well her as another.

The tyranny of tying anything an artist might do or say to his or her own life, to give it the weight of the real, and switch off the lights on the weightlessness of the imagination—a philistine fear of art that found its most spectacular form in the JT Leroy hoax, which only seemed to convince people that while taking fiction for autobiography remained the highest form of understanding, it was worth making sure that the person whose autobiography one was plumbing actually existed—was summed up all too well by John Irving in 1979. We were talking about the scene in *The World According to Garp* where Garp's son Walt is killed, and about the many readers who'd written to him, saying, "I lost a child, too"— believing that any story that hit them so hard had to be true. "How do you respond to those letters?" I asked him. "Do you have any answer to those letters?" "I always answer those letters," he said. "Those are the serious ones; those are the ones that matter."

I have had two or three friends who went through that, and their reactions were very matterful to me—and I guess the letters that I really felt drawn to respond to were those from people who, in that old way, again, would write me one letter, *assuming* that this had to be my experience, too. And when I would write back—sort of a condolence and a thank-you for responding to the book—I felt I had to *say*, no, this is not my misfortune. Then I developed a number of ways of saying, well, it's enough to have had children to imagine what it would be like to lose them. But this, of course, assumes an imagination of immense paranoia on the part of everyone, which everyone may not have.

I found people writing back to me a second time, some of them unable to conceal their resentment: they felt tricked. They felt they had been *taken in* by the book. They came to the book with open arms, saying this is genuine, this is true, that hurt in all the real ways—and then to find out that it was only imagined—

I *live* by my imagination, and yet even I can be influenced by how the imagination is mistrusted by the rest of the world, by the way fiction is discredited by *non*-fiction. I've been on airplanes and people say, "Hi, Ken, Kansas City, what do you do?" I say, "Oh, I write." "Oh, what do you write?" "Novels." "Oh, ah, *fiction* . . . " Immediately: you know what I mean! It's just this *shitting on from the word go.*

In Mary Gaitskill's novel *Two Girls Fat and Thin*, a writer takes up the challenge of imagining whole worlds out of glimpses, out of a walk down the street:

The evening was cool and vague. Justine watched everyone who walked past her, and irksome tiny acts about them entered her orbit and clustered about her head. A young couple approached her, the man with his square pink head raised as if he were looking over a horizon, his hands thrust angrily in his pockets, his slightly turned-out feet hitting the ground with dismal solidity, his cheap jacket open to his cheap shirt. The woman on his arm crouched into him slightly, her artificially curled hair bounded around her prematurely lined face, her pink mouth said, "Because it's dishonest to me and to everybody and even yourself." Justine looked headlong into the open maw of their lives; they passed, and the pit closed up again.

It doesn't matter if Gaitskill actually walked down a street where someone said the words that in her paragraph appear in quotation marks. A moment this closely observed has already gone beyond the limits of observation; it is already imagined. That is why any talk of the real, the lived, the experienced as a legitimation or validation of aesthetic response—really, nothing more than a permission for us to be moved by what we are in fact moved by—is a red herring at best. There are only two reasons people try to track Ma-

dame George down, to link her to a real person: because the
character is itself powerful, full of allure, and because of our
own fear of the imagination, our fear that we are vulnerable
to some trifle somebody else merely thought up. But Morrison's translation is better: are you letting the song sing you,
or are you trying to sing the song?

So let your imagination open up and drift. Let Madame
George tell you who she is. Who do you think of? I think of
Michael Jackson. I think of Marianne Faithfull, telling the
same sixties stories—the sixties as the New Jerusalem, and
she its consort, mother, and Merlin—over and over again,
always with a glamour that is both grimy from use and full
of its own imperious light, qualities you can hear in Faithfull's own recording of "Madame George." I think of the
mother of one of my eighth-grade classmates. With her
daughter as a front, she would hold parties for the class, fifteen of us from a Quaker school on the San Francisco Pen-
insula. She was the first bohemian I ever encountered: a
single mother, when that was strange, if not a scandal, who
dressed in silk, in long, loose dresses. She was heavily made
up. While she never gave us alcohol, it was all around, fancy
bottles displayed on tables and in cabinets, like a hint of future pleasures, and she always seemed drunk. She showed us
her gun. She seemed to need to be around young people. At
thirteen in 1958 this was seductive—and a relief to leave behind, to move on to high school, where, a few years later,
one or two of my new classmates found their way to Ken
Kesey's acid farm, just up the road in La Honda, as she
might have also, unless she faded away, chasing her own
daughter's youth until it too was used up.

Morrison first recorded "Madame George" for Bert Berns's Bang label in November 1967, as *Blowin' Your Mind!* was climbing its way to #182 on the charts—a version not released until long after Berns's death, and until long after the song, as it appeared on *Astral Weeks*, had achieved the kind of hermetic glow that transcends fame. Here it's a production, as if at a party or a nightclub, with dead-end ambiance. Morrison is sarcastic, even sneering; behind him the Sweet Emotions do "the colored girls go" exactly as Lou Reed always heard it. The people in the audience, if this is a club, or on the couches and in the kitchen or in the doorways if it's an apartment, are distracted, ignoring the singer, everyone talking and drinking. There's bass, tambourine, and an electric guitar playing stripper blues like something out of the roadhouse scene in *Twin Peaks: Fire Walk with Me*, where women wander through the crowd naked and the floor is covered with a layer of cigarette butts that except for the dancers' feet hasn't been disturbed since the place opened. Morrison fights for space, draping cool over himself like an overcoat. It's as if he needs to satirize the material to protect himself from it—or to protect the song from the crowd, which is to say the producer. "Then your self-control lets go / Suddenly you're up against the bathroom door," he says in lines that would be gone by the time he sat down with Connie Kay, Richard Davis, Lewis Merenstein. The crowd is egging him on, then yelling and shrieking. The music is busy and burdened. "We know you're pretty far out," Morrison says, as if his stand-up act is just about to completely dry up, as if all he's really doing is schmoozing music business hustlers, as if he'd rather be anywhere else. "I've got a tape in Belfast with all my songs on that record"—from *Blowin' Your Mind!*—"done the way they're supposed to be done," he said after a show in early 1969, at the Avalon Ballroom in San Francisco. That night his own acoustic guitar completed a combo of a stand-up bassist and the *Astral Weeks* hornman John Payne; Morrison sang every song from *Astral Weeks* along with "Who Drove the Red Sports Car" and "He Ain't Give You None" from *Blowin' Your Mind!* which now took on drifting, *Astral Weeks* rhythms. "It's good and simple, it doesn't come on heavy. 'T. B. Sheets' isn't heavy, it's just quiet. It was the producer who did it, and the record company. They had to cover it with the big electric guitar and the drums and the rest. It came out wrong and they released it without my consent."

Morrison and Berns had been fighting over the record, and everything else—*Blowin' Your Mind!* advances eaten up by expenses, royalties deferred against returns, management contracts, publishing contracts, production contracts—when Berns dropped dead of a heart attack at the end of 1967. There were people who thought Morrison had yelled him to death. There were threats from people who knew how to make good on them,* and there was the demand from Berns's widow that Morrison produce the thirty-six new

---

* A photo taken at a Bang Records launch party for Morrison—a launch party held on a boat—shows a tipsy Morrison, a beaming Janet Planet, the Brill Building songwriter and Berns associate Jeff Barry, Berns himself as a ringer for Gene Vincent, and a big man with a bigger cigar sticking out of his mouth like a screwdriver—the most mobbed-up-looking picture of the New York record business I've ever seen.

songs he had owed Berns's publishing company, and that he now owed her.

Thus one day in 1968, not long before he began recording *Astral Weeks*, in order to escape his contracts with Berns and retrieve the freedom to record again on his own terms,* Morrison sat down with his guitar and Lewis Merenstein and taped thirty-one numbers, seemingly in approximately the thirty-five minutes it takes to play them: "Twist and Shake," "Shake and Roll," "Stomp and Scream," "Scream and Holler," and "Jump and Thump," five variations on Berns's Isley Brothers hit "Twist and Shout"; "Hang On Groovy," a flip of the bird to Berns's hit "Hang On Sloopy" with the McCoys; the likes of "Just Ball," "Ringworm," "Blow in Your Nose," "Nose in Your Blow," "You Say France and I Whistle," "I Want a Danish," and "The Big Royalty Check." But there are two performances that don't parody themselves. One is "Goodbye George," if only for the stately "Like a Rolling Stone" chords that open it. "Goodbye, George," Morrison sings soulfully. "Here comes—" The song seems about to turn into a farewell to Berns himself—until "Here comes" is followed not by "the night" but "number forty-five, in Argentina."

But with the next cut, "Dum Dum George," the melody of "Madame George" as it would emerge on *Astral Weeks* is instantly and completely in place. This and the real song begin in the same mood, with the same count—even if

---

* While agreeing to include two Berns estate–owned compositions, which turned out to be "Madame George" and "Beside You," a version of which Morrison had also recorded with Berns, on any new album.

Morrison is dismissing Lewis Merenstein's entreaties before either had the chance to make anything more of them than this. "This is the story of Dum Dum George," Morrison says as the theme continues. "Who came up to Boston, one sunny afternoon"—and there is that "Madame George" minor-key drop. "He drove up from New York City . . . and he was freaky. And he wanted to record me. And I said, 'George, you're dumb.' And he said, 'I know. Why do you think I make so much money? I want to do . . . a record . . . that'll make number one.' Dumb dumb." Ilene Berns listened to the tape and let the other five compositions Morrison owed her slide.

It's spooky to hear the song find its voice ahead of the moment when that voice would take shape. "That's what we got on tape," Morrison said in 2009 of the *Astral Weeks* sessions that followed. "Another performance might have been totally different. That was that performance, on those days." That sense of accident and serendipity takes over. "Madame George" as one can hear it today sounds most of all unlikely, not something that could be traced to anything in the singer's immediate circumstances, his past, his idols (though Lead Belly's "Alabama Bound" is here too, as it is all over Morrison's music). The possibility that the throwaway one minute and twenty-seven seconds of "Madame George" that Morrison recorded before encountering musicians with whom he would make *Astral Weeks* might be all there was hits home in the same way that one might worry that the day would come when one would put on "Madame George"—or any song one thought was as rich as life itself—and it would turn up dead.

For me there is always a sense of worry when I put the album on again. Will it sound as true, will it sound as good as before, will there come a time when I will be listening to the end of "Madame George" and suddenly it's already there, I've heard it, it has nothing left to tell me—and that has never happened. It has never worn out. It's never given itself up.

Is that because it has no ending? When I think idly about *Astral Weeks*, walking down the street, something in the air or in the carriage of the person next to me reminding me of a turn of phrase or a pause somewhere on the album, it doesn't end with "Slim Slow Slider," the last song of the eight that comprise it. It ends with "Madame George," which is only the fifth song—and that is because of what happens after Richard Davis hits that note that, for him, has said all the song had left to say.

The scene has been set, and all the players have wandered into it. In George's apartment, with the frayed damask cushions and the heavy drapes making the air close, the boys watch as George changes the LPs and 78s on the box, handling each so carefully, thumbs never touching the grooves, strange records by Billie Holiday and Charlie Parker that speak a different language, they watch as George turns her Ouija board, they watch her smoke, they watch when in panic she thinks the police are near and rushes to throw her dope out the window—"down into the street below." Even when the boys are doing all these things themselves—playing with the Ouija board, speaking the secret jazz language, which in this place is their language, the language they speak to each other as if "Kokomo" or "I Cover the Waterfront" are clues to real life and a code to keep the square world at bay, smoking dope, gathering it up to toss it away—they feel as if they're watching.

There is the long section when all the boys turn their back on her and walk away—into adulthood, responsibility, idleness, dope-dealing, addiction, wealth, respectability, renown, and, never, what she already represents, with the makeup caking on her eyes, the sweat rotting the foundation, the wig slipping, her speech slurring, the laughter too loud, the need in the way she waves you goodbye ("Hey love, you forgot your glove") too obvious: death. The singer has to get all the way away, taking a train out of the city, maybe even leaving the country, the pennies he throws out of the window onto the bridges below at once a way of pretending he's still a little boy and an echo of George's dope falling to the street, all one long fall. Here are the great passages of repetition, where you cannot imagine the song can end. *Dry your eye dry your eye dry your eye dry your eye dry your eye dry your eye dry your eye* and on thirteen times, more, as if it's all been a breath being drawn, a pause to launch the more bitter, withdrawing, fleeing *And the love that loves the love that loves the love that loves the love that loves to love the love that loves to love the love that loves the glove*, all with the burr of a trumpet coming down like an execution, the blade of the guillotine raised and dropped again and again long after the head has been passed from hand to hand in the crowd. And this is only prelude to what Morrison will do with the word "goodbye," what he will do murmuring, singing ooos and woos as if he's found them on the copy of "Earth Angel" that one day a DJ forgot to take off the turntable, a record that played on after the DJ was fired and after the station shut down, a signal in the ether sustained by its own power.

One day in 2000 I walked into the Portland Art Museum to find the Dick Slessig (as in dyslexic) Combo—Carl Bronson, bass, Mark Lightcap, guitar, Steve Goodfriend, drums—half an hour into a performance of what would turn into ninety minutes before I realized that the nearly abstract, circular pattern they were offering as the meaning of life—it was all they were playing, anyway—was from George McCrae's 1974 Miami disco hit "Rock Your Baby." Or rather the pattern wasn't from the tune, it was the tune, the thing itself. Variation was never McCrae's point (the big moment in "Rock Your Baby," the equivalent of the guitar solo, is when he barely whispers "Come on"); finding the perfect, self-renewing riff was. "I could listen to that forever," I said to Bronson when he and the others finally stepped down for a break. "We'd play it forever if we were physically capable," he said.

They were also playing "Madame George." When Morrison dives into the words, the syllables, that will seem to divest him of flesh, leaving only a word, the word repeating until it has remade a body of flesh to hold it, until it can walk like a man, the feeling is that the singer has lived this out many times before, the word always evading him, until the day when it happened that certain people came together in the right place at the right time and the body was, for the ten minutes it took to play the song, found.

The ending, as it begins again with Davis's moral exit, is so long, so drawn out, so dramatic and scary, I get chills thinking about it, let alone listening to it. As the train pulls off, it seems a whole body of memory is dropping away, has been cut off to drift away on the sea. In the trick your mind plays on you, the drama "Madame George" enacts might be the end of the record because nothing could follow it. That's the end of the story—and yet because of the way that ending is so drawn out, each repeating word or syllable doubling back on itself, the song doesn't ever really end, and in fact the ending is false. As you listen you hear that no one present, not the singer, the producer, the musicians, not even Richard Davis can actually make the song stop, and so as you listen, and reach the end, and there is a pause before the next song, "Madame George" seems to be still playing. When you merely let the song play in your mind, catching perhaps for the first time that at the very end the boy remembers that it was Madame George herself who put him on the train, telling him, so flatly, as if she herself has to return him to whatever life it is he'll lead, "This is the train," him crying out to her, long after the train last left the city behind, then telling himself to say goodbye, *say goodbye goodbye goodbye goodbye goodbye goodbye goodbye goodbye, say goodbye, get on the train*, but always commanding himself to say it, saying it always to himself, never to Madame George, and because he cannot say the words out loud, she can't hear them, so he has to keep saying it, and in that way too the song doesn't end. Is it any wonder that people try to fix something so unfixed, so free of its own body as the Dick Slessig Combo's version of "Rock Your Baby" is free of "Rock Your Baby," that people have tried for more than forty years to contain it, to say exactly what it is, who it is, and what it isn't—which is to say whatever it might be to whoever might hear it? "I can remember to the day when I stopped teaching Virginia Woolf's *To the Lighthouse*," John Irving said in 1979. "I loved that little part called 'Time Passes.' . . . It's the difference between a novel of manners and a novel of *weight*, a novel of some kind of history, where it says, 'Hey look, "time changes."'"

I became so angry when I had to teach that book after Quentin Bell's biography came out. Not because the book is lousy. It *isn't*. But because the students were so willing to use that biography as an explanation for everything they read—and so many people read fiction that way it nauseates me.

It's difficult to tell people what the reason for that is without insulting them—because the real reason is that people with limited imaginations find it hard to imagine that anyone else has an imagination. Therefore, they must think that everything they read in some way *happened*. For years, I've sat with students, knowing full well that the worst, most *dreck-ridden* piece of their story is in the story because "That's just the way it happened." And I say, "Why is this dreadful scene, why is this stupid person here?" And the student says, "Oh, that's not a stupid person, that's my mother, and that's exactly what she said."

"They felt they had been *taken in*," Irving had said. But that's what art does—that's how it takes you somewhere else. And the phrase has its meanings. To be taken in means to be accepted into the brotherhood, the secret society, where all recognize the same signs. It means to be bereft, helpless, and then to be received off the street into a place where you will be cared for. It means to be fooled. And that is the bedrock meaning, the speech "Madame George" speaks: if you don't make the song happen to the person who knows nothing, who has never heard of your characters and has no reason to care about them, no matter how real they might be, the song didn't happen. And if you do make it happen, it did.

Josh Gleason, "Van Morrison: *Astral Weeks* Revisited," *Weekend Edition*, NPR, 28 February 2009.

Happy Traum, interview with Van Morrison, *Rolling Stone*, 9 July 1970, 33.

Jonathan Cott, "Bob Dylan," *Rolling Stone*, 26 January 1978, in *Bob Dylan: The Essential Interviews*, ed. Cott (Wenner Books, 2006), 187.

————"Van Morrison: The *Rolling Stone* Interview," *Rolling Stone*, 30 November 1978, 52.

"The original title was 'Madame Joy'": Ritchie Yorke, *Van Morrison: Into the Music* (London: Charisma, 1975), 60–61.

"It may have something to do": John Collis, *Inarticulate Speech of the Heart* (New York: Da Capo, 1996), 107.

Tom Nolan, "Who Was Madame George?" *Wall Street Journal* online, 14 April 2007.

Van Morrison and automatic writing, Jonathan Taplin, audio commentary, *The Last Waltz* DVD.

"John Irving: The *Rolling Stone* Interview," GM, *Rolling Stone*, 13 December 1979, 75, 71.

Mary Gaitskill, *Two Girls Fat and Thin* (New York: Poseidon, 1991), 225.

Marianne Faithfull, "Madame George," on *No Prima Donna: The Songs of Van Morrison* (Polydor, 1994). Produced by Van Morrison and Phil Coulter—whose theme music is all over *Breakfast on Pluto*.

Dick Slessig Combo—included as *Jessica Bronson and the Dick Slessig Combo present for your pleasure* . . . as part of the exhibition "Let's Entertain: Life's Guilty Pleasures" (Walker Art Center, Minneapolis; Portland Museum of Art, Portland, Oregon; Musée national d'art moderne, Paris [2000]; Museo Rufino Tamayo, Mexico City; and Miami Art Museum [2001]). From the exhibition catalogue (Minneapolis: Walker Art Center, 2000): "Working with Carl Bronson, [Jessica Bronson] has designed a curvilinear bandstand that is lit from below so that it appears to float in a pool of light. The band will perform on-stage on the opening night of the exhibition, leaving behind the lights and a looped compact disc of the performance for the duration of the exhibition. This empty stage with disembodied voices evokes notions of virtual pleasure and performance, the empty dreams of Hollywood, and the underbelly of spectacle. The machinery of fame—illumination, spectacle, performance—is laid bare, and the lack of a nice Hollywood ending suggests a disrupted narrative." Not to me—or, I think, the musicians. Other Dick Slessig Combo performances include versions of Kraftwerke's "Computer Love" and Bobby Gentry's "Ode to Billie Joe"; a 2004 single (dickslessig.com) was made up of a forty-two-minute dreaming-and-waking drift through Jimmy Webb's "Wichita Lineman" paired with a twenty-two-minute trudge through Crosby Stills & Nash's "Guinnevere."

Van Morrison, "Madame George" (November 1967), plus "Goodbye George," "Dum Dum George," and other demo recordings (fall 1968), collected on *Payin' Dues* (Charly, 1994).

———"Madame George," *Astral Weeks* (Warner Bros.–Seven Arts, 1968).

SAINT DOMINIC'S PREVIEW. 1996

On the album of the same name, released in 1972, the year of Bloody Sunday in Belfast, there was no escaping the immediacy of the song. Saint Dominic's Preview—was it a mass held for those who wouldn't see the next year? A special invitation-only pre-sale sale to empty Northern Ireland of everything it ever was before and was now ? For all that the phrase explained itself it might as well have been the Veedon Fleece, and that probably would have been in one of the sale bins if you knew how to look.

The cover of *Saint Dominic's Preview* featured a theatrical shot of Morrison sitting on what might have been church steps, holding a battered guitar. Save for an oddly dandyish kerchief around his neck his clothes were worn, with even a gaping hole in one pant leg, a street singer playing for coins and truth, his head slightly lifted toward the sky, his face sad but thoughtful, you could even say wistful, philosophical, his eyes gazing into the future, into the past: *Will this war never end?* You could buy a photocopied broadside called "The Troubles" off him for a dollar.

Even though Van Morrison has never written or sung a song with the phrase in it—no blues song, not even the cabaret blues "Trouble in Mind," planting the probably nineteenth-century southern verse "Sun gonna shine in my back door some day, wind gonna rise up, blow my blues away" in a twentieth-century New York penthouse—the portrait was as corny as it was contrived, and more fake. Morrison had worked for years to say nothing about the Troubles. The Sex Pistols might use the letters "IRA" in "Anarchy in the UK" like a bomb, but the acronym had never passed Morrison's lips in public, and for all one knows never will. In *In The Name of the Father*, Daniel Day-Lewis's Gerry Conlon is an out-of-control prankster IRA hanger-on in Belfast sent to London by his father because the IRA will kill him for his unreliability, then falsely imprisoned for an IRA London bombing. He has a poster on the wall of his cell to keep him alive, to affirm his innocence and his defiance: Johnny Rotten, not Van Morrison.

Whatever the intentions behind it, the cover of *Saint Dominic's Preview* worked as a setup, convicting the album's title song of falsity and bad faith—a song that in fact would name Belfast, and with a bitter regret weighting the word with all of its history, which is to say all of its killings—in advance. But the song was written and recorded before the cover was made, and it had fixed the game in advance: there was no false face it could not erase.

The song was stirring. It was exhilarating. The singer's commitment to his every word passed over to the listener even if the listener had never wasted a thought on Northern Ireland; there was a sense of engaging with the world on your own terms. As the scene shifted from Belfast to San Francisco to New York, shifted in phrases that barely made more narrative than a single word, as the story went from people being shot down in one street to people looking away from others as they walked down another to a rock 'n' roll singer at a party to promote his new album, what could have been felt as a slide from the profound to the trivial remained a story that stayed on its feet, that surrendered not a single measure of moral right from one side of the story to the other. When the song ended, you could feel you'd been around the world.

The specificity of the bare nod to Belfast went off like a gun. If, as more than one person has written, the title of Seamus Heany's 1975 poem "Whatever You Say, Say Nothing" summed up both the aesthetic and the everyday life of avoidance in Northern Ireland in that time, when the cause writing your name on a bullet could as well be that of your presumed fellows as of your fated enemies, if not chance itself, could Morrison's work up to this moment have been a version of that poem itself, with "Whatever You Say, Say Nothing" boiled down, in the manner of a song, to nothing more than its phrase, sung over and over in endless variation? "Is there a link between that attitude, which Morrison seems to embody," a friend wrote, "and the yarragh? Can't we understand aspects of the yarragh as being at once a safe place beyond language"—when the wrong words could get you killed, or, with you safe at home in Marin County or New York or England, get someone who sang your song in the wrong place at the wrong time killed—"and an attempt to stretch for the sublime when the world, and Belfast is a world whether you're there in the flesh or not, is crowding you very tightly, and even a gut cry, a howl beyond words, is an embrace of the failure of language, a celebration of the faith that some things not only should not but can't be spoken of or even named?"

When Morrison performed the song on television twenty-four years later, the context was no longer clear. In 1972, the description of life in the Bay Area that Morrison offered in "Saint Dominic's Preview"—a utopia of sun, sloth, and solipsism, where nothing was more important than a refusal, in his words, to feel anybody else's pain, where the best struggled to get outside their empty shells, and failed—was so acute it wrote the script for a movie that wouldn't be shot for six years. Asked in 2000 why in 1978 he'd chosen to remake Don Siegel's 1956 *Invasion of the Body Snatchers*, and why he'd set it not in the film's original California Valley town but in San Francisco, Phil Kaufman, the director, didn't hesitate for a second: "I was living in San Francisco, it was the beginning of the New Age movement, and all I saw were pods." But in 1996 that was all a long time ago—even if the British torture of IRA militants, IRA bombs in London and UDA bombs in Belfast, each side executing not only the enemy but its own suspects, informers, collaborators, unreliables, anyone unlucky enough to have joined the right side at the wrong time, went on. For that matter, it had been awhile since a record company had put on a big bash for Van Morrison. The song had to make its own stage and raise its own curtain.

In 1996, the piece begins with a guitarist picking out a modal theme, a minor key that quickly loses itself in all that it might say: this could be the beginning of anything, a train song, a cowboy ballad, "Little Maggie." When Morrison begins to sing, about cleaning windows in Belfast, about Edith Piaf, a violin comes in, and the territory opens up—to San Francisco, then immediately across the country, in the old folk phrase "A long way to Buffalo," then across the ocean to Belfast again, and without your noticing the journey has turned strange, and the stakes have been raised. You can't tell when it was that Morrison began to push, when his voice lowered, when he began to play with the harsh vowels of his own gruff tone, when a hint of violence crept in—so that when he caught the history of a country as he pushed down with "Hoping that Joyce, don't blow the hoist," you realize you know exactly what he was talking about, even if time and place were now unfixed, even if you couldn't have explained "don't blow the hoist" to save your life.

The song went on, with horns, another guitar, maybe a mandolin, backing singers coming across with a quiet sympathy. The story went on. And yet, by the end—when the singer went from the record company party to an interview with a rock critic to another party in a fancy apartment on Fifty-Second Street—the shift in the song that in 1972 was lost in a mass finale, everyone playing at top volume, now came to the fore. After everything—after murder, after indifference, after flattery, after a no to all of it—everyone in the song turned to their windows, shocked, as perhaps they never were before, to see that the streets were now filled with people, people neither killing each other nor avoiding each other but marching as one, shouting for freedom, in the moment celebrating the truth that they already had it. Morrison looked out his window, surprised, confirmed, but most of all happy. "Can I get a witness!" he said, as if the words were no less a folk theme, part of the collective imagination, the common memory of anyone who might have already passed through the song, as Lead Belly testifying that "They was driving the women, just like the men" or Frank Hutchison promising "I won't be dead, just won't be here no more" when you came looking for him and he wasn't there.

Saint Dominic's Preview (Warner Bros., 1972).

"Saint Dominic's Preview" (1996), collected on *Catalog Strays 1965–2000* (Wild Card bootleg).

SWEET THING. 1968

The music strides into its field like fate, and there are no
obstacles: at the start, at the end of each phrase, the ping of a
triangle marks the next step in the flight. It's the strangest
thing—in this song, which I've never been able to play only
once, that tiny moment can become the axis on which the
whole piece turns. At first there's only Morrison's strum and
Richard Davis's bass; as the arrangement takes full shape, as
strings come in to take the measure that that ping once did,
the chiming sound disappears. It's easy to forget—there's no
triangle-player's wing in the Rock & Roll Hall of Fame. But
when the song starts again, there it is, signaling a simplicity
that the singer will soon leave behind. You can always recover it—you can even drag the song back and wait for the
sound over and over again. You can't tell if the singer would
even want to. Moving fast, he may have already forgotten
the place in the song you don't want to leave.

After two and a half minutes, Davis seems to want to shut the song down. His bass makes a clacking sound, as if to put the brakes on the rhythm as everyone else rushes ahead; the brakes don't hold. *My my, my my, my mmm-my my, my my my*, Morrison muses; he takes a breath, and in one of the highest points in a song made of high points— "And I will run my merry way and jump the hedges first," is the first line; the image is so thrilling you never lose sight of it as the song moves on, and the singer never does stop jumping—he shifts into a higher gear. He finds an image that is as adult as the first is childlike, carrying specters the grown man cannot gainsay, an image that is less abandoned, more determined, but as much a sign of freedom, saying "And I will raise my hand up into the nighttime sky"—

> And I will raise my hand up into the nighttime . . .
> *skyyyyyyyyyy*

—and like the sound of the triangle, which is the song itself pausing for an instant to draw a breath, the moment of suspension is everything.

A minute later, Davis makes the same clacking sound again. This time he does take the reins of the music, and Morrison begins to drift away from the song. "Sweet thing," he says, as he's said throughout, but now that changes into "Sugar baby"—"Sugar baby, sugar baby," a phrase from before the blues, a phrase that helped shape it, a face hiding inside all the songs Morrison grew up loving, a phrase that now belongs to him as much as it ever belonged to Lead Belly or Dock Boggs.

Van Morrison, "Sweet Thing," *Astral Weeks* (Warner Bros.–Seven Arts, 1968).

TAKE ME BACK. 1991.
JENNIFER JASON LEIGH, 1995

Nostalgia pulls down like quicksand, and it's always had Van Morrison in its grip. He was twenty when he made "The Story of Them," about the band's days in Belfast at the Maritime Hotel, but the scene as he looked back was so perfect, the long-lost names and faces standing out so clearly through the haze of the intervening decades, or rather year, that he might have been eighty—even though, as he wrote and recorded the song, Them had yet to put out its second album. "Gotta walk away," he sang, tailing off, as if leaving the past behind was the same as building a palace for it.

All through his working life Morrison has fixed touchstones, talismans, charms—as if, from the time he was a boy, he saw the future as a forest, a wilderness of tangles and snares, and so like Hansel scattered crumbs that he might find his way back to a true home, except that his crumbs were old Ray Charles records. As the years have gone on he has turned ever more frequently to songs he treasured as a boy—not for lack of his own songs, or even for fun or out of affection, but as if to validate his own songs, anchor them, or test the truth of his songs against songs that, the feeling must be, can't lie. Even as his musical heroes have appeared in his songs as characters—Ray Charles, Lead Belly, Jackie Wilson, Billie Holiday, Sonny Boy Williamson, Charlie Parker, Sonny Terry, Brownie McGhee, Mahalia Jackson, Elvis Presley, Fats Domino, Lester Young, Lightnin' Hopkins, Jay McShann, John Lee Hooker, Jerry Lee Lewis, Muddy Waters—he has covered John Lee (the first Sonny Boy) Williamson's "Good Morning Little Schoolgirl" and "Take Your Hand Out of My Pocket" by Rice Miller, the second Sonny Boy Williamson, Bobby Bland's "I'll Take Care of You," Waters's "I Just Want to Make Love to You," Sam Cooke's "Bring It on Home to Me," Charles's "Lonesome Avenue," "Georgia On My Mind," and "I Can't Stop Loving You," but most often in a bland, passive way, as if to take nothing from them. And that is to say nothing of *How Long Has This Been Going On*, Morrison's 1996 album with Georgie Fame, filled with compositions by the jump blues king Louis Jordan, King Pleasure and Lester Young, Mose Allison, Harold Arlen and Johnny Mercer, and Ira and George Gershwin's title song; from the same year, *Tell Me Something*, an entire album of Mose Allison numbers; *You Win Again*, his 2000 album with Lynda Gail Lewis, shooting back and forth between covers of records by Hank Williams, John Lee Hooker, Bo Diddley, Smiley Lewis, and Jerry Lee Lewis; and, with *The Skiffle Sessions*, recorded at

Whitla Hall in Belfast in 1998, Morrison's reunion in spirit and flesh with Lonnie Donegan, with Dr. John and longtime British jazzman Chris Barber along for the ride, Lead Belly everywhere: "Alabamy Bound," "Frankie and Johnny," "Good Morning Blues," "Goodnight Irene," "Midnight Special."

Walking side by side in this never-ending stroll through the bowers of days when all was cool, when the sound of another voice, a young person's first apprehension of art, could make it seem as if he and the world were one—when the terrors of childhood and the alienations of adolescence disappeared in that moment when you understood just how Ray Charles pressed down so hard on the chorus of "Lonely Avenue," and why—is the alienation that will not disappear: the alienation from the world in which you have to live. It's the cheats and liars and frauds and thieves and parasites and writers and suck-ups and managers and promoters and record companies and the people you called friends, all of them, but more than anything it's the so-called modern world, throwing itself in your face every day, so proud of itself, so sure of itself, so sure and proud that it has left the past behind, and you with it, unless you're ready to play a game you don't remotely comprehend.

It's no secret that when one reaches his or her forties, maybe fifties, almost certainly his or her sixties and seventies, the world as it presents itself in advertisements, talk, technology, dress, movies, music, money, and perhaps most of all manners, the way in which people walk down the street, the way they say hello or goodbye or don't bother to do either, becomes an affront to one's entire existence. One may reach a point, as the historian Robert Cantwell puts it

so gracefully, when one's "life begins to go into the past"—
that, or your whole fucking frame of reference.

Morrison has sung about the parasites in song after song,
from his whole string of demos in 1968 to "The Great De-
ception" in 1973, across the last twenty-five years in the likes
of "New Biography" (someone's written another book about
him), "A Town Called Paradise" ("copy cats stole" his words,
songs, melodies), the self-explanatory "Big Time Operators"
and "They Sold Me Out," and the no-one-listens-anyway
anthem "Why Must I Always Explain," which is a good song.
But he has sung far more powerfully about escape, about
running from the modern world, vanishing from it as if you
were never there. On *Hymns to the Silence*, a twenty-one song
set illustrated with photographs of grubby Belfast streets released in 1991, the theme was as ever-present as Lead Belly
on *The Skiffle Sessions*—or rather it was Lead Belly, Lead
Belly changed from flesh to idea. "I'm Not Feeling It Anymore," with "Have to get back," sung with bitter acceptance,
as if there's nothing left to feel; "On Hyndford Street," with
"Take me back, take me way, way, way back" the opening
for an entire catalogue of a teenager's discovery of the world,
reading "Mr. Jelly Roll" and "Mezz Mezrow's 'Really the
Blues,'" and "'Dharma Bums' by Jack Kerouac / Over and
over again." But none of that is really any preparation for
Morrison's nine minutes and eleven seconds of "Take Me
Back." Wait, wait, you could be forgiven for asking, didn't we
already hear that?

Morrison opens with a few seconds of harmonica so wistful you might be tempted to shut the song off right there, but
the pace is too slow, already too distant—the music is not

giving itself away. The harmonica continues to push, as if through fog. There's a sense of defeat. "Well, I remember," the singer says. "When life made more sense." Morrison will sing variations on this line ("Take me back, take me back, take me back, take me way, way, way back, way back, to when, when I understood") across the length of the song, and it's more painful every time. The singer has been forced to make this confession: to admit that the world no longer has a place for him, a place he may not deserve. He has made a wasteland, alluring, even beautiful, and dead; that is where the yarragh is in this song.

He drops down into a whisper, only a hint of piano and guitar behind him, and the music, now in a realm the modern world can't enter, a place of almost silence, ends without a marker, a note to tell you it has ended; it merely isn't there anymore. And it's as if you've fallen asleep for less than a second; nothing close to nine minutes seems to have passed.

But that was only the song's first life, and not its real life. That comes five years later, in the movie *Georgia*.

Released in 1995, the film pits Jennifer Jason Leigh's no-talent junkie punk singer Sadie against Mare Winningham's Georgia, Sadie's sister and a folk singer all but worshipped by her legions of fans. Georgia's voice—which is also that of Winningham, who has made her own albums—is all mellifluousness to Sadie's—Leigh's—horrid cracks and discords. The heart of the picture comes at a big AIDS benefit. Winningham appears to sing "Mercy," an uplifting ballad; her simple, modest "Hello" to the crowd brings a torrent of applause. "Mercy will you follow me," she sings, and the audience knows the answer: how could it resist? Then comes Sadie with nine drunken minutes of Morrison's "Take Me Back"—weirdly, exactly nine minutes and eleven seconds of "Take Me Back." Her seizing of the stage for an endless, no-range, flat, mindless assault on the defenseless song is presented in the film not as music but as a psychotic breakdown. It's meant to be as excruciating for the audience in the movie theater as for the people in the movie's concert hall; plainly, Sadie will keep singing until she or the song drops dead. Ultimately her sister appears on the stage like a fairy godmother, softly strumming her guitar, easing the madwoman off the stage.

Watching this car crash, you can't tell if this is the actor Leigh singing as Sadie or simply Leigh doing the best she can, and it doesn't matter. Sadie has nothing to bring to the song but the death wish that Morrison's song as he wrote it contains, something which, as Morrison recorded the song, is smothered by artistry, by a voice that cannot hide either the imagination inside of it or the command behind it. Leigh has nothing to bring to the song but will: no lift, no tone, no tricks. In Jonathan Lethem's phrase, she's an animal wandering through a karaoke machine, tangled in the gears and wires. All she can do is turn a concert hall into the street behind it where a junkie like her shows you her teeth as she asks for change, and then if you stop tries to tell you the story of her life. But she sings with the same up-and-down, back-and-forth refusal of time that women have always brought to songs, specifically work songs—and as the late musicologist Wilfred Mellers wrote of such music,* "Through repetition it carries the singers beyond the body's thrall. It at once affirms and transcends the physical, inducing a state of trance, even ecstasis, when the women begin to yell a magical 'music of the vowels,' which is beyond literate sequence and consequence."

What a remarkable thing to say: beyond consequence. But once the idea is there, you can hear Leigh travel beyond consequence—or rather, when the consequences of her performance arrive, they seem false, perhaps because Leigh's Sadie has touched the ecstasy Mellers calls down. Railing her takemebacks like someone hammering a single nail so many times she's now hammering through the wood, there are moments when the words come loose from themselves, and the singer is loosed from meaning, from purpose, from having to justify her existence to anyone at all—for seconds as the song grinds on, she is free. The song cracks open; a horde of beetles swarms out of it, and behind them all the naked, tortured men and women out of *The Garden of Earthly Delights*. Then Winningham's Georgia finally gets her sister to finish the song, to shut up. There's the barest ripple of clapping, no more than a sign of relief. Leigh—Sadie—immediately falls back into her crazy-pathetic persona, but in a way you don't want to believe, as if she's ashamed of

---

* Specifically "Robh thu 'sa' bheinn? (Were You in the Mountains?)," a Gaelic waulking song from the isle of Barra, off the coast of Scotland, sung by one "Mary Morrison and a group of old women": "They sing to aid their labour as they pound homemade cloth, 'waulking' it round in a sunwise direction against a board."

what she's done. "Thank you!" she says, her words smeared. "God bless! You're the real goods! Keep drinkin'—around the edges—I love you. I love you, Georgia," she says, sounding as if she's begging forgiveness for burning Georgia's doll collection in the fireplace when they were kids—and with the mere mention of Georgia's name there's lots of applause.

For nine minutes and eleven seconds, though, in a trance of terrible singing, Leigh has taken you right out of her not-very-good movie. While you were out, you were somewhere oddly quiet—a place that with "Take Me Back" Van Morrison marked on a map and Sadie the punk found.

Robert Cantwell, "Twigs of Folly" (1997, unpublished).

Wilfred Mellers, *A Darker Shade of Pale: A Backdrop to Bob Dylan* (New York: Oxford, 1985), 32, 33.

Jonathan Lethem, "The Fly in the Ointment," in *Best Music Writing 2009*, ed. GM (New York: Da Capo, 2009), 186.

Miss Mary Morrison and Calum Johnston, Kate Buchanan, and Flora Boyd, "Robh thu 'sa' bheinn?" on *Scottish Tradition 3: Waulking Songs from Barra* (School of Scottish Studies: University of Edinburgh, Greentrax, 1993, recorded 1965–1967). Earlier traditional recordings by Mary Morrison, made by Alan Lomax in 1951, can be heard, along with contemporaneous recordings by Penny Morrison, on *World Library of Folk and Primitive Music: Scotland* (Rounder, 1998).

Jennifer Jason Leigh, "Take Me Back," from *Georgia—Original Soundtrack* (Discovery, 1996). Also includes covers by Sadie's punk band, which includes Joe Doe of X, of the Velvet Underground's "There She Goes Again" (Doe) and "I'll Be Your Mirror" (Doe, Leigh, and Smokey Hormel), and of Lou Reed's

"Sally Can't Dance" (Doe and Leigh), plus, most startlingly, Stephen Foster's "Hard Times (Come Again No More)" by Mare Winningham (at the beginning, making you feel they never arrived) and by Leigh (at the very end, as if there'll never be anything else, and shouldn't be).

Them, "The Story of Them" (Decca, 1967, UK), included on *The Story of Them Featuring Van Morrison* (Polydor, 1998).

Van Morrison, "Take Me Back," *Hymns to the Silence* (Polydor, 1991).

——with Georgie Fame & Friends, *How Long Has This Been Going On* (Verve, 1996).

——*Tell Me Something: The Songs of Mose Allison* (Verve, 1996).

——and Linda Gail Lewis, *You Win Again* (Virgin, 2000). "Sometimes you make mistakes," Morrison said to Dave Marsh in 2009 when Marsh asked about the Fame and Allison and Lewis albums. "And sometimes you're bored."

——and Lonnie Donegan and Chris Barber, *The Skiffle Sessions—Live in Belfast 1998* (Virgin, 2000).

MYSTIC EYES. GREEK THEATRE, BERKELEY. 2009

At a concert where Morrison has played his way through all of *Astral Weeks*, surrounded by a four-person string section with a lead violinist, two drummers, guitarist Jay Berliner from the original sessions in 1968, an electric guitarist, a bass player alternating between bass guitar and bass fiddle, keyboard player (piano, organ, harpsichord), two female backup singers, a one-man horn section, a woman on acoustic guitar and steel guitar, with Morrison himself moving between alto sax, piano, acoustic guitar, harmonica—he finishes "Madame George," the last song of *Astral Weeks* as he will present it tonight, and floats into fragments of "Listen to the Lion," that long, speaking-in-tongues song from 1972. "All . . . my . . . love . . . comes tum-bling down," he chants. Suddenly it seems to be absolutely clear, the most obvious thing in the world, that from its first notes to its last *Astral Weeks* is nothing

more than a version of Wilson Pickett's "In the Midnight
Hour": "Not a song, but an epic," Jon Landau wrote in as
good a line as music writing has left behind. Nothing more,
and perhaps nothing less. I thought of the film of Roddy
Doyle's novel *The Commitments*, the story of a teenage
Dublin soul band, taking their stand in the late 1980s, when
nobody knows and nobody cares, but the Commitments will
make them care. (Morrison himself was solicited for the role
of Joey "The Lips" Fagan, an old trumpeter the kids bring in
to have someone to look up to, some link to a past they can
create but not remember.)* Now it's the night of their big
show, Wilson Pickett himself is in town, they do everything
they can to get him to come to their show, to bless them with
his presence, to give them a face to look into that they will
never forget as surely as Wilson Pickett will forget theirs. The
show ends; he isn't there. But it was a great show. The boys
and girls in the Commitments justified their existence—their
existence on earth, not merely their momentary existence as
a soul band. And as they scatter, as they raise their glasses, the
film finds Mr. Pickett—no actor, the man himself. His own
show is done; tells his limo driver to take him to this other

---

* The movie was directed by Alan Parker and produced by Lynda Myles,
who, when in 2009 I asked about Morrison's involvement, wrote: "VM
came over to see Alan and met in Alan's hotel room in London. He arrived with his manager, having been sent pages of the script in advance.
The manager said that VM required a club sandwich. There was no
small talk while this was delivered and VM ate the sandwich. The manager kept saying how keen VM was to be in the movie. Van continued to
eat the sandwich. He was asked to read but refused. When Alan asked
why not, VM said 'because it's shit.' The meeting was then basically
abandoned."

show, this band, what are they called? Of course he'd sung "In the Midnight Hour" that night. Where else would Van Morrison have first heard *Astral Weeks*?

The thought passed in an instant as Morrison sang "And my love comes tumbling down" one more time, now no distance at all between that and Pickett's deliberate, unstoppable pledge:

> I'm going to wait til the midnight hour
> That's when my love comes tumbling down

It was the sort of reverie that comes at those times in a show when in the audience you feel as if you are seeing all around the event as it happens, the past not past at all, more voices than those on the stage singing the song. Then Morrison raised his harmonica, as if to ornament his words, and flew like his own missile into "Mystic Eyes." It was shocking, blood in the sylvan glade, the headless horseman in the Kentucky Derby riding the wrong way, and it lasted only long enough for it to be uncertain if it had happened at all.

Roddy Doyle, *The Commitments* (Dublin: King Farouk, 1987; New York: Vintage, 1989).

The Commitments, dir. Alan Parker (1991, DVD 1999, 20th Century Fox). Johnny Murphy played Joey "The Lips" Fagan.

Wilson Pickett, "In the Midnight Hour" (Atlantic, 1965).

BEHIND THE RITUAL, 2008

"Don't need no juice to unwind," Van Morrison says in "Don't Go to Nightclubs Anymore," early on on *Keep It Simple*, his last album of new songs to be released as I write. Then he says the same thing in different ways three more times. *Go ahead, knock this bottle off my shoulder!* But the only song on *Keep It Simple* that makes its own time and place is anything but simple.

"Behind the Ritual"—you could make up a picture of Morrison as Michelangelo's Adam holding out his hand to God's, with the opposite of Adam's cool gaze on his face, and get away with using it for the cover of a third of all the albums he's ever made. The religious yearning in his music that first surfaced explicitly in "Astral Weeks" has been a constant ever since, like references to backstreet jelly roll or gardens all wet with rain. It can be as airborne as it is on "Full Force Gale" in 1979—when Morrison says, "I've been lifted up again / By the Lord," Toni Marcus's fiddle can make it feel as if you've been lifted high enough to at least glimpse what the singer is seeing—or as entombed as it is all over *Avalon Sunset* ten years later, an album that leads off with a duet with the 1950s British rock 'n' roll pioneer and noted evangelical Cliff Richard. It smothered Morrison's voice for nearly two decades. But here it's never clear what the ritual is or what it promises.

"Behind the Ritual" takes seven minutes to end the album—to inhale it like smoke and make it disappear. It starts with Morrison strumming a ukulele and the drummer moving slowly from a woodblock to traps. The words are slurred, or maybe it's that the old man singing them is singing them as clearly as he can, testing his tongue against his pursed lips, like someone whose fingers are so webbed with arthritis he has to draw words instead of writing them. Morrison lifts his saxophone, and gets the lucidity he can't find on his own.

It all burns off like fog. He's taken you into an alley, the same alley, he seems to be saying, where Uncle John met Long Tall Sally, but also a place where boys just into their teens once gathered to do all the things the stolid singer in "Don't Go to Nightclubs Anymore" says he doesn't do, doesn't want, doesn't need: drinking, smoking, bragging about girls they haven't touched and the snappers they're going to give them, talking jive, saying *fuck* and *shit* when someone mentions church. Now that stolidity—the granite face on the front of the album that has "Behind the Ritual" on it—has been replaced by desire, and desire bleeds all over the music. "Given the courage, we live by moments of interference between past and present, moments in which time comes back into phase with itself," the historian Roger Shattuck wrote in 1958. "It is the only meaning of history. We search the past not for other creatures but for our own lost selves."

It is the deepest nostalgia, where some things you did, some things you saw, and some things you heard about replace any sense of life as it is, its true burdens, struggles, paradox, failures, betrayals. You can argue against the idea, but you can't argue against music if it moves you, you can only listen or change the station or turn off the radio and say you don't do that sort of thing anymore. But you can also get the feeling, as Morrison leads his old self back into the alley, sits down with the boys, drinks their wine, offers them his, whispering, because what they do is secret, not the act so much as the warmth of friendship and of the forbidden that the act leaves in the air like perfume, that *this* is the mystic, this is the astral plane, nothing given by God or located in another dimension, but memory, true or false.

It's true if the singer can make it true. Morrison circles the words like faces that are slipping their names, bits of tunes that won't let you sing them. He circles the people he finds in the alley in the same way, talking them into being. What he's summoning is all in the past, but you can sense that the drama has yet to play itself out. It's an adventure, and no one knows, no one could understand. "We few, we happy few, we band of brothers," says one of the boys out of *Henry V*, and Morrison answers him out of *Julius Caesar*: "How many ages hence / Shall our lofty scene be acted over / In states un-born and accents yet unknown?"

The theme takes shape in steps. There is drinking in the alley, there's making time with Sally, there's dancing drunk in the alley, there's making up rhymes in the alley, there's turning and spinning in the night, verse after verse, each one a slight variation, a tiny step past the one before it. From the old man sharing a secret there's another man, per-haps no less old but stronger, less afraid of himself, singing as if hoping someone outside of the alley will hear him, or to make certain the buildings rising up from the alley hear him and never forget. But he also wants to explain. It's all one quest: behind the ritual, he says, you find the spiritual.

"Behind the ritual" now become the key words on which all other words turn, around which all the rhythms of the song will shape themselves. And as always in Van Morrison's highest moments, the words come loose from their own song and remake it, leading the singer down their own path. "The only time I actually work with words is when I'm writ-ing a song. After it's written, I release the words"—and now the words circle the song and choose the words they want to marry. At one point, as if to free the words from their own bodies, to divest them of any chance to signify, to let the word begin again in sound and find its own way out, Morri-son throws away them all—

Blah blah blah blah blah blah
Blah blah blah blah blah blah
Blah blah blah blah blah blah

> Blah blah blah blah blah blah
> Blah blah blah blah blah blah

—but it doesn't work, and it doesn't work because it isn't needed. By now the words themselves are rituals. The words are already free, and immediately as they regain their form they cast their spell again: *Getting hiiiiiiiiiiiiiigh, behind the ritual, so high—behind the ritual.*

Behaaaaaand the ritual, the singer twisting the word, making it gnarled and threatening—behind the ritual, the singer wanted to tell you, is the spiritual, but now the ritual, gathering every Saturday night in the alley with a bottle of sweet wine, is the spiritual, and the spiritual, that state of grace, is this tawdry ritual. The words begin to come apart, away from the transcendent, from that sense that there is always something unknown, a revelation that will leave you changed, behind the holiest rituals: isn't that what the church is for? No, it's life and what you want from it between the time you wake and the time you sleep.

The song pulls the singer farther and farther away from the truths it's rightfully his duty to tell you, the lessons you can learn from his mistakes, the peace of mind that is his and can be yours. But the voice is so expressive, so contained within itself and capable of going anywhere: "this music," the director and one-time rock critic Wim Wenders wrote about Morrison in 1970, "gives you a feeling and a notion of what films could be like: *perception* that doesn't always jump blindly at meanings and assertions, but rather lets your senses extend further and further."

You never do get out of the alley with this song. You never get back to the rest of the album, or for that matter to the rest of Morrison's career. It could stop right here. But over the course of that career one might have said the same thing a dozen times.

Roger Shattuck, *The Banquet Years: The Origins of the Avant-Garde in France, 1885 to World War I* (1958; rev. ed. New York: Vintage, 1968).

"The only time": Jonathan Cott, "Van Morrison: The *Rolling Stone* Interview," *Rolling Stone*, 30 November 1978, 52.

Wim Wenders, "Van Morrison," *Filmkritik*, June 1970, collected in *Emotion Pictures* (London: Faber and Faber, 1989), 53–54.

Van Morrison, "Behind the Ritual," on *Keep It Simple* (Lost Highway, 2008).

ACKNOWLEDGMENTS

My thanks go to Dave Marsh, William, Paula, and Erik Bernstein, Jon Landau, Jonathan Cott, Ben Schafer of Da Capo, Clinton Heylin, the indefatigable Toby Gleason, Danielle Madeira of Another Planet, Joel Selvin, Josh Gleason, John Elrod, Lynda Myles, Marc Smirnoff, Devin McKinney, Scott Foundas, David Patton, and the gracious and forthcoming Michael Sigman; to Jann Wenner at *Rolling Stone*, Marvin Garson and the late Sandy Darlington at the San Francisco *Express-Times*, the late Lester Bangs and the late Barry Kramer at *Creem*, Jon Carroll, Bill Broyles, and Nancy Duckworth at *New West*, David Frankel at *Artforum*, Bill Wyman at *Salon*, Graham Fuller at *Interview*, Alice O'Keefe at the *New Statesman*, and Jeffrey M. Perl of *Common Knowledge*; and to Emily, Cecily, Steve Perry, and Jenny, for the night at the Avalon Ballroom where this book first took shape.

INDEX

Greil Marcus is the author of *The Shape of Things to Come, Like a Rolling Stone,* and *The Old Weird America*; a twentieth-anniversary edition of his book *Lipstick Traces* was published in 2009. With Werner Sollors, he is the editor of *A New Literary History of America,* also published in 2009 by Harvard University Press. Since 2000 he has taught at Berkeley, Princeton, Minnesota, and the New School in New York; his column "Real Life Rock Top 10" appears regularly in *The Believer*. He lives in Berkeley.

PublicAffairs is a publishing house founded in 1997. It is a tribute to the standards, values, and flair of three persons who have served as mentors to countless reporters, writers, editors, and book people of all kinds, including me.

I. F. STONE, proprietor of *I. F. Stone's Weekly*, combined a commitment to the First Amendment with entrepreneurial zeal and reporting skill and became one of the great independent journalists in American history. At the age of eighty, Izzy published *The Trial of Socrates*, which was a national bestseller. He wrote the book after he taught himself ancient Greek.

BENJAMIN C. BRADLEE was for nearly thirty years the charismatic editorial leader of *The Washington Post*. It was Ben who gave the *Post* the range and courage to pursue such historic issues as Watergate. He supported his reporters with a tenacity that made them fearless and it is no accident that so many became authors of influential, best-selling books.

ROBERT L. BERNSTEIN, the chief executive of Random House for more than a quarter century, guided one of the nation's premier publishing houses. Bob was personally responsible for many books of political dissent and argument that challenged tyranny around the globe. He is also the founder and longtime chair of Human Rights Watch, one of the most respected human rights organizations in the world.

·　　·　　·

For fifty years, the banner of Public Affairs Press was carried by its owner Morris B. Schnapper, who published Gandhi, Nasser, Toynbee, Truman, and about 1,500 other authors. In 1983, Schnapper was described by *The Washington Post* as "a redoubtable gadfly." His legacy will endure in the books to come.

Peter Osnos, *Founder and Editor-at-Large*

Catherine Aird

Chapter and Hearse

 St. Martin's Minotaur ✻ New York

www.minotaurbooks.com

ISBN 0-312-29084-5

First published in Great Britain by Macmillan an imprint of Pan Macmillan Ltd

First St. Martin's Minotaur Edition: February 2004

10 9 8 7 6 5 4 3 2 1

Dedicated to

Peter Lucas

of happy memory

Contents

CONTENTS

Chapter and Hearse

A Change of Heart

'There's a girl downstairs, sir,' reported Detective Constable Crosby, 'who is saying that the hospital's killed her granny.'

'They've been killing grannies over there for years,' responded Detective Inspector C. D. Sloan drily. 'Par for the course, if you ask me.'

'No, no, sir, it isn't like that at all.'

'You mean granny wasn't one of Dangerous Dan's patients?' said Sloan.

The worryingly high casualty figures for Mr Daniel McGrew's surgical operations at the Berebury and District General Hospital were a byword throughout the county of Calleshire, but not a police matter. So far, that is.

'No, sir. One of Dr Edwin Beaumont's.'

'Ah, that's different.' Sloan frowned. 'He's one of the physicians, isn't he?'

'One of their top ones . . .' began Crosby.

'I'd always heard,' mused Sloan, 'that he was one of their good ones too.'

'Nothing known against,' responded the constable promptly, police-fashion. He hastily amended this to,

'I mean, yes, sir. They say over there that he's very highly thought of in his own line.'

'Which is?'

'Hearts,' said Crosby succinctly. It seemed appropriate for the time of year. The constable was still debating the wisdom of sending a Valentine Day's card to a nubile young lady on the police station's switchboard. 'And this is all about hearts.'

'And her granny's heart in particular?'

Unlike most of the rest of the police station, Sloan had refused to be drawn on the matter of the Valentine. As a happily married man, 14 February no longer held any terrors for him and he meant to keep it that way.

'Too right, sir.' He glanced down at his notebook. 'A Mrs Hilda Galbraith. The granddaughter is called Susan Merton and she insists her grandmother had always wanted to live.'

'Don't we all, miss?' Detective Inspector Sloan asked Susan Merton gently. She was young and pretty and very upset.

'I didn't mean Granny wanted to live for ever,' said the girl carefully, 'or that we wanted her to, even though she brought me up after my parents died. Of course she knew she would die one day. Everybody does . . .'

Sloan nodded sympathetically.

'And there's that bit in Shakespeare saying golden lads and girls all must come to dust, isn't there?' Her eyes began to mist over. 'Granny loved Shakespeare.'

'Yes?' said Sloan encouragingly. The Immortal Bard

was particularly good on the subject of death, but he didn't think this was the moment to say so.

'She'd known for ages that she could die suddenly at any time. She'd even told us where her will was and what sort of funeral she wanted and everything. You see, she had had a bad heart for ages.'

'Ah . . .'

'Besides, Inspector, she'd slid back from Thomas Hardy's "all-delivering door" more than once.' She frowned. 'Granny used to say that that poem of his called "A Wasted Illness" described what was happening to her very well.'

'Really, miss?' As far as Detective Inspector Sloan was concerned, poetry – however distinguished – was not usually something that was given in evidence. And evidence was what counted in police cases, not allegations.

'Anyway, Inspector, she'd had it spelled out by Dr Beaumont when she asked him – and we all knew it, anyway. You'd only to look at her blue lips. And she kept on having these terrible attacks of breathlessness.'

'I see,' murmured Detective Inspector Sloan, although he wasn't at all sure that he did. Mrs Hilda Galbraith's number sounded to him to have been pretty nearly up anyway. Not, of course, that it should make any difference to a potential murder inquiry. On the other hand, it did add to the statistical likelihood of a natural death . . .

Susan Merton said, 'Her son – that's my uncle Colin – came back to see her whenever he could, of course, but he's been through a nasty divorce and only just got married again, so it isn't easy for him to get down here now . . .'

Sloan made a mental note.

'And he's had to start a new job up in the north. His own firm went bust, you see . . .'

Quite automatically, Detective Inspector Sloan made a written note of the name Colin Galbraith.

'Although – ' Susan Merton's face started to crumple into tears – 'I'm afraid he didn't get here in time today.'

'Ah . . .'

'He's on his way back now and I know he'll be very upset when he arrives.'

'I'm sorry,' said Sloan simply.

The girl took a deep breath and tried to steady herself. 'But Granny always wanted to go on living as long as she could. I know she did.'

'Don't we all?' said the policeman again.

'Oh, no, Inspector.' She stared at him. 'A lot of the patients in the hospital don't . . . especially the old ones who are very ill.'

As Sloan turned over a page in his notebook, he was reminded of an ancient character in one of Geoffrey Chaucer's *Canterbury Tales*. He was the old fellow in 'The Pardoner's Tale' who spent his days searching for Death without being able to find him. Now, their Mr Daniel McGrew, decided Sloan, could probably have done something for him . . .

'Sometimes they even ask you straight out when you're admitted there,' Susan Merton was saying.

Sloan came back to the present, keeping his pen at

the ready. 'They ask you if you want to die? Are you quite sure of that, miss?'

'They ask you if you want to be actively resuscitated,' said the girl spiritedly, 'which comes to the same thing, doesn't it?'

'Well . . .' It wasn't only lawyers who could split hairs, of course. Doctors could be sophists, too.

'And sometimes if you're really ill, they don't ask you at all,' declared the girl. 'They just let you die.'

Sloan made a noncommittal noise well down his throat while he thought about this. Crosby appeared to be concentrating his mind on a pair of shapely ankles. If it hadn't been for the tear stains, the girl's face would have been really striking too. It was oval-shaped, with eyes of a deep, deep brown and hair to match. He couldn't see any young man hesitating about posting any number of Valentines in her direction tomorrow.

'I don't mind that,' said Susan Merton more matter-of-factly. 'In fact, sometimes I think it's better if the doctors do do the deciding themselves . . .'

Detective Inspector Sloan mentally reserved judgement on that too. He wasn't either a medical man or a theologian and these were muddy waters for a mere policeman.

'Those who aren't ever going to get better, for instance,' went on Susan Merton. 'The hopeless cases.'

Sloan made a note. Hopeless cases or not, policemen – mere or not – had a duty to see that the law was kept. And killing was unlawful. Not keeping alive might be something different, but that was not for him to say. He was, after all, only a policeman.

'Sometimes those who are in what they call

intractable pain too,' continued Susan Merton, twisting her handkerchief into a damp knot.

'Like your grandmother?' Sloan suggested tentatively.

'No, not like my grandmother,' she said at once. 'She wasn't in great pain.'

'Are you then alleg— That is, miss, are you then suggesting,' he asked, 'that your grandmother's life-support machine was switched off without consultation?' His knowledge of the law on this point was a bit shaky. If someone was going to say that the patient had been thus intentionally killed, then 'F' Police Division at Berebury stood a good chance of making legal case history.

'No,' responded Susan Merton promptly. 'She wasn't on a life-support machine.'

'So, miss,' asked Sloan, his pen still hovering above his notebook, 'what exactly is the problem, then?'

She sniffed and said in a muffled voice, 'They – Dr Dilys Chomel, that is . . .'

'And who might she be, miss?'

For the first time something approaching a smile flitted across Susan Merton's face. 'Uncle Colin calls her God's representative on the ward, but she's actually Dr Beaumont's house physician.'

Detective Constable Crosby lifted his eyes from his study of Susan's ankles. 'Who's God?'

She looked at him, surprised. 'Dr Edwin Beaumont, of course. He's the consultant in cardiac medicine there.'

Detective Inspector Sloan, who was older and thus

more experienced in the obeisance exacted by the medical hierarchy, hadn't needed to ask.

'Dr Chomel's very nice,' went on Susan Merton, 'but she was actually off duty when Granny... when ... when it happened.'

Sloan made another note.

'Dr Beaumont,' said the girl, 'had already asked Granny whether or not she wanted to be resuscitated if she had yet another heart attack ...'

'And?' asked Sloan, leaving aside Dr Chomel's niceness as not really germane.

Susan burst into tears. 'And Granny had said she did want to be. Definitely. I know, because I was there when Dr Beaumont and Dr Chomel discussed it, and so was Uncle Colin. He'd come down specially to see Dr Beaumont about Granny.' She swallowed visibly. 'Neither of us wanted her to die either.'

'So why, may I ask,' said the police inspector sternly, 'are you now saying that the hospital killed Mrs Hilda Galbraith?'

'Because they didn't even try to save her,' she sobbed. 'That's why.'

Sloan stiffened. 'I must remind you, Miss Merton, that it is a very serious accusation to make.'

'They just let her die,' insisted the girl flatly, 'and I think that's the same as killing her, whatever anyone else says.'

At the Berebury and District General Hospital Dr Dilys Chomel did her best to cast a professional gloss over Mrs Galbraith's death.

'We have a policy here, Inspector,' she hastened to assure him, 'of taking the patient's wishes into account in our decision-making processes as well as our own medical view of their future quality of life.' She added the latest medical mantra: 'Illness is a partnership, you know.'

Sloan ignored this fashionable concept and got straight down to the tried and tested police agenda of first checking what he had been told. 'Could you then, doctor, tell me exactly what Mrs Hilda Galbraith's own wishes were in this respect?'

'Ah . . .' began Dr Chomel.

'I take it you did know them?' He must remember that the old lady hadn't been on oath when she told her family she wanted to live. She might, he thought sympathetically, actually have wanted to be allowed to turn her face to the wall in peace, untrammelled by oxygen masks, needles and tubes, leaving herself undisturbed by the distress of her nearest and dearest, yet letting them happily believe that all that was medically necessary was being done for her.

It was what he himself would have wanted.

'I think,' said Dr Chomel cautiously, 'she may have changed her mind about the whole thing. At first she told us that, if it was ever called for, she wanted us to attempt resuscitation.' The house physician always put in that little rider about *attempting* resuscitation rather than just doing it. The popular view was too optimistic a one.

'Ah . . .'

'It isn't always successful, you know, in spite of what you usually see on television,' she sighed, 'and after being on the ward for a little while, I'm afraid the patients do get to realize this.'

'I can see that might be the case,' agreed Sloan, bearing in mind that Mrs Galbraith also might have said one thing and later agreed to another. After all, it was a free world – even in hospital. 'But after that?'

'She must have told – er – someone else on the staff here that she didn't want it tried after all.'

'What makes you say that, doctor?'

'Her notes.' She hesitated. 'As you will see, Inspector, they're quite clearly marked and that's why the crash team wasn't sent for. Look, there . . .'

Both policemen peered at the patient's records.

'You will observe,' said Dr Chomel, 'that we had her down as a "122".'

'Meaning what exactly?'

The house physician explained that the figures had succeeded the letters 'DNR' on the admission records of patients at the Berebury and District General Hospital. 'In most hospitals, Inspector,' she said awkwardly, 'those letters stand for "Do Not Resuscitate".'

'I see.' Sloan thought he was beginning to see quite a lot now.

'And some people,' the young doctor said ingenuously, 'take exception to that decision being visible on the chart at the bottom of the bed.'

Detective Inspector Sloan said that he could see that they might.

Detective Constable Crosby said that he would have done.

'So now we write "122" instead,' she finished lamely.

'One, two, that'll do,' chanted Crosby insouciantly.

Dr Dilys Chomel, who came from a culture that did not encompass English nursery rhymes, looked bewildered. 'That way,' she said, 'now only the medical and nursing staff know.'

Detective Inspector Sloan, for one, did not for a single moment believe this; but then, he was in the disbelieving business. Any half-intelligent patient or visitor could have worked it out for themselves.

Dr Chomel wasn't in the disbelieving business. Not yet, anyway.

'And if a visitor should ask what the "122" means,' she went on hastily, 'they're told that it's the extension number of the doctor who has to be informed of any emergency.' Active medical resuscitation was not a problem in her own country. Few people there lived to their three score years and ten, let alone any longer. They also shared an unshakeable belief – completely at odds with contemporary Western medicine – that 'what will be, will be'.

'But I take it they weren't told that the patient would be dead by the time that doctor was contacted?' enquired Detective Inspector Sloan. Hippocrates, he decided, would be surprised at quite how far medical ethics had come since his time. 'If he or she was ever to be contacted, that is . . .'

'No,' she said, looking uncomfortable.

'The best of both worlds,' he murmured.

'This and the next,' remarked Crosby incorrigibly.

Sloan resolved that as soon as they got back to the police station he would give his assistant something more serious to think about than the sending of a

Valentine. Such as when to keep quiet during an investigation . . .

Unfortunately the detective constable had more to say. 'Do they have a secret sign too, doctor, when they want to reuse your liver and lights?'

Dr Chomel's command of English, though good, was not up to this. 'No, no,' she said when Crosby explained. 'For organ transplants we need the written consent of the relatives.'

'I can see that your resuscitation procedure looks good on paper, though,' said Sloan absently, his mind now elsewhere.

Dr Chomel still looked uncomfortable.

'Having to be good on paper,' Sloan said kindly, 'is half the trouble these days.'

Dr Chomel looked even more uncomfortable.

'So who,' piped up Detective Constable Crosby helpfully, 'wrote this number "122" on the patient's notes, then?'

'I'm not entirely sure,' Dr Chomel said with obvious reluctance, 'but it does explain why the crash team wasn't summoned.'

'Someone must have put the number there,' said Sloan ineluctably.

'Yes, Inspector.'

'Someone who knew what the numbers meant,' concluded Sloan aloud.

'Yes, Inspector.'

'Narrows the field a bit, doesn't it?' said Detective Constable Crosby chattily.

'Ye-es,' she agreed, her uncertainty now patent.

'Someone must have done it here, in the hospital, too,' continued Sloan.

'Yes.' She gulped and suddenly blurted out, 'I'm afraid that it's written in green ink.'

'Is that significant?'

Her voice fell to almost a whisper. 'Dr Beaumont always writes his patients' notes in green ink.'

Sloan nodded. Idiosyncrasies were important in establishing the pecking order. 'To be different?'

She shook her head. 'No, Inspector. He says it's so that there can't be any doubt who's written them.'

Dr Edwin Beaumont treated the police visit to his home as a tiresome interruption. 'Don't tell me that the relatives are complaining the patient wasn't well treated,' he began testily.

'Only in a manner of speaking,' said Sloan, explaining.

'If you think,' the consultant said crisply, 'that I am going about administering a *coup de grâce* to every very old patient blocking one of my beds, Inspector, you are mistaken. And I have statistical records to prove it.'

'It seems that someone did,' said Sloan mildly. 'In green ink.'

'Clever,' conceded the medical man. 'Very clever. But not done by me.' He took out his pen and wrote down the numbers on a sheet of paper. He handed pen and paper to the policeman. 'Or with my Waterman pen nib. Check with your tame specialists if you like.'

'I doubt if that will be necessary, sir,' said Detective

Inspector Sloan. 'But if I might just borrow your telephone to talk to Dr Chomel . . .'

The physician pushed it towards him.

'Dr Chomel? Inspector Sloan here. There's something I want you to do for us. Now, listen very
carefully . . .'

The two policemen were back at Berebury police
station with a surprised Colin Galbraith under arrest
on suspicion of causing unlawful death before Sloan
expanded further.

'What counts in police work, Crosby, is evidence –
hard evidence – not just suspicion.'

'Yes, sir, but . . .'

'What we needed to do was to get the old lady's
son to write down those letters in the presence of an
impeccable witness . . .'

'Dr Chomel,' said Crosby, faint but pursuing.

'The courts trust medical doctors,' said Sloan ellipti-
cally, 'even if all their patients don't.' ·

'Yes, sir, I know that, but . . .'

'So we had to get Colin Galbraith, who after all
must have needed his share of his mother's money
after a contested divorce, a new marriage and a failed
business if anybody did . . .'

'I'll say,' said Crosby, who had had the perils of
matrimony spelled out to him in the canteen by the
cohort against the sending of the famous Valentine.

' . . . to write the letters "122" down without sus-
pecting that we knew anything was amiss.'

'But what I don't see, sir, is why you got Dr Chomel

to get Galbraith to sign a statement that he didn't want a post-mortem performed on his mother. That's got nothing to do with it.'

'Nothing,' agreed Sloan cheerfully. 'What was important was getting him to date it.'

Crosby frowned. 'What's the date got to do with it?'

'With today's date, of course,' said Sloan.

'Today's date?' said Crosby, adding after a moment's thought. 'The 12th of February?'

'The graphologists don't mind if you use letters or figures,' said Sloan. 'Or which pen.'

'So . . .'

'Whether you write down 12 February or 12.2 and the year, you've got to use the figures 1 and 2.'

'One, two, that'll do . . .' remarked the constable.

'Exactly. Anyone can use a green pen but your handwriting characteristics can't be disguised. Distance-killing, you could call it, writing in that death warrant. By the way, Crosby . . .'

'Sir?'

'If I were you, I think I'd send that Valentine card for 14 February after all . . .'

Due Diligence

'I must say I don't like the idea at all myself,' said Simon flatly. 'Otherwise, of course, I can see that it would be a very good place to live.'

'Quite,' said Kenneth Marsden, the estate agent, patently unperturbed. The word was one he was very fond of using with his clients. It implied agreement without actually spelling it out. 'Quite.'

'Nor me,' chimed in Simon's wife, Charlotte, quickly.

Too quickly.

'Quite,' said the estate agent again. Kenneth Marsden had found that this all-purpose word equally usefully concealed disagreement without actually spelling out the fact to prospective purchasers of attractive properties newly on the market in rural Calleshire. 'I do understand, naturally. It was all very, very unfortunate.'

'I mean,' said Simon Cullen, 'it's not every day that something like that happens in someone's house.'

'Quite so.' The man from Messrs Crombie and Marsden, Estate Agents and Valuers, paused and then said judiciously, 'On the other hand, it has at the same time to be remembered – ' Kenneth Marsden was also

in the habit of making all unwelcome pronounce-
ments in the impersonal tense – 'that there are very
few domestic properties in this country – especially
genuinely old ones such as the Manor at Cullingoak –
in which, over the years, somebody has not died . . .'

'Naturally,' agreed Simon, 'but this death was really
only the other day, wasn't it?'

'Which is why the present owner wishes to dispose
of it so quickly,' said the estate agent smoothly. He
changed the subject with the skill born of long practice.
'By the way, how did you happen to hear about the
Manor being up for sale? We shan't be advertising it
until the end of the week.'

It was Charlotte Cullen who answered him. 'Somebody at work mentioned it to me, and I rang my
husband and got him to collect the key when he was
in Berebury so we could see over the house while
I could fit it in. I've got to go abroad for the bank
tomorrow.'

Kenneth Marsden translated her coded message
without difficulty. There would be no problems over
money or mortgage with any purchase was what she
was actually telling him.

'But the lady of the house didn't just die, did she?'
persisted Simon.

'My husband meant houses in which there has
been a fatal accident,' spelt out Charlotte for him.
'Didn't you, Simon?'

Simon Cullen did not respond to this.

'I do understand,' Kenneth Marsden hastened to say
soothingly. Actually he understood a great deal more:
he now knew which of this couple it was who meta-

16

phorically wore the trousers. This knowledge was something that was as important to him now as it would be to any experienced negotiator.

'The publicity,' pointed out Simon.

'Unfavourable,' conceded the estate agent immediately. He allowed a little pause to develop before he said obliquely, 'You yourselves would, of course, be benefiting from this to the extent that the property has been placed on the market at a substantially lower price than it would have been had the – er – unfortunate accident not occurred.'

'We do appreciate that,' murmured Charlotte Cullen. 'It is an important factor in our even considering purchasing a property such as this. I must say, though, that I agree with my husband that it is a very nice house.'

Within the privacy of the partners' room of Messrs Crombie and Marsden, Kenneth Marsden had described this particular instance of his lowering of his valuation of the house as 'blood money'. To his eternal credit, the vendor had not demurred at his suggested figure. Indeed, for a money man – he was a stockbroker – Mr Wetherby had shown very little interest in the prospective sale, only in disposing of the property at the earliest possible moment.

Needless to say, Kenneth Marsden did not say either of these things now. Instead, he nodded his agreement with Charlotte. 'Yes, indeed, Mrs Cullen,' he said easily. 'It's a very fine example of its period.'

Charlotte, who was rising rapidly through the upper-middle echelons of the Bank of Calleshire, where she worked, leaned forward and said, 'Actually it was the price which first attracted my husband.'

'I'm sure,' said Kenneth warmly.

Simon said nothing.

'I hesitate to use the word "bargain" in these particular circumstances,' went on Kenneth Marsden, matching spurious frankness with superficial – if seemingly transparent – honesty, 'but there's no denying that if it weren't for the – er – tragic incident there, the Manor at Cullingoak would be much more highly priced than it is today.'

'My husband,' began Charlotte again, 'was quite taken with the actual property too . . .' She turned towards Simon and said, 'Weren't you, dear?'

Simon had long ago decided that Charlotte must have read in a women's magazine that where the wife was the money earner, it was important that she deferred to her husband on each and every occasion when this was at all possible. And that her constant litany should be, "I'll have to ask my husband." That this should only be when his answer wasn't important went, Simon knew, without saying.

'The kitchen needs a bit of work doing on it . . .' said Simon spiritedly. 'And the larder window needs fixing.'

He made both statements without any fear of being described as a 'house husband'. Charlotte had never ever brought herself to tell the world that her husband had been made redundant from his job at the metal works in Berebury and therefore that he stayed at home while she made the money – and quite a lot of money it was these days too, to be sure. He wasn't complaining about that. It was her end-of-the-year bonus, she had told him, that was going to make buying the Manor at Cullingoak possible.

When asked what her husband did, Charlotte always replied with perfect truth that he was a bi-metallist. Since she moved in the world of corporate banking, this was almost always taken by her office colleagues to mean that Simon was an economist who was concerned with the monetary system in which two metals are used in fixed relative values and not – as he actually was – someone trained in the coefficients of expansion of all metals.

Charlotte never disabused them of this misappre-hension, and when the more knowledgeable responded with remarks such as, 'Gold and silver, I suppose,' she would say uncertainly, 'I think so, but I'm afraid it's not really my field . . .' That people did not talk much about their work went without saying in all banking circles, and the conversation would move on.

'I dare say that the owner might agree to that sort of repair being taken into account,' the estate agent was saying to Simon, without for one moment revealing how very useful it was in a negotiating situ-ation to have a few small bones to chew over. The smaller the bone, the better, of course. In the world of the estate agent, work on a larder window was easily conceded, and the cost of an upgraded kitchen some-thing to be wrested from the owner after a nominal struggle.

'Who is the owner anyway?' asked Charlotte casu-ally. 'He wasn't around.'

'A Mr Wetherby,' replied Kenneth Marsden, adding, 'He's naturally still very shocked at losing his wife, you know, and not too keen on going back to the house.'

'I'm not surprised,' said Charlotte Cullen. 'Poor man.'

Simon gave Marsden a hard look. 'And I take it that the whole place has been rewired?'

The estate agent looked pained. 'I can assure you that the house's electrical system was the very first thing that was checked after the accident. It was found to be all in good order – ' he gave a slight cough – 'in spite of everything.'

'Everything?' queried Simon.

'Mrs Wetherby's electrocution seemed quite inexplicable. Mr Wetherby was at work when it happened and so wasn't able to help much with the coroner's enquiries.'

'Then there shouldn't be anything for us to worry about, should there?' said Charlotte in the same decisive tones as she had used to wind up many a meeting at the bank.

'No,' said Kenneth Marsden automatically.

She raised an enquiring eye in her husband's direction and went through her usual routine. 'What do you say, Simon? It's up to you, of course, but I must say I like it . . .'

'Me too,' he said meekly.

'Right.' She turned to Kenneth Marsden. 'You can tell Peter Wetherby that we'll take it.'

'I don't think you'll regret it,' said the estate agent heartily, shaking hands as they left.

Simon Cullen was inclined to agree with him when, six weeks later, he and Charlotte had duly moved into the Manor at Cullingoak. The larder window had been fixed and the men were due to come that Monday morning to improve the kitchen layout. Simon had no hang-ups about doing the cooking, belonging as he did to the very workman-like 'if you can read, then you can cook' school of *haute cuisine*, but equally he saw no point in ever working under less than optimum conditions. Actually he brought to the task of cooking the same attention and care that had served his previous employers very well until the advent of the world decline in the heavy metals industry.

'Now, then, Mr Cullen,' said the foreman, 'before we get started, can you just check that this plan here is how you want it all doing? Measure twice and cut once, as my old boss used to say.'

Simon switched the electric kettle on as a gesture of good intent before he joined the man peering over the drawings laid out on the kitchen table. 'That's right,' he said after duly studying the design. He pointed to the larder door and with his hand sketched an imaginary journey round the kitchen in the direction of the stove via the work surfaces and the kitchen sink. 'Store, wash, prepare, cook, serve . . . that's how it should be.'

The foreman scratched his head. 'I hadn't thought of it like that.'

'Only if you're right-handed,' said Simon. 'The lady who lived here before must have been a southpaw.'

'Both her hands had burns on them,' the man informed him ghoulishly.

'Though they never did find out how she got them,' chimed in his mate, Fred.

'Electrocuted in the utility room, she was,' said the foreman lugubriously. 'But don't you let that worry you. They went over that room with a fine-tooth comb after it had happened.'

'Couldn't find a thing amiss, though,' said Fred in his role as Greek chorus. 'They never did work out what went wrong.'

'Really?' said Simon, absently moving in the direction of the worktop. The kettle had come to the boil and switched itself off. 'Tea?'

'Milk but no sugar for me,' said the foreman, undiverted. 'Thought it must have been something to do with the ironing board, they did, because that was lying on the floor beside her when her husband found her. There was a pile of nearly dry washing in the laundry basket beside her too.'

'And,' supplemented his assistant eagerly, 'because she always did the ironing while she watched her favourite afternoon programme on television.'

'My wife too,' said the foreman. 'Thanks,' he added, cradling the mug between his large, dirt-ingrained hands. 'I don't know which channel, though,' he added in the interests of accuracy, 'because I'm not there then.'

Simon decided that this was not the moment for quoting that famous question, 'But what was the play like, Mrs Lincoln?'

'Two lumps for me,' said his mate, stretching his hand out for his tea. 'They thought she died just before the programme came on at four o'clock . . . and that's what the man who did the post-mortem said too.'

'Pathologist,' supplied Simon.

'But they never found out how she came to be electrocuted,' repeated the foreman, addressing himself to his drink. 'Never.'

'Funny, that,' murmured Simon Cullen.

'It said in the paper that her husband was at work at the time it happened,' expanded the foreman.

'At a meeting all afternoon,' chimed in Fred. 'It said that too. About a dozen people there with him all the time.'

'My wife spends a lot of her time at work in meetings,' said Simon. 'I know, because she tells me when not to ring the office.'

'If you ask me,' opined the foreman, pushing back his chair, 'most meetings are a waste of time. Let's get started here, Fred.'

Simon swept up the empty mugs and drifted off to take a look at the utility room with new eyes. It was situated off the kitchen and housed the central-heating boiler and the washing machine, as well as all the impediments associated with living in a sizeable house in the country – including Simon's new green wellies. The Wetherbys' ironing board had gone and Simon had stood the Cullens' one there in its place, but otherwise the room looked very much as it must have done in the days of the previous occupants.

Propped up beside the ironing board and the radiator was the clothes horse which Simon and Charlotte had brought with them from their old house. In fact, the only relic of the Wetherbys' regime was one of those old-fashioned wooden airers, which could be lowered by a thin rope, loaded with damp washing and then hoisted back up to the ceiling above the boiler to dry.

Simon examined everything in the room with his customary care but was no wiser at the end of his survey. In fact, had he but known it, he reached the same conclusion as the investigating authorities had done – that something had electrified the metal of the ironing board.

When he gave the men their tea in the afternoon he said, 'You might just put a lick of paint on that small scratch on the radiator in there next time one of you has a paintbrush in his hand.'

'No problem,' said the foreman. 'No sugar, thanks.'

'Two lumps for me,' Fred reminded him. 'Worked out how it was done, have you?'

'Done?' said Simon.

Fred gave him a knowing wink. 'They said the husband had got a lady love tucked away somewhere.'

The foreman set his mug down and said sapiently, 'What he had got was an unbreakable alibi, so you mind what you say here, Fred.'

Fred bridled. 'There's no smoke without fire. Besides, don't forget that most murderers are widowers.'

'Because they've killed their wives.' Simon nodded. 'I've heard that one before.'

'Remember,' pronounced the foreman magisterially, 'it didn't say anything about that in the newspapers – not even the Sunday ones.'

'What else did it say?' asked Simon, adding in spite of himself, 'I suppose it is theoretically possible that the ironing board was live – electrified, that is – a long time before Mrs Wetherby touched it.'

'Not before one o'clock it wasn't, insisted Fred vigorously. 'Ivy Middleton was here all that morning. She put the dirty washing in the machine and started it up before she went home, like she always did, dinnertime.'

'That's right,' said the foreman. 'I was forgetting about Ivy. She touched that ironing board and she didn't get an electric shock, did she, Fred?'

Simon and Charlotte hadn't kept Mrs Ivy Middleton on to do the rough housework. As Charlotte had put it so pithily when she – they – paid for the Manor, 'They could afford Cullingoak Manor – just – but not the extras as well.' Ivy had rated as an extra and so Simon saw entirely to the running of the house.

'There could have been some cable and a time switch,' he said in spite of himself. It was just as well Charlotte was at work. She wouldn't have approved of his wasting the workmen's time – let alone his gossiping with them – like this. 'You know, an electric wire from the nearest power socket to the ironing board timed to come live after Mrs Middleton had left.'

'Now, if I may say so, that's where you're wrong,' said the foreman placidly. 'The police thought of that too.' He took a swig from his mug. 'It so happens that there wasn't any such timer in the house or garden, and, believe you me, they searched for it.'

'I can quite see that they would,' murmured Simon.

'And,' the foreman added, tapping the table with his forefinger for greater emphasis, 'they had a witness that the husband – Peter Wetherby, that is – didn't leave the house before the police arrived, so he couldn't have hidden a timer anywhere outside the house.'

'Got it in for him, haven't you,' said Simon, 'this Peter Wetherby?' Suddenly something about the name jarred in his mind. He couldn't quite place the memory but it was there, somewhere.

'Ironing boards don't become live on their own.' The foreman shrugged, starting to get to his feet.

'I reckon,' said Fred, 'it was suicide.'

'Suicide?' echoed Simon.

Fred nodded. 'I think she connected a wire from the socket to the ironing board herself and her husband came home and found her and removed the evidence pretty quickly. Didn't want anyone to know she'd done it because of this other woman, see?'

The foreman said, 'You're a great one for your theories, Fred, but it don't get the work done . . . Come along now, let's get started here or we'll never be done.'

Over the next few weeks Simon had to agree that Fred's suicide theory was the most tenable. Something like a kettle flex could have been plugged into the nearest power point and bare wires at the other end made to touch the metal of the ironing board. Turn the switch on, clasp the ironing board and Bob's your uncle. A married man becomes a widower in no time at all.

And all that the husband would have had to do before he rang the police was put the proper plug back on the appliance – the work of a moment – and no one would be any the wiser. Oh, and perhaps change the face of the plug in the wall in case there were burn marks there too.

He gave this thought whenever Charlotte was away – she was away rather a lot these days for the bank. At least he thought it was for the bank until the bank telephoned urgently one weekend to talk to her and he referred them to their conference and they said they weren't having one.

That was when he remembered what it was about the use of Peter Wetherby's Christian name that had bothered him. Charlotte had known it even though the estate agent had only given them his surname.

Now he came to think of it, she had known too about Cullingoak Manor being for sale for a low price before it had been advertised . . .

It still didn't explain how Mrs Wetherby had died while her husband was well away from the action unless it had been by her own hand.

Simon Cullen was rapidly coming to the conclusion that it hadn't been.

That was when he laid his plan.

'Darling,' he said to Charlotte the next evening, 'I think I'm going to have to have a couple of nights away next week. Uncle George wants me to go up to Yorkshire to see him.'

'Fine,' she said. 'Remember me to the old boy. Not that I've seen him since the wedding.'

'No more you have,' he said, since his relations weren't much liked by Charlotte. 'I'll go on Tuesday and be back Thursday evening. That all right?'

'Fine,' she said. 'By the way, before I forget, I may be a bit late back on Friday – we've got a big meeting at the bank Friday afternoon.' She smiled. 'Salary review committee – mustn't miss that.'

'Not on any account,' he agreed gravely.

Simon studiously avoided the utility room when he got back to the Manor on the Thursday evening – he and Charlotte had a quiet evening together.

'You might switch the washing machine on first thing, Simon,' she said as they went upstairs. 'I went through my summer things while you were away ready for the autumn.'

'They'll be all beautifully ironed,' he said, 'by the time you get home.'

'It's getting too chilly to wear them now. I must say I was quite glad of the central heating when I got in yesterday.'

'The afternoons are getting cooler,' he agreed amiably.

As soon as Charlotte had left for work on the Friday morning – the day of her big meeting – Simon entered the utility room very carefully. He didn't switch on the washing machine, though. Instead he examined the room with extreme caution. There was indeed a plug in the power socket and a length of flex tucked away behind the radiator and then running, almost out of sight at ground level, to the nearest leg of the ironing board. Fred had been right about that anyway.

But he wasn't into metals and Simon was.

Also behind the radiator, firmly taped to it, was

what he had been looking for – that which would make the whole thing live.

But not just yet. Not until the central heating warmed the radiator.

'Clever,' he murmured to himself appreciatively. 'Very clever.'

It was a short metal bar which neither the police nor anyone else would have looked at twice had they noticed it lying around. It was half copper and half steel lengthways – the principle on which thermostats often work. And it was pressed firmly against the back of the radiator, the copper part set alongside – but not touching – one of the two wires in the flex.

This had been scraped bare. He checked that the central heating was set to come on at three o'clock as usual – Simon thought it would take about an hour to warm up enough to make the copper expand and complete the electrical circuit. Then he went back to the kitchen to wait for something to happen to establish that he was alive and well before lunch.

At twelve o'clock their next-door neighbour came to the door. 'Your wife has just rung me, Mr Cullen, to say she thinks she can't have put the telephone back on its hook properly because she keeps getting the engaged signal.'

'I'll check,' he said, knowing it would be so. 'Thanks for letting me know. Like a coffee?'

'Some other time, if I may.'

'I'll look forward to that,' he said, and meant it. His neighbours really were very agreeable people indeed. Getting to know them in future was going to be a pleasure.

When Charlotte got back at six o'clock he was out of sight, behind the utility-room door. She went straight there, calling out his name as she did so. He did not answer, but when she was right inside the room and standing, puzzled, in front of the ironing board, he stepped out quietly from behind the door and gave her a gentle push towards it. She put out her hands to save herself, and screamed as she touched the ironing board.

At the trial, before pronouncing a life sentence, the judge described Peter Wetherby as a clever, calculating and callous killer of the two women in his life.

Time, Gentlemen, Please

'I don't like it, Sloan,' declared the Superintendent heavily.

'No, sir.' Detective Inspector C. D. Sloan hadn't for one moment imagined that he would. Change was undeniably in the air and, just like the Victorian hymn writer, Superintendent Leeyes invariably associated change with decay.

'In my young days,' Leeyes was rumbling on, 'the police force was the police force and MI5 and MI6 were the secret services.'

And, exactly as it said in the old hymn, the Superintendent always saw change and decay all around him too.

' "And never the twain shall meet",' muttered Sloan under his breath. 'Like East and West.'

'What's that, Sloan? I didn't quite catch . . .'

'Nothing, sir.' The Inspector coughed. 'You were saying that in your day . . .'

'Then the police did their job and the secret services did theirs.'

'I'm sure, sir.'

The news that it had been ordained from on high that in future members of secret services MI5 and MI6 were to work hand in hand with the police in the tracking down of major criminals had been received at Berebury police station with what a professional diplomat would have called 'some considerable reserve'.

'Moreover,' said Leeyes flatly, 'when that lot got up to something in the course of their activities which wasn't legal, we weren't told.'

'Quite, sir.' Metaphorically, Sloan averted his eyes too.

'Not that we wanted to know, of course,' he added hastily. 'At least they spared us that.'

'Not our problem,' agreed Sloan.

'Now,' he said morosely, 'if they overstep the mark, we'll get the blame too. Bound to.'

'Clandestine operations usually make for difficulties,' said Sloan sagely. In his opinion they were almost as risky as stings.

'And why, Sloan, they should imagine for one moment that a bunch of out-of-work old cloak-and-dagger merchants should be able to nail our drug traffickers and big-time fraudsters any better or quicker than we can beats me.'

'Yes, sir. Me too,' said Sloan, noting with detached interest that the Superintendent's famous territorial imperative extended to Calleshire criminals as well as to its good citizens.

'Which is not to say,' pronounced Leeyes trenchantly, 'that I am suggesting for one moment that the Serious Fraud Squad couldn't do with some proper help.'

'No, sir . . . I mean, yes, sir, I'm sure it could.'

He opened his hands in gesture. 'I ask you, Sloan, what *is* the force coming to?'

Detective Inspector Sloan, who from bitter experience knew better than to attempt to answer his superior officer's rhetorical questions, made no reply to this.

'I suppose they haven't got anything else better to do these days,' carried on Leeyes ruminatively. 'Not now, seeing that the Cold War is over.' He sniffed. 'I understand that today it's not so much a case of "know thine enemy" as knowing who on earth your enemy is in the first place.'

For one wild moment Sloan considered mentioning that in an international context this fragile state was known as 'peace', but he soon thought better of it.

'The secret services just don't think they've got any real enemies left,' insisted Leeyes. 'That's their trouble.'

'Well, we have.' Detective Inspector Sloan was under no illusions about this. 'More than enough of them.'

'Oh, yes,' Leeyes unhesitatingly concurred with him. 'There are still plenty of bad boys around in Calleshire. No doubt about that.'

'And so these – er – secret services want to borrow our enemies so that they can keep going, do they, sir?' asked Sloan, aware that even in these politically correct times 'enemy' and 'criminal' were still always spoken of as male.

'Right first time.'

'And we,' ventured Sloan carefully, letting several

tricky revolutionary situations abroad pass unmentioned, 'at least have the benefit of usually knowing who our enemies are.'

'You name it, Sloan, and we've got them on the job. Fraudsters, drug dealers, confidence tricksters, car criminals – the lot.'

'Quite so,' said Sloan. Like change and decay, criminals were all around. And with them always too.

The Superintendent pushed a directive across his desk. 'According to this, Sloan,' he quoted mincingly, 'we've got to feel free to enlist the aid of MI5 and MI6 in our struggles with serious crime whenever we may want their assistance.'

'Right, sir,' he responded neutrally. Detective Inspector Sloan was head of the tiny Criminal Investigation Department at Berebury police station and such serious crime as there was in this corner of Calleshire usually landed on his desk first. He got up to go. 'I'll remember that.'

'Wait a minute.' Leeyes stayed him with a raised hand. 'I'm afraid the Assistant Chief Constable wants to put in his ha'p'orth too.'

'Yes, of course, sir. When are you going to see . . .'

'Oh, not me, Sloan.' The Superintendent looked out at a clear, golfing sky. 'I'm going off duty now. You.'

The Assistant Chief Constable, who was both a police officer and a classicist, welcomed Sloan with a genial, 'Ah, Inspector, come in and hear what our secret services are up to . . .' He waved Sloan into a chair the other side of his desk. 'Sit yourself down.'

'Thank you, sir.'

'I'm not sure all this isn't in direct contravention of the Civil List and Secret Service Money Act of 1782 – as revised in 1978, of course – but ours is not to reason why.'

'Probably repealed by now, sir.' As far as Sloan was concerned, the older the statute the better. Laws that had stood the test of time were usually good ones.

'I'm afraid that MI5 and MI6 are taking this business of closer cooperation with the force quite literally.'

'Really, sir?' responded Sloan. 'I must say, myself I don't quite see how they can help us. Not in the short term, anyway.'

'Help us, Sloan?' echoed the Assistant Chief Constable stoutly. 'I should think not, indeed! The very idea . . .'

'Sir?'

'I can assure you that the boot is quite on the other foot.'

'Sir?'

'You've got hold of the wrong end of the stick, man. They want us to help them.' The Assistant Chief Constable fingered the message sheet before him and frowned. 'At least, I think that's what they mean. Their prose is what you might call a trifle opaque.'

'They've got a problem?'

He smiled thinly. 'Yes, I think we may say that. Of course, I'm only reading between the lines, which I understand is what you do with their messages before you swallow them.'

'On our patch?'

'Four times over so far.'

'I see, sir.' Sloan leaned forward. 'They need our help, do they? Might I ask in what way?'

'In the matter of establishing the assignation procedure of certain enemies of the state.' The Assistant Chief Constable suddenly looked remarkably cunning. 'Unless, of course, Sloan, they are just testing us out. Seeing if we are any good at playing their sort of wide games – that sort of thing . . .'

'A dummy run?'

'Quite possibly.' He tapped his desk with an elegant gold pen. 'Except that I wouldn't like this force to be thought of as dummies in any sense – if you take my meaning.'

'No, sir. Naturally not.'

'What they have said to me – ' the Assistant Chief Constable contrived to project doubt into every word – 'is that they have two suspects – that is to say, two people with – er – different loyalties from ours . . .'

'Spies . . .' supplied Sloan, wondering if this term too had now become as politically incorrect as almost every other expression in hitherto common usage.

'Shall we say "agents of another power", then?' suggested the Assistant Chief Constable helpfully.

'Very well, sir.'

'And that they, whoever they are, are meeting,' said the Assistant Chief Constable, 'somewhere in your manor here for the exchange of – er – of whatever it is secret agents hand over these days . . .'

Sloan nodded. With Kipling it had been letters for a spy; with Sherlock Holmes it had been plans – the Bruce-Partington Plans; with John Buchan it had been something to do with the Thirty-nine Steps . . .

'Money?' he hazarded, coming fully into the twenty-first century.

'That's quite possible, Inspector. As even infant criminals seem to know these days, money leaves too much of an audit trail if you transfer it by any other method than hard cash in the good old brown envelope.'

'So what exactly is their problem, sir?' Detective Inspector Sloan knew a good deal more about the importance of audit trails now than he had done before money-laundering had joined the older, simpler crimes in the Newgate Calendar.

The Assistant Chief Constable tapped the message sheet. 'How the two parties – whoever they are – get in touch with each other to arrange the handover.'

'So that they can be stopped?' enquired Sloan diffidently.

'So that their communications can be intercepted,' the senior officer amended, suddenly looking very cunning again. 'And, for all we know, tampered with and sent on.'

'And when they do meet,' hazarded Sloan, 'it will presumably then be established who they are? I take it identities are wanted . . .'

'Got it in one, Sloan.' He frowned. 'No, that's not quite right.' He fingered the message sheet again. 'They know who one of them is.'

'Ah . . .'

'What they don't know is who she's meeting.'

'She?' said Sloan.

'Codenamed Mata Hari,' the Assistant Chief Constable said apologetically. 'These people haven't got any imagination, you know.'

'And what they want to know, you say, sir, is who she's meeting . . .' It sounded all very *Boy's Own Paper* stuff to Sloan.

'That and how they make their – er – '

'Assignations, sir?'

'Exactly.'

'Not by telephone?'

'Tapped.'

'Letters?'

'Intercepted.'

'E-mail?'

'Don't ask me how, Sloan, but these clever johnnies tell me that they've got that sussed out too.' No one, except perhaps Superintendent Leeyes, remained more Luddite in his attitude to computer technology than the Assistant Chief Constable.

'Coded advertisement?'

'Apparently their code breakers can't work out anything in the daily newspapers that could possibly mean "Meet me outside St Ninian's Church in Berebury at eight o'clock on Friday morning", or words to that effect.' He twitched his lips into a grin. 'And I'm told it wasn't for want of trying either. For their sins, they even went through all those Baucis and Philemon advertisements.'

'Beg pardon, sir?'

'Baucis and Philemon were Ovid's couple to whom the gods gave the gift of growing old together like entwined trees.'

'Ah.' Sloan's brow cleared. He should have remembered that the Assistant Chief Constable was a classicist first and a policeman a long way second. 'I'm with you, sir. The "Lonely Hearts" columns . . .'

'I understand there was no shortage of volunteers for the research,' said the Assistant Chief Constable drily, 'but much good it did 'em . . .' He paused and then, scholar that he was, added punctiliously, 'In that respect anyway.'

'Radio transmitter?' suggested Sloan.

'First thing they looked for.' The Assistant Chief Constable wrinkled his nose. 'Old hat anyway, these days.'

'Internet?' Sloan made another effort to come into the twenty-first century.

The Assistant Chief Constable said 'They're quite sure that Mata Hari – sorry, but that's how they will refer to their female suspect – doesn't have access to it.'

'Don't they have Internet Cafes now, sir?'

The Assistant Chief Constable said gloomily, 'They've been tailing her for weeks . . . Mata Hari, indeed. You'd have thought they'd have been a bit more original, wouldn't you?'

'And her opposite number?'

'Always male so far.'

'How do they refer to him?'

'You're not going to like this either, Sloan.'

'Sir?'

'They're calling him George.'

'They do have a precedent,' Sloan conceded stiffly. The boundaries between spy, traitor, defector and double agent were something that in the ordinary way he didn't have to explore. But, like those between crime and sin, they were as intertwined as that couple with the odd names whom the Assistant Chief Constable had just mentioned.

'And they've seen him once – but so briefly that it didn't help much.' The Assistant Chief Constable waved a memo in the air. 'They got a camera shot of his back, here in Berebury, that's all.'

'But they exchanged something?' Detective Inspector Sloan, like most policemen, remained ambivalent in his attitude to criminologists, but Loccard's famous exchange principle that all contacts left traces on both objects, inanimate and otherwise, had been ground into him when a young constable as firmly as the twelve times table.

'He came up behind her and took something out of her hand without speaking or looking at her, and then walked on without a pause or looking back either.'

'So he knew where she would be and when,' concluded Sloan without difficulty.

'And conversely, presumably she knew when and where he would come,' said the Assistant Chief Constable, 'because I gather she didn't even look up as he lifted whatever she had for him . . . She just went on strolling along.'

'But what nobody knows is exactly how they made the arrangements . . . Is that it, sir?'

'The problem in a nutshell, Sloan.'

'And,' pointed out the Detective Inspector, 'they think that George was probably aware that she – er – Mata Hari, that is – was being kept under close observation.'

The other man nodded. 'That's right. Because by approaching her from behind, he didn't let our people

40

see his face.' He straightened up. 'Except we must remember that they're not really our people, Sloan.'

'No, sir.' That was the trouble with the secret services. No one was ever really sure whose people they were . . .

'How they think we can help, I don't know.' The Assistant Chief Constable scratched his chin. 'I can't see the point of waiting by the spot where the exchange happened to see if it happens again, can you?'

'No,' said Sloan, adding vigorously, 'and in any case, sir, if that's what these types want, I can see no reason why they shouldn't do the surveillance themselves. It's the force who are short of man power.'

'Quite, quite,' said the Assistant Chief Constable pacifically. 'On the other hand, it would be good to get them off our backs so that we could all return to proper policing.'

'So it therefore follows,' said Sloan, in the manner of a schoolboy proving a theorem, 'if the secret services are so sure that Mata Hari and this character whom they call George haven't been in touch by any other means, that there must have been a sign or a plan, separately visible to them both, bringing them together in some other way.'

'We're all agreed on that, Sloan, but their people have looked everywhere and can't find one.' The Assistant Chief Constable squinted modestly down his aquiline nose. 'That's why they've come to us, and we don't want to let them down, do we?'

'So when and where did all this happen, sir?' enquired Sloan stolidly. The larger question of whether or not the police wanted to help the secret services, he left unanswered.

The Assistant Chief Constable waved the message sheet in his hand. 'Outside St Aidan's Church at ten o'clock on Tuesday morning last week . . . and I may say they mounted a watch there too on Tuesday this week.'

'No joy?'

'Not there. All the action was over at St Barnabas's at twelve noon instead.'

'The other side of town.'

'That's what's irking them, Sloan. As you know, Berebury's by no means short of churches. Comes of being an old medieval settlement, I suppose.'

'And their next encounter?'

'Just in front of St Ninian's at nine yesterday morning.'

'That's my mother's church,' remarked Sloan absently, his mind elsewhere. 'I suppose they could be going through all the churches in Berebury alphabetically. That would be easy enough for anyone to arrange.'

'They'd thought of that. You're forgetting St Catherine's.'

'So I am, sir.'

Detective Inspector Sloan had been doing his best to forget the ultra-modern St Catherine's Church ever since it had reared its ugly metal spire in the middle of the old market town. Even worse than the tower was the series of shiny spikes where a traditional church would have had flying buttresses.

'But it was the rendezvous at St Peter's at nine this

morning that got the secret service boys really wound up, Sloan. You know, that old church down by the riverside that isn't used any more . . .'

'Redundant,' said Sloan pithily, 'although if you ask me there's more sin down in that part of the town than anywhere else.'

'Quite so. Well . . .'

'If ever a patch needed a church,' averred Sloan feelingly, 'it's the Water Lane district.'

'Perhaps.' The Assistant Chief Constable frowned. 'They tell me Mata Hari and someone else . . .'

'Who wasn't George?'

'A new face – or, rather, a new back. They did their exchange dead on the first stroke of the church clock.' He scratched his chin. 'From all accounts it went like clockwork too, which is more than it did one day last week . . .'

Detective Inspector Sloan looked up. If there was one thing every police officer found worth investigating it was a deviation from the norm. 'What happened last week?'

'Apparently, Mata Hari was outside St Olave's all that morning, but no George. It was raining and she got soaked, but he never showed and neither did anyone else.'

'And next time?'

'Your guess is as good as mine, Sloan.'

'Actually, sir, the time and place might be a guess,' said the Detective Inspector, 'but, if past performance is anything to go by, the meeting will be outside a church.'

'Ye-es, I suppose that's so.'

'And on the hour.'

'That too, Sloan, now you come to put it like that.'

'On past performance alphabetically, saving St Catherine's – ' Sloan knew what it was those high spikes there reminded him of, so many mantraps – 'it should be St Thomas's . . .'

'Mata Hari and her friends do seem to need a church, all right,' agreed the Assistant Chief Constable pensively, 'which is funny, when you think about it.'

'They seem to need the outside of one, sir, anyway,' amended Sloan.

'And something by way of a clock.'

'St Ninian's doesn't have one,' said Sloan, almost without thinking. His mother's arrival there went by the sound of the church bells. All he ever had to do was to get her to the church door on time. She was always telling him it was an interesting church doorway, but he couldn't for the moment remember why.

'Right.'

'And it can't be the church bells,' said Sloan knowledgeably, 'because St Olave's doesn't have a ring any more.'

'Nowhere near enough young bell-ringers coming forward these days, Sloan. Too much like hard work – pulling a rope and counting.'

Sloan paused. 'There's one more thing, sir . . .'

'What's that?'

'All these meetings you've told me about have been in the morning.'

'So they have, Sloan.' He tapped his pen on his desk. 'Now, why should that have been, I wonder?'

'Perhaps this precious pair need daylight to come together, sir.'

'Good point, Sloan.' The Assistant Chief Constable leaned back in his chair. 'But not for recognition . . .'

'The recognition would seem to be a bit one-sided, sir. That's if Mata Hari only has something lifted out of her hand from behind.'

'True, but – er – George must know whose hand from which to do his taking.'

Sloan wrinkled his brow. 'On the other hand, she may not need to know who's coming up behind her to collect the – er – dibs. It might even be safer that way.' Dibs wasn't a word he relished using. Like the name Mata Hari, it smacked of an earlier, more melodramatic era.

'Perhaps, Sloan, there's something else they need . . .'

'Fine weather?'

The Assistant Chief Constable nodded. 'Could be, Sloan. Now what sign, I wonder, could there be which doesn't work in the rain.'

'There must be something,' said Detective Inspector Sloan. There was a pair of tribes in Borneo he'd read about which only went to war in daylight – that was because they were frightened of the dark – and in fine weather because the rain spoiled their martial feather head-dresses. 'They'll have a reason for using the front of all those churches . . . bound to.'

'Something which needs the sun perhaps?' The Assistant Chief Constable frowned. 'There can't be that number of handy sundials in the middle of Berebury, though.'

'And the sundial only tells the time, sir. It wouldn't

tell them when to meet.' The rim of the sundial in the municipal park said something sententious about its only recording the sunny hours, but he did not say this. 'These meetings, sir, that the secret service said were all outside churches . . .'

'Yes?'

'Did they mean outside the church doors?'

'I'm not sure if they were as precise as that, Sloan.' The Assistant Chief Constable peered at the notes on his desk. 'Why?'

'Churches usually face east . . .'

'Agreed. So?'

'So their entrance doors are usually on the south and north sides.'

'Granted.'

'Although sometimes, of course,' went on Sloan, 'they have a west door too . . .'

The lean, intelligent face of the Assistant Chief Constable took on a look of close interest. 'Are you telling me, Sloan, that none of the action will have been on the north side of any of these churches?'

'If that is the case, then it might perhaps indicate that we are thinking along the right lines, that's all, sir.'

A little smile played along the other man's lips. 'Am I then right in thinking that an extension of this proposition would be that our two suspects wouldn't have met on the west side of any of the churches either?'

'Yes, sir. Not if the meetings all took place in the morning, sir, which you said they did. The west side only gets the afternoon and evening sun and the north side none at all.'

'I did say they were in the mornings,' said the Assistant Chief Constable. 'All of 'em.'

'And if their signal needs the sun, that would explain why the meeting outside St Olave's was fouled up by the rain.' Like the warriors of Borneo, Mata Hari's contacts too would have had their reasons for not liking bad weather.

The Assistant Chief Constable stroked his chin. 'Go on.'

'But if they're working their way round the Berebury churches alphabetically, it wouldn't explain why they left St Catherine's out,' said Sloan. He'd learned long ago not to bend facts to suit a theory. Defence counsel always found a chink in faulty armour.

'They didn't leave St Peter's out though,' remarked the Assistant Chief Constable, 'just because it's not being used now.'

'So, sir, it wasn't something hidden in the church notices in the porches . . .' His own mother, now, was always able to draw accurate conclusions from innocent-looking flower rotas.

'That follows, Sloan. St Peter's in, St Catherine's out . . .' He sat back and regarded his notes with a pensive air. 'Doesn't make sense, does it? We're like those chaps looking for a sign from the East.'

'The Three Wise Men . . .' There was something beginning to niggle at the back of Sloan's mind now.

'Well, it looks as if we two wise men can't help our – shall we say our "confrères"? – with the answer to their little problem after all.'

The niggle at the back of Sloan's mind was turning into a positive irritant.

'Pity, that, Sloan,' murmured the Assistant Chief Constable wistfully. 'I should have liked the force to have come up with . . .'

'St Catherine's Church is post-war,' Sloan said suddenly.

'The 1960s architects have a lot to answer for,' observed the classicist urbanely.

'But the other churches are all old and Anglican,' said Sloan.

'I don't know that that gets us very far, Sloan . . .'

'Before clocks, sir, churches had to have ways of telling folk when to come to services . . . those who couldn't read anyway.'

'Agreed, but what about it?'

'They had something called mass clocks on the church masonry.' The niggle in his mind had clarified into a memory. 'Usually on the porch door.'

'Well?'

'The priest put a little wooden peg into a hole in the stone and then scratched a line outwards from the hole.'

'But I don't see . . .'

'The congregation would know it was time for church when the shadow from the peg fell on the line.'

'Are you telling me that there's one of these mass clocks on all these churches?'

'There's one at St Ninian's,' said Sloan. 'Scratch dials, they're sometimes called.' He paused and then said, 'It would be easy enough to make a little hole and draw a line on the stonework of the others if they hadn't got one already.'

'Except St Catherine's, which hasn't got any stone-work.'

'All metal and glass,' agreed Sloan, 'more's the pity.'

'And no one would ever notice something like that on an old church, would they?' The Assistant Chief Constable reached for the telephone. 'Right, Sloan, we'll tell these intelligence types where the next meeting will be . . .'

'And when, sir . . .'

'Amazing where a bit of ratiocination can get you, isn't it?'

'Sir?'

'A Latin word,' said his superior officer airily, 'for a conclusion reached by reasoning.'

Cold Comfort

Sixteenth-century Scotland

Sheriff Macmillan hadn't at first heard the sound of the approaching bagpipes but the hall-boy at Drummondreach had. Upon the instant, the lad uncurled himself from the rush-strewn floor and reached for his own set of pipes, listening intently the while. He began to pump up the bag under his arm even as he scrambled to his feet, making ready to carry out his duty of first identifying and then heralding any new arrivals at the policies of Rhuaraidh Macmillan, Sheriff of Fearnshire.

Cocking his ear in the direction of the distant pipes, the boy echoed his response with the preliminary notes of a lament. That sound, though, brought the Sheriff to the entrance hall of his dwelling place quickly enough, even though the other bagpipe players were still a mile or more away.

'They're playing "The Fearnshire Lament", my lord,' said the boy, his own acute hearing demonstrating one of the many advantages of youth to the older man. 'I ken it well . . .'

'Aye,' said the Sheriff crisply. 'I hear it quite clearly myself now . . .'

COLD COMFORT

Rhuaraidh Macmillan stepped back more than a little thoughtfully while the hall-boy took up the bag-pipes' chanter again and made to answer those heard from afar but as yet still unseen. The playing of that melancholy tune carried its own sad significance to the Sheriff. It meant not only that those coming near approached in sorrow rather than in anger but that a man was untimely dead somewhere nearby and within his jurisdiction.

It meant more than just dead, of course.

That particular lament told both Sheriff Macmillan and the hall-boy at Drummondreach that the death being announced by the playing of the dirge was of a known clansman. It was not some enemy or stranger of no consequence who was being thus sung. It foretold rather that a man had died from within the tight little circle which comprised the close-knit aristocracy of the Fearnshire clans.

'Who'll it be this time?' he pondered aloud. The Sheriff's writ ran among clansmen all tied by gener-ations of auld alliances and ancient fealties. Rumour had it that the new Queen in Edinburgh – she who had lately come over from France – had referred to them as unruly tribes, but that was not to understand their allegiances to the land and its people, both of which had been established in these northern parts for time out of mind.

'I think I can see them now, my lord,' said the boy.

And it must be said, the Sheriff admitted fairly to himself, there were men around too who were locked together by equally ancient enmities. Memories in the

Highlands were long and unforgiving. Perhaps this was what Her Majesty at Holyroodhouse had been told . . .

Perhaps too it was different over in France.

'There's three of them, my lord,' announced the hall-boy, peering out.

Sometimes, of course, the Sheriff reminded himself as he scanned the horizon, the enmities were still red and raw, just like the scars on Murdo Ross's face. These were still livid from an altercation at hogmanay with Black Ian – Ian Tulloch – of Eileanach. The man had drawn his dirk at Murdo Ross – kinsman and friend – over the delicate matter of which of the pair should at the turn of the year first-foot a certain young lady at Achnagarron, and Ian Tulloch hadn't been seen at Eileanach or anywhere else in Fearnshire from that day to this.

The pipes were calling to each other now like urgent vixens . . .

Moreover – and this was where the Sheriff's responsibilities came in – that lament also meant that the death was of a Fearnshire man who should not have died: that is to say that he – whoever he was – had not died in his bed of a sore sickness or old age.

Thus, according to the old custom of the country, it followed ineluctably that the Sheriff of Fearnshire had duly to be told, and that he had a duty to enquire, had to inspect, had to pronounce and – if it were then proved that the death had been unlawfully at the hand of another – had to punish. What happened in France might well be different, but this was Scotland and, as far as Rhuaraidh Macmillan himself was concerned, this was how things were going to stay, new Queen or not.

The drone of the other pipes could be heard quite clearly now and soon a little gaggle of men hove into view, hurrying down over the brae.

The hall-boy, the keener-eyed of the two, took his lips off the chanter long enough to say, 'Angus Mackintosh of Balblair, my lord, and a Mackenzie . . .'

'Colin of that ilk,' observed the Sheriff without enthusiasm. The man was a troublemaker.

'And Merkland of Culbokie, Younger,' said the hall-boy, resuming his pipes.

Rhuaraidh Macmillan advanced towards the threshold and waited for the men to reach him, sniffing the air as he did so. It was a little warmer today and not before time. Spring, he decided, must really have come to the Highlands at long, long last – and that after one of the darkest, coldest winters in living memory. It was the same each year, though, he conceded to himself. He always began to doubt the return of warmer weather and then, suddenly, like the midges, it was upon them.

The drone of the pipes died away as the three visitors drew near. Colin Mackenzie stood forward as self-appointed spokesman, while Angus Mackintosh and young Hugh Merkland kept a pace or two behind him.

'We've found Black Ian,' announced the man Mackenzie breathlessly. 'Ian Tulloch . . .'

'Dead,' added Hugh Merkland.

'Long dead,' supplemented Angus Mackintosh.

'And Murdo Ross is away over to the west,' said Mackenzie, adding meaningfully, 'today.'

'Just as soon as he heard Black Ian had been found,' chimed in Angus.

Colin Mackenzie said, 'You'll no' have forgotten, Sheriff, that it was Ian Tulloch that struck Murdo Ross.'

'I remember,' said the Sheriff shortly.

Striking any man was bad, striking a relative or friend much worse. Doing it with a weapon in the hand was never likely to be forgotten, still less forgiven. Even worse was the crime of following a man to his own dwelling place and assaulting him there – otherwise known as hamesucken. And that was what Ian Tulloch had done.

'Murdo Ross was off like the De'il himself was chasing him,' contributed Hugh Merkland, 'as soon as he was told the news.'

'Perhaps the Devil was chasing him,' said Mackintosh insouciantly. 'How can any man tell what Satan looks like?'

Merkland ignored this and went on eagerly, 'Will we be going after him for you, Sheriff?'

'You will not,' said Rhuaraidh Macmillan firmly. 'You will be first telling me where you found Black Ian dead.'

'In a barn at Eileanach.'

'More bothy than barn,' put in Angus Mackintosh.

Merkland said, 'The men were taking the sheep up to the hills for the summer . . .'

Sheriff Macmillan nodded. The annual movement of the sheep to the higher ground was a late spring ritual in Fearnshire. The French had a special word for it – *transhumance* – not that the new Queen would be likely to know about it, for all her regal French connections. Summer pasture for sheep would not be one of the concerns of her world . . . She had others, though, from all accounts. Mostly to do with the heart, he had heard.

' . . . and when they got up there the drovers tried to open up the place as usual but they couldn'a get in,' Merkland was saying.

'How did you know he was dead?' asked the Sheriff.

There was a pause while Mackenzie shifted from foot to foot. 'He was hanging from a beam.'

'We saw him through the cracks in the wood,' vouchsafed Colin Mackenzie. 'We couldn'a get in either, you see.'

'Dead long since, with a bang-rape round his neck,' supplied Angus Mackintosh.

'Someone must have been after the hay,' said the Sheriff.

A bang-rape was a rope with a noose used by thieves for carrying off corn or hay. It would do fine for hanging a man too.

'Maybe so, Sheriff, but they didn't steal what hay was there,' said Angus Mackintosh. 'It's still strewn about in the bothy.'

'Ian's axe is there too,' said Mackenzie. 'It's standing against the wall.'

'Nobody could get in to take it, you see,' contributed Hugh Merkland. 'The door was barred on the inside.' He waved a hand. 'It still is.'

'So why then did Murdo Ross go away to the west when he heard?' asked the Sheriff, not unreasonably. For a man to take his own life in these parts was rare enough, but a man who had harmed friend and family might well feel that he should. 'If the door had been barred on the inside by Ian Tulloch . . .

'Anyone,' sighed the Sheriff, 'who had reached man's estate could have told Black Ian that remorse was the most difficult – in fact, the only intolerable – emotion with which to live.'

There was an uncomfortable pause and an uneasy shuffling of feet as it became apparent that not one of the three wished to answer his question about Murdo Ross.

'Well?' demanded Rhuaraidh Macmillan.

Eventually Colin Mackenzie said uneasily, 'We couldn'a see anything there, Sheriff, that Black Ian could have been standing on . . . before . . .'

'Nothing at all,' said Merkland.

'Not a thing.' Mackintosh of Balblair endorsed this. 'We looked.'

'Whoever had put him there must have taken it away with them,' said Hugh Merkland, adding, 'Whatever it was.'

'I see,' said the Sheriff.

'Now shall we go after Murdo Ross for you, Sheriff?' said Merkland impatiently. 'He'll be well away by now.'

'No,' said Rhuaraidh Macmillan at once. 'You'll come with me back to Eileanach. First I must see the body.'

Now, *super visum corporis* was a phrase Her new Majesty at Edinburgh, a daughter of Mary of Guise or not, would surely understand. They said she was good at the Latin as well as at the French. It was her lack of comprehension of the Gaelic, indeed of nearly all matters Scottish, that was the worry . . .

*

Mounted on his palfrey, his clerk riding a little behind him, the Sheriff led the party out towards the broad strath above which lay Ian Tulloch's lands. The journey took time. The bothy was far away up in the hills, alongside the route of one of the old coffin roads over to a clan burial ground and already halfway to the west as it was.

His mount stumbled and slipped from time to time as it tried to pick its way over the bare stony track towards the rough building. What was possible for men on foot and hardy sheep was not so easy for a horse. Spring might have come to the lower-lying ground, but higher up winter had only just left. Rhuaraidh Macmillan could see that even higher there was still snow and ice lying on the side of the ben. On a north-facing hillside, both could linger all summer.

'There, Sheriff – ' Colin Mackenzie pointed. 'You see yon bothy over there?'

'Aye,' agreed Macmillan, automatically noting that any footprints in the snow leading to the building were long gone. And so were any footprints in the snow leading away ... Equally, any marks made by footprints on the ground since the thaw would have been overlaid by those made more recently by men and sheep.

'Look, Sheriff, through this gap here ..' Colin Mackenzie already had his eye to a crack in the door.

Rhuaraidh Macmillan reluctantly brought his horse to a standstill on the track. There would be those – and plenty – who held that Murdo Ross had been well within his rights in exacting his revenge on Ian Tulloch for raising his weapon – if he had, that is – against

Murdo in anger, let alone in jealousy; who would insist for all time that Black Ian had received only his just desserts for an attack on a life-long friend – to say nothing of one with blood ties.

That, however, was not the law and the law must be served above anger and jealousy. This applied in Fearnshire if not any longer in Holyroodhouse in Edinburgh. Aye, there was the rub. Rhuaraidh Macmillan straightened himself up in the saddle. The difference was that he himself was responsible for the upholding of law and order in Fearnshire. Who exactly it was who was responsible for law and order and not anger and jealousy triumphing at the Scottish court today was not for him to say . . .

The Sheriff dismounted and bent his eye – albeit unwillingly – to the crack in the wooden door of the bothy.

What the three men had told him was true. Swinging from a high beam without handholds to reach it was a body. That it was of Ian Tulloch he was in no doubt. 'Black' might have been how the man had been known in his lifetime; it was assuredly an accurate description of how he now looked many weeks after his death.

The Sheriff's gaze travelled down from the suspended body to the floor. What the men had told him about that was true too. There was nothing at all there which Black Ian could have climbed on or kicked aside to jump to his death. All that was visible was a large damp puddle on the floor, surely greater by far than could have come from the body above. He put his shoulder to the door of the bothy and found, as the others had done, that the entrance was still firmly barred against them.

'Shall we batter the door down, Sheriff?' asked Hugh Merkland, always a man of action rather than thought.

'No,' said Rhuaraidh Macmillan sternly. 'Wait you all over there while I take a look around.'

He walked slowly and carefully round the outside of the bothy. Ramshackle it might be, but it was still proof against the elements and animals. Deer would not have been able to get in there any more than the four men could. The primitive building had never boasted windows or a chimney.

'Murdo Ross'll be away over the hills by nightfall,' murmured Merkland restively. 'We'll no' catch him now.'

'And Black Ian didn't have any other enemies,' said Colin Mackenzie with emphasis. 'None at all.'

'Och, one enemy's enough for any man,' put in Angus Mackintosh of Balblair, stroking his chin sagely. 'Isn't it, now?'

'Black Ian was his own worst enemy,' said the Sheriff, stepping back to examine the roof. 'He didn't need others. You all know that.'

'Aye, that's true,' conceded Colin Mackenzie, nodding. 'The man should never have taken cold steel to a kinsman right enough . . . What is it that you're seeing on the roof, Sheriff?'

'Nothing,' replied that official with perfect truth. 'It's quite sound.'

'It would need to be up here,' observed Angus Mackintosh, looking round the bleak countryside. 'If the wind had once got under it, yon roof would be away up over Beinn nan Eun in no time at all.'

'Or down in the loch,' said Merkland.

Colin Mackenzie pointed down the hill. 'It's a wonder Black Ian didn't just jump into Loch Bealach Culaidh there – if he had a mind to make away with himself, that is.'

'It's hard to drown if you're a swimmer,' remarked the Sheriff. 'Or if the water's frozen.'

'It's hard to hang yourself from a high beam without having anything to hold on to or stand on to get you there,' said Hugh Merkland. 'I still think we should be away after Murdo Ross . . .'

'No,' said the Sheriff quietly. 'Tell me, is that Ian Tulloch's own axe I saw in there?'

'It is,' said Mackenzie.

'Ah . . .'

'Man,' exploded Merkland, 'you dinna need an axe to hang yoursel.'

'Ian Tulloch did,' murmured the Sheriff.

'But . . .' Merkland's eyebrows came together in a ferocious frown.

'He couldn't have done what he did without an axe,' said the Sheriff. 'Or something like it.'

'But it's rope you need to hang yoursel,' protested Colin Mackenzie. 'We all know that.'

'Mind you,' said Rhuaraidh Macmillan, 'I'm not saying that Black Ian didn't need the rope as well as his axe.'

'But . . .' Hugh Merkland began his objection in turn.

The Sheriff said, 'He needed the rope afterwards.'

'Afterwards?' echoed Merkland.

'After he had used the axe.'

'But . . .' began Colin Mackenzie.

'And the rope together,' said the Sheriff.

'I still don't understand,' said Colin Mackenzie.

'Neither did Murdo Ross,' said the Sheriff, 'and that's why he's away to the west in such a hurry.' Rhuaraidh Macmillan gave the door of the bothy another great shake. 'It's barred right enough and by my reckoning it was Ian Tulloch himself that put the bar on the inside there.'

'And so,' demanded Colin Mackenzie truculently, 'how did he get himself high enough to hang himself from that beam without anything to stand on?'

'Ah,' said the Sheriff neatly, 'he did have something to stand on.'

'But there's nothing there,' said Colin Mackenzie. 'Nothing at all.'

'There's nothing there now,' said the Sheriff patiently. 'There was something there that he could stand on at the time.'

'That's taken itself away?' growled Colin Mackenzie derisively.

'In a manner of speaking, yes,' replied the Sheriff. 'But it was brought there by Ian Tulloch himself using the bang-rape and his axe.'

Colin Mackenzie drew himself up and said with dignity. 'I'm thinking that you are for making fools of us, Sheriff.'

'Is it the Little People we're going to have to thank for killing Black Ian, then?' chimed in Hugh Merkland scornfully.

Angus Mackintosh asked instead, 'What is there, then, Sheriff, that Black Ian could have brought here with an axe and a noose that's gone away on its own after he used it?'

'A block of ice,' said Rhuaraidh Macmillan, pointing to where some still lay unmelted further up the hillside. 'Now will you be away, all of you and find Murdo Ross and tell him to come back?'

Chapter and Hearse

'Sloan,' barked Police Superintendent Leeyes down the telephone, 'you're wanted, and quickly!'

'I'll be right over, sir.' Detective Inspector C. D. Sloan didn't exactly click his heels together, but he did get to his feet pretty smartly.

'No, not by me. Don't come to my office.'

'Sir?'

'It's the Assistant Chief Constable who's asking for you.' The Superintendent didn't even try to keep his amazement at this unlikely event out of his voice. 'Don't ask me why.'

'Me, Sir?'

Detective Inspector Sloan did a rapid mental revision of his past week and work. As far as he knew, he hadn't blotted his copybook in any way, but you never knew. With the Police and Criminal Evidence Act in operation, even not offering a suspect a cup of tea was capable of being misconstrued by a defence solicitor.

'You, Sloan. He says,' said Superintendent Leeyes, 'that it's a sudden emergency.'

'I'm on my way.'

*

The Assistant Chief Constable – a gentleman copper if ever there was one – received him with his customary courtesy.

'Ah, Sloan, there you are . . .' If there was anything urgent pending, it certainly didn't show in his manner. 'Take a seat.'

'Thank you, sir.' It wasn't going to be a disciplinary matter, then: rebukes were delivered to a man standing. On the carpet, if there was one.

'A little problem has cropped up this morning in connection with the Minster.'

Sloan sat down. That explained one thing anyway. Calleford Minster was not in Superintendent Leeyes's 'F' Division and the Superintendent took as narrow a view as did the Coroner as to what was and what was not within his jurisdiction.

'And,' continued the Assistant Chief Constable unhurriedly, 'it's got to be resolved before tonight.'

'I see, sir.'

'By half past seven, actually,' said the Assistant Chief Constable.

'Time is of the essence, then, is it?' ventured Sloan.

'It was and it is,' said his superior enigmatically.

'And the problem?'

'There are two problems,' said the ACC, 'and one of them is murder.'

'Ah!' And the victim, sir . . .' Every case had to begin somewhere and every case – every murder case anyway – had a victim. 'Do we know . . .'

'Oh, yes, Sloan. There's no doubt about that. The man's name was Lechlade. Walter Lechlade. Exact age unknown. Probably about forty.'

'And his occupation?' If unemployment carried on on its present-day scale, a man's occupation – or lack of it – would soon cease to be worth recording.

'Precentor and prebendary,' said the ACC.

'So this Walter Lechlade was a clerical gentleman, then, was he, sir?' Sloan wasn't quite sure of his ground here, but the words sounded ecclesiastical enough and they were talking about cathedrals.

'That's the whole trouble,' said the ACC gently.

'The Church looking after its own?' suggested Sloan. It had, after all, been known to happen.

'Well,' conceded the ACC, stroking his chin, 'I must say it was all hushed up at the time. Nothing written down and so forth.'

'People will always try . . .'

'Until Peter Quivel – he's the Bishop in the case – started making a fuss.'

'Ah,' said Sloan. 'Truth will out.'

'I'd very much like to think so, Sloan, but I'm afraid the bishop had his own axe to grind.'

'It happens,' said Sloan, without thinking. He pulled himself together and got down to business – he wasn't here to philosophize. 'And the time of this murder, sir?' After all, the ACC had said himself that time was of the essence, hadn't he? 'Is it known?'

The ACC looked down at a pile of notes on his desk. 'Between one and two o'clock in the morning.'

'And where exactly?' Detective Inspector Sloan opened his notebook from sheer force of habit.

'Between the cathedral and Lechlade's own house nearby. That is, in the lane between the Bishop's Close and Canon de Derteford's house at the corner of Bear Lane.'

'Not a very usual hour for a clergyman to be out and about, sir, if I may say so.' Sloan tried not to sound at all censorious. Time was when it would have been relatively safe to be abroad at that time of night, but not these days. Small wonder, though, that someone had wanted the whole matter hushed up.

'Oh, yes, it was,' said the ACC unexpectedly.

'Not a sensible hour even so, though,' insisted Sloan.

'He was in the Cathedral Close,' the ACC reminded him.

'But was it secure?' said Sloan, unimpressed.

'Well, no, it wasn't actually. That's the whole point. But it ought to have been, Sloan, and I must say you've got to the heart of the matter very quickly.'

'Thank you, sir.'

'You see, the gates to the Close should have been shut at curfew . . .'

'It's good that these old customs are kept up, sir, isn't it?' put in Sloan. 'It's still done at eight o'clock every evening at the Minster, I believe.'

'Yes,' responded the ACC briskly. 'But what happened the night Walter Lechlade was murdered, Sloan, was that not only was one of the gates – the south gate – left open for his murderers to come in, but it was also left open for them to get out.'

'Murderers?' Sloan sat up. 'Was it a gang-killing, sir, then?' They didn't have a lot of those in the mainly rural county of Calleshire, thank goodness, but the ways of the city were bound to reach them in the end.

'I suppose you could say that it was, Sloan,' agreed the ACC thoughtfully. 'I must say I hadn't thought of it in that light myself . . . More of a conspiracy, you might say.'

'And the gateman given something for his – er – forgetfulness?'

'He was indeed,' said the ACC warmly, 'and probably not what he expected either.' He prodded the pile of papers in front of him. 'He – the gateman, name of Stonyng, Richard Stonyng – said that the Mayor hadn't told him to shut the gate.'

'What had it got to do with the Mayor, might I ask?' Criminal investigation and local government usually met head on over fraud and planning law, not murder.

'Quite a lot. The cathedral had been in dispute with the civil authorities about their boundaries for years.'

'It's not unknown, sir.' It had always been a great relief to Sloan that property disputes were civil not criminal matters. He added a trifle sententiously, 'Good fences make good neighbours.'

'Good neighbours the city and cathedral weren't,' said the ACC emphatically, 'In the old days, men on the run from the Mayor and commonalty used to jump over St Peter's churchyard wall and take sanctuary in the cathedral – much to the city's annoyance.'

'Men have always tried to escape from justice,' observed Sloan, who carried several scars on his person to prove it.

'I suppose,' said the ACC, who had been at school at Eton, 'that you could call it a sort of Wall Game. Anyway, it seems that the man on the gate . . .'

Sloan glanced at his notebook. 'Richard Stonyng . . .'

' . . . took his orders from the Mayor that night.'

'And the Mayor's name, sir?' prompted Sloan, his pen poised. Office holders always had recorded names.

'Alfred Duport.'

'And where, sir, does he come in, or don't we know?'

'Good question, Sloan. First and foremost, he seems to have been in cahoots with the Dean against the Bishop.'

'That's bad.' It sounded an unholy alliance to Sloan.

'Very. But not unknown in English history,' said the ACC grimly. 'In this instance, the *casus belli* . . .'

'Beg pardon, sir?'

'What? Oh, sorry, Sloan. The cause of their dispute was the appointment of John Pycot as Dean of the cathedral . . .'

'Not popular?'

'Not with Bishop Peter Quivel anyway. He said the election had been rigged.'

'And as it was the Bishop who – er – blew the gaff, do I take it the Dean had something to do with the death of the pre . . . the other clerical gentleman, sir?' Rigged elections were not usually the province of a detective inspector, but murder was.

'You've got it in one, Sloan,' said the ACC, beaming.

'Not a lot of brotherly love lost?' observed Sloan. That, at least, could be safely said about most murders.

'None.'

'But why should it have been Walter Lechlade who got killed, then?' asked Sloan, anxious to get at least one thing clear.

'Pro-Bishop, anti-Dean,' said the ACC succinctly.

'So where does the Mayor – Alfred Duport – come in, then?' asked Sloan for the second time.

'Friend of the Dean,' said the ACC.

'But the Dean wasn't the murderer, surely, sir, was he?' ventured Sloan, although he was naturally prepared to concede that it wasn't what you knew that mattered but who.

'John Pycot didn't kill Walter Lechlade personally, if that's what you mean,' said the ACC, 'any more than Henry II actually killed Thomas à Becket on an earlier and much more celebrated occasion.'

'That, sir,' observed Sloan, greatly daring, 'is a fine point.'

'Oh, the King was morally guilty,' conceded the ACC, who didn't have to deal with split hairs on a daily basis in court. 'No doubt about that.'

'And did penance,' said Sloan. There had been a picture in his history book of a barefoot Henry, in sackcloth and ashes, making his way to Canterbury in the snow to be flogged that had stayed in Sloan's mind since he was a small boy.

'The Dean did penance too,' said the ACC.

'For helping get rid of another turbulent priest?' asked Sloan, his memory stirred now.

'For getting rid of a priest,' amended the ACC.

'Really, sir?' Sloan's mother, who was a great churchwoman, was forever insisting that she didn't know what the Church was coming to. It was beginning to sound as if she might be right.

'From all accounts,' said the ACC drily, 'it was the Dean who was turbulent.'

For reasons that Sloan had never enquired into, his

mother always blamed any present-day trouble in a cathedral on Thomas Cranmer and his statutes – perhaps he should have listened to her more. Detection was a more arcane business than it seemed at first sight.

The ACC was still talking. 'History, Sloan, says that Walter Lechlade was a peaceable enough fellow. Not that that saved him, of course.'

Detective Inspector Sloan nodded. Being peaceable was no insurance against being murdered. 'How was he killed?' he asked, the policeman in him taking over from the erstwhile schoolboy and the inattentive son. There had, he remembered, been another Archbishop of Canterbury as well as Thomas à Becket who had been done to death in office. His name had stayed in Sloan's memory from his history lessons purely because of the manner of his murder.

The ACC consulted his papers again. 'Two blows on the skull and the arm from knives, swords and Danish axes.'

'Not a lot of those about, sir.' With that other archbishop, St Alphege, it had been ox bones.

'There were then, Sloan.'

'Then?' Sloan's pen stayed suspended above his notebook, a suspicion confirmed. 'Do I take it, sir, that we're not talking about the here and now?'

'Yes and no,' said the ACC, quite unabashed. 'More of the there and then, perhaps, than the here and now, but some of both.'

'Might I ask where?'

'Exeter, Sloan.'

'And when?'

'November 1283.'

'When the Mayor and the Dean murdered this Walter Lechlade . . .'

'The Precentor . . .'

'With a Danish axe?' Their pastry must have come later.

'No, no, Sloan. The actual murder was done by others, orchestrated by three vicars and a canon . . .'

With Thomas à Becket, thought Sloan, it had been four knights, but the end result had still been the same spilling of brains.

'In fact,' murmured the ACC, 'one commentator called 'em satellites of Satan.'

Sloan said he wasn't at all surprised.

'Henry de Stanway, clerk in holy orders, John de Wolrington, Vicar of Ottery St Mary, John de Christenstowe, Vicar of Heavitree, and Canon Reginald de Ercevesk,' recited the ACC. 'Almost the Four Horsemen of the Apocalypse, you might say.'

'Caused a bit of a flutter in the dovecotes, that, I dare say, sir.' There had been other clergymen who had hit the headlines, but Sloan didn't think this was the moment to mention them.

'The Bishop appealed to the King for justice.'

'And which King would that have been, sir?'

'Edward I of blessed memory.'

'The Hammer of the Scots?' More of those history lessons had stuck than Sloan had appreciated.

'He was known as the English Justinian,' said the ACC, who had had a classical education.

'I didn't know that, sir.'

'And he came down to Exeter at Christmas 1285.'

'Two years later?' In Sloan's book, justice delayed was justice denied.

'This is where it gets interesting, Sloan.'

'Really, sir?' Interesting, he decided, it might be; urgent – today, this minute, urgent – he couldn't see how it could possibly be.

'The case was begun on Monday 24 December . . .'

'Christmas Eve?'

'Christmas Eve – the judges were Roger de Loveday and Richard de Boyland – and then it was adjourned for Christmas.'

' "The hungry judges soon the sentences sign",' said Sloan, quoting Alexander Pope, ' "And wretches hang that jurymen may dine".' They had that piece in their speeches each time at the Berebury Magistrates' Annual Dinner.

'It wasn't like that at all,' said the ACC a trifle plaintively. 'No, they all kept Christmas Day in high old style and then, on St Stephen's Day . . .'

'Boxing Day.'

'They found Richard Stonyng . . .'

'The gatekeeper . . .'

' . . . guilty of murder.'

'For not shutting the gate?' Sloan was sensitive about gates. There had been one terrible week in his schooldays when the boy who had been detailed to play brave Horatius, Captain of the Gate, had gone down with mumps. Sloan had been the unwilling understudy and anything to do with gates, fearful odds, ashes of his fathers and temples of his gods still struck an unhappy chord.

'For opening the gate to let the felons in before the

murder and for not shutting it after the deed was done to keep them in.'

'I see, sir.' Dereliction of duty or complicity he would have called that himself, but apparently the judges had reckoned it murder. 'An accessory before and after the fact,' he said neatly.

'And as for "Mr Mayor, sirrrr" . . .' baaa'd the ACC in the tones of Larry the Lamb.

'Alfred Duport,' supplied Sloan. The ACC's literary background had obviously been broad enough to have included *Toytown*.

'Found guilty of consenting to and planning the felony and receiving and harbouring the felons.'

'Aiding and abetting,' translated Sloan.

'And then on Holy Innocents' Day . . .'

That, thought Sloan, couldn't have been judicial irony, surely?

' . . . all those who had pleaded benefit of clergy . . .'

'That, sir,' said Sloan, 'was some sort of establishment cop-out, wasn't it?' He knew that, like sanctuary, they didn't have it any more, although it was true to say that the only criminal clergymen to come his way officially had certainly been attempting – one way and another – something for their own benefit.

'A way of exculpation of men of the cloth grounded in a text in the First Book of Chronicles,' said the ACC, admitting that he'd looked it up. 'Chapter sixteen, verse twenty-two.'

Sloan decided he really would have to pay more attention to his mother's interests in future.

The ACC shuffled the notes on his desk and read out, ' "Touch not mine anointed and do my prophets no harm." And all they had to do to prove they were clerks in holy orders was to be able to read the first verse of Psalm fifty-one. The Miserere.'

'So the clerical conspirators got off?' concluded Sloan doggedly.

'Handed over to their bishops, except the Dean, who was sent to a monastery.'

'And the actual murderers, sir?' Sloan knew who he meant – the ones with blood on their hands, which was as good a definition as any he knew.

'Escaped abroad.'

Detective Inspector Sloan, currently coming to terms with the vagaries of the Crown Prosecution Service, sighed and said, 'Not a very satisfactory outcome, sir.'

'There was one more puzzle.'

'Sir?'

'The records are a bit shaky, but afterwards they wrote down that the Mayor had been hanged on St Stephen's Day.'

'But,' said Sloan, frowning, 'surely that was before he was tried?'

'It has been known.'

'Lynch law.' That was the only law the police were pledged not to uphold.

'Actually, Sloan, it was known as Lydford law. Punish first and try afterwards.'

Sloan said he thought 'Try first and don't punish afterwards' was more the vogue these days.

The ACC said, 'What they meant was that the prisons were so awful that often those who were accused died from gaol fever before they could be brought to trial – which is rather different.'

'Yes, sir.' Sloan paused. 'I take it that this has all been written up somewhere?'

'Admirably.'* The ACC patted a thin, square grey book on his desk. 'I can't think why no one's made a play out of it.'

What Detective Inspector Sloan couldn't help but wonder was how something that had happened in the year 1283 could suddenly become enough of an emergency this morning for him to have been summoned post-haste from dealing with latter-day criminals who only ever pleaded broken homes and unhappy childhoods.

'You think it hangs together all right, Sloan, do you?' asked the ACC.

'Yes, sir.'

'I've made myself quite clear, I hope?'

'Perfectly, sir.'

'And you found it an interesting case?'

'Yes, sir.' He ventured a modest pun. 'What you might call a top-brass rubbing-out.'

'The difficulty is,' said the ACC, surreptitiously making a note of this, 'that they have a literary and historical society attached to Calleford Minster. I belong myself.'

'Really, sir?'

'And they've got a bit of a problem.'

'Sir?'

'Yes, indeed.' The ACC leaned back in his chair.

* Frances Rose-Troup, *Exeter Vignettes* (Manchester University Press, 1942).

'Their secretary's just rung me to say that tonight's speaker has been taken ill and would I step into the breach with something suitable.'

'I see, sir.' The quotation 'Once more unto the breach, dear friends, once more' could, Sloan felt, safely be left to the Chairman in his introduction.

'I thought I would tell them about this murder,' said the ACC.

'The cathedral interest.' Sloan nodded.

'I'm calling my talk "Another Exeter Riddle", Sloan, because there were some famous medieval Exeter riddles . . .'

It all seemed quite open and shut to Sloan. He said restrainedly, 'Should go down very well, sir.'

'It was helpful to rehearse it with you,' said the ACC unblushingly.

'Thank you, sir.'

'I thought I would begin with a quotation.'

'It's often done, I understand, sir.' It was always done at the Berebury Magistrates' Annual Dinner.

'From Shakespeare.'

'Naturally, sir.'

'This one.' The ACC squinted modestly down at his notes. ' "Some men are born great, some achieve greatness, and some have greatness thrust upon them . . ." '

The Widow's Might

Anthony Mainwaring Heber-Hibbs knew to a nicety the moment at which to step out from under the shelter of the canopy outside the airport lounge and into the hot sun of Lasserta. It was immediately after the aeroplane had trundled up the runway, come to a final standstill and been linked to the landing steps.

And not a moment before, the heat of the sun in Lasserta being what it always was.

He stood forward now but doffed his topi only as the cabin door opened and the first of the passengers began to stumble out into the open air after their long journey from England.

It wasn't by any means every visiting group that the Ambassador turned out for in this manner. There had been a party of archaeologists the month before that he hadn't so received and last week a posse of forensic accountants had similarly landed at Lasserta airport without being officially welcomed. They had arrived to look into the flourishing money-laundering industry for which the sheikhdom was renowned, Lasserta being one of the most efficient of the world's rapidly diminishing number of tax havens, while the archaeologists had been searching for signs of a really ancient civilization in this antique desert land.

Her Britannic Majesty's Ambassador had allowed both those other parties to touch down without affording them any diplomatic niceties. The East Calleshire Regimental Association – in this instance, a group of widows and orphans – came into a rather different category. The accountants had talked about 'widows and orphans' as well, but they had referred to them in a financial context as potential assets for someone – he wasn't quite sure whom. His secretary too sometimes spoke of 'widows and orphans' when she was producing reports, but why he never knew or asked.

These widows and orphans – the Calleshire ones – were quite different. And something had given him cause to think that they weren't going to be exactly assets either . . .

The people coming off the aeroplane now were real widows and real orphans from an ill-fated Anglo-Lassertan military campaign of some twenty years ago which had come to be known as the Engagement at Bakhalla. This disastrous action had strayed uncomfortably near the Sheikh's palace at Bakhalla, hence its name.

Anthony Heber-Hibbs had deemed it appropriate – the words 'appropriate' and 'inappropriate' were much used in diplomatic circles – that he give this particular tour a polite reception.

He therefore advanced, a model of civility, right hand outstretched, towards their leader as she reached the bottom of the steps. Mrs Norah Letherington, a woman clearly born to command and looking every inch the late Colonel's lady, responded with a firm – albeit slightly damp and sticky – grasp.

'Is it always as hot as this here?' she asked faintly as the heat rising from the airport tarmac hit her in an advancing wave for the first time.

'I'm afraid so, madam,' he said, replacing his formal headgear before the sun got at what was left of his hair.

Mrs Letherington blinked in the glare of the sun and beckoned her trusty lieutenant forward to be introduced. 'This is my deputy, Miss Ann Arkwright.'

The Ambassador bowed towards a sandy-haired woman whose freckled skin would doubtless soon begin to suffer from the sunlight.

'And – ' Mrs Letherington half turned as a young man in crumpled jeans and grubby T-shirt appeared at her elbow – 'this is Colin Stubbings, who is acting as our military adviser for the tour.'

Only years of training in the diplomatic service kept the Ambassador's eyebrows in place rather than raised to his hair-line as he surveyed an unattractive youth who had not quite outgrown acne. Anthony Heber-Hibbs charitably attributed the incipient beard to the difficulties of shaving on a long-haul flight, but not even charity could cause him to forgive the libidinous logo on the young man's T-shirt.

'Your adviser?' he asked politely.

'Colin has made a special study of the Anglo-Lassertan campaign,' she explained quickly, sensing his reaction, 'especially the Engagement at Bakhalla.'

'Has he?' responded the Ambassador without enthusiasm.

'He's a student of military history at the university,' she went on, 'and naturally, since he lost his father out here – George Stubbings was a Sergeant in the action – he's always taken a particular interest in what went on in the campaign.'

'Quite so,' said Heber-Hibbs, hastily pulling himself together. 'Well, I mustn't keep you standing here in the sun. Very bad for you all, especially if you're not used to it. Now, I understand that you're staying at the Coningsby Hotel in Gatt-el-Abbas, so . . .'

'That's where the general staff holed up during the Bakhalla campaign,' Colin Stubbings informed him. 'Miles behind the firing line. And well out of danger, of course.' He shrugged. 'Lucky for some, you might say, but not for my mother.' He hitched his shoulder in the direction of a large woman in a floral dress now descending the airline steps as if her feet hurt. 'Most of dad's platoon got wiped out.'

'Colin,' Mrs Letherington informed Heber-Hibbs, perhaps feeling some further explanation was warranted, 'was awarded the Tarsus College History Prize for an essay on what Anthony Eden should really have done when Nasser annexed the Suez Canal.'

'Did he indeed,' murmured the Ambassador.

'Instead of what he did do,' added Colin Stubbings gratuitously.

'Naturally,' said Anthony Heber-Hibbs at his smoothest. 'It wouldn't have been a matter of speculation otherwise, would it? Only fact – which always gives one so much less scope, don't you think?'

'I don't mind telling you that it's fact that we've

come out here for,' announced Stubbings bluntly. 'To find out what really happened at Bakhalla.'

'Ah,' said Anthony Heber-Hibbs.

' '"Theirs not to reason why"', of course, '"Theirs but to do and die"', quoted Stubbings, 'and die they did.' He sniffed. 'Not much of a poet, Tennyson, but at least he got Balaclava right.'

'Yes, indeed,' agreed the Ambassador, hoping that there had been no other parallels in the Engagement at Bakhalla with the ill-fated Charge of the Light Brigade, or, come to that, with the Charge of the Heavy Brigade either.

'Someone had blundered,' declared Stubbings firmly.

'The Earl of Cardigan, I think,' murmured Heber-Hibbs. 'Or was it Lord Lucan? I'm afraid I'm not an authority on the Crimean War.'

'I meant someone had blundered here in Lasserta,' asserted Stubbings. 'And we don't know who.' He paused and then added ominously, 'Yet.'

'It's too soon for us to be able to examine the official records, you see,' murmured Mrs Letherington obliquely. 'The thirty-year rule and all that.'

'We have to wait another ten years before we can look at them,' put in Ann Arkwright from the sidelines. Her voice quavered slightly. 'I lost my brother out here and I'd really like to know how and why before then.'

'It's ten years to wait only if the records aren't embargoed for another fifty years after that,' said Colin Stubbings. He sniffed. 'I wouldn't put it past them to do that either, things being what they were at Bakhalla.'

'I quite understand,' said Heber-Hibbs readily. Like

almost everyone else he knew, the Ambassador considered thirty years much too soon for official records to be available to the general public. He did his best to sound sympathetic. 'Difficult for you.'

Personally Heber-Hibbs favoured a hundred-year rule, and, given the choice, he would have advised the authorities to leave records undisturbed for at least another hundred years after that for the dust from any battle to settle. Mercifully the Anglo-Lassertan campaign had been only twenty years earlier – well and truly inside the thirty-year rule. This, he was now beginning to realize, was something to be profoundly thankful for.

'It's what they usually do with official records when there's something they want to hide,' asserted Colin Stubbings trenchantly. 'Mark them down as not to be opened for another fifty years.'

Mr Anthony Heber-Hibbs, a man grown old in the Diplomatic Service, decided against enlightening the lad with the truth. What actually happened to records that might damage the reputations of either the living or the great and dead was much simpler than merely placing them under a dated embargo.

They were lost.

Without trace.

Accidentally on purpose, you might say.

'And we shall want to visit the cemetery, of course,' Mrs Letherington was saying, her face clouding. 'My husband's grave . . .'

'I quite understand,' responded Heber-Hibbs gently. 'And naturally if there's any way in which my staff and I can be of assistance to your party . . .'

The Ambassador summoned his Military Attaché as soon as he got back to the Embassy.

'Christopher,' he said, 'you'd better fill me in. I have a feeling that this party means business. What exactly went wrong at Bakhalla?'

'Nobody really seems to know, sir.' He frowned. 'That's the whole trouble.'

'Which is why the widows and orphans have come out here with their battle guru,' deduced Heber-Hibbs. 'To find out. Go on.'

'It would appear that one platoon of the East Calleshires suddenly wheeled away from the main action and disappeared out of view.'

'Never seen again?'

'Not alive,' said Christopher Dunlop ominously.

'It's happened before, of course,' remarked the Ambassador. 'It's not the first time.'

'Sir?'

'The lost Legion of the Ninth. Went missing north of Eboracum – that's York to you and me – around AD 117.'

'Never seen again?'

'Neither dead nor alive,' said Heber-Hibbs. 'Like the lost army of Cambyses. That disappeared in a desert too.'

'Cambyses, sir?'

'King of Persia. Herodotus tells us that the king lost thirty-thousand men who'd been sent out to occupy an oasis in the desert. Never seen again either, not one of 'em.'

The Military Attaché coughed. 'They found this platoon of the East Calleshires all right, sir, but dead.

They'd suddenly moved out of range of the covering fire, but no one could say why.'

'Strange,' mused Heber-Hibbs.

'Wiped out to a man,' the Military Attaché said. 'At the time it was put down to lack of intelligence, but they weren't really sure.'

'Never a good thing,' agreed Heber-Hibbs gravely. 'Not having enough intelligence, I mean. Always makes for difficulties.'

'I was talking in the military sense, sir,' said Dunlop hastily. 'I meant a lack of good intelligence.'

'Ah . . .'

'There were plenty of well-trained brains about at the time,' Dunlop assured him. 'No doubt about that.'

'Which is something,' said Heber-Hibbs, who had served in several foreign stations where there hadn't been.

The Military Attaché forged on. 'It seems that the Colonel did all the right things – went by the book and all that – but he was blown up early on, visiting an observation post.'

'Did the wrong thing for the right reasons, I expect,' said Heber-Hibbs with a touch of melancholy.

'As did his successor after he'd been killed – an officer called Arkwright, I believe. He very bravely went off into the desert in an armoured car after the missing platoon.'

'The legion of the lost ones, the cohort of the damned,' said Heber Hibbs, misquoting Kipling, 'the poor little lambs who lost their way . . .'

'Ye-es, sir. I suppose you could put it like that. But I fear it didn't do any of them any good.'

'And I dare say,' sighed Heber-Hibbs, 'there were good reasons for our involvement in this débâcle?'

'Yes, sir.' The Military Attaché cleared his throat. 'As you know, sir, we have this long-standing defence treaty with the sheikhs of Lasserta . . .'

'A half-baked agreement,' responded Heber-Hibbs spiritedly, 'hatched up between Sheikh Ben Mirza Ibrahim Hajal Kisra's great-grandfather and Queen Victoria's ministers . . .'

'To come to the aid of the sheikhdom of Lasserta . . .'

'A benighted country that was only a half-baked protectorate at the time,' swept on Her Britannic Majesty's Ambassador to the state in question with some vigour.

'To come to their aid against their ancient tribal enemies if we deem it necessary,' finished the Military Attaché. 'I think that's the exact wording.'

'In exchange for what?' demanded Heber-Hibbs rhetorically. He, of all people, was well aware of there being no such thing as a free lunch, in the world of international diplomacy as everywhere else.

The Military Attaché took this question literally. 'In theory, sir, in exchange for the Lassertans permanently keeping the Sultan of Zonaras at bay.'

'Say no more,' growled the Ambassador.

There was, in fact, no need for either man to say anything. What had really been being defended at Bakhalla was the only known seam of queremitte ore in the free world. The hard-wearing qualities of this rare mineral had long been much prized by the armaments and space industries, as well as by more ordinary manufacturers. The Sultan of Zonaras was by no means the only man who would have liked to get his hands on queremitte twenty years ago – or now.

'Not so much a case, sir, of trade following the flag,' ventured the Military Attaché with an ironic smile, 'as of the flag following trade.'

'But we still don't really know what made the Engagement at Bakhalla such a disaster, then?' persisted the Ambassador.

'No, sir.'

'I suppose I should have known myself, but I was Third Secretary in Chile at the time, with other things on my plate, and anyway Lasserta was a long way away.' He frowned. 'Surely, man, it shouldn't have been too difficult to see off the Zonarans?'

'It shouldn't,' replied Christopher Dunlop cautiously, 'but it was.'

'Well, let me tell you, Christopher, that there's a cocky little lad staying at the Coningsby Hotel who intends to find out why it was.' The Ambassador stroked his chin. 'That is, if he doesn't know already.'

Colin Stubbings didn't know.

But as a student of military history he did know that time spent in reconnaissance is seldom wasted. While the remainder of the party from Calleshire was bathing and resting, he slipped out of the Coningsby Hotel and made his way to Bakhalla in one of the battered vehicles that in the town of Gatt-el-Abbas constituted cars for hire.

He found the site of the battle easily enough – a stretch of desert leading towards the Kisra Pass. It was this which had had to be held against the warring Zonarans in their advance southwards if Lasserta was to be saved. Tidily to one side lay the white-walled military cemetery, its occupants as neatly ordered as on the parade ground, but he would pay his respects there later – after he had found out what had gone wrong at the Engagement at Bakhalla.

All he had to go on was what a surviving mate of his father had told him. 'I couldn't see what happened all that well, lad,' the old soldier had said, 'because I was over on the west flank with a bunch of Lassertans – not that they were up to much. Couldn't really call 'em fighters. That's why we were there, I suppose.'

'Dad's lot . . .' Colin had prompted him.

'It was a funny thing.' The man had frowned. 'Suddenly your dad's platoon just wheeled away from the main advance and set off into the desert to the east, your dad leading. For no reason at all that anyone could see.'

'But under orders surely?' Colin had said, mindful too of *The Charge of the Light Brigade* and the disputed blame for giving the orders there.

'Not that anyone would admit to giving,' the old soldier had said carefully. 'Proper Valley of Death it looked from where I was, and hellish hot. Didn't stop the Adjutant going after them in an armoured car to see what they were up to.'

'Leading from behind, I suppose.' Colin Stubbings hadn't forgotten 'the sneer of cold command' either.

He'd got the shake of a grizzled head for an answer. 'He bought it too.'

'Communications all gone?'

'There was strict radio silence. We'd got orders to advance and take up our positions behind a good layer of trees and scrub well up the wadi to the north – that's where the blighters were coming from. There was nothing to the east but open ground. "B" platoon must have been a sitting target out there.'

Stubbings could see the scrubland himself now. It constituted a broad band of low but thick growth to the north. He turned his head and looked east, and rubbed his eyes . . . To the east there was rather more in the way of trees, and much better cover than ahead. No wonder his father had led his men that way . . . it must have seemed like Sanctuary Wood in a wilderness.

Puzzled, he went forward.

His father's friend had said there had been nothing to the east but he could see trees in plenty, and established scrub vegetation much more than – as the boys' book had it – 'twenty years a'growing'. Tall, well-grown trees . . .

It was nearing noon now and the desert was at its hottest, shimmering in the heat of the midday sun. He advanced over the rough ground as quickly as he could in that oven-like temperature but seemed to get no nearer to the trees. Muttering under his breath something about mad dogs and Englishmen, he forged on. He got no nearer, though, to the thick band of growth to the east.

Perspiring heavily, he was aware that the ground was falling away a little now, giving a better view of the heights of the Kisra Pass. That meant that 'B' platoon would have been especially vulnerable to fire from the north . . . 'If you can see them, they can see you' was a hard lesson learned in the First World War.

So was 'Know Thine Enemy.'

He was still no nearer the trees.

He stumbled on, weary now and more than a little thirsty. There was a disturbing heat haze coming off the desert and soon the broad swathe of trees ahead began to dance before his eyes. He would go as far as the trees and then turn back.

But walk as far and as fast as he could, he couldn't get to them.

It was then that he stumbled and almost fell. That stopped him for a moment, and when he looked up again the trees had gone.

All of them.

He rubbed his eyes.

There was nothing ahead but sand and desert.

Nothing at all.

Yet he hadn't been dreaming.

He was quite sure about that.

He stood stock still while he gave the matter thought.

His father – that unknown figure in a hallowed photograph, and dead before his son was born – could well have led his platoon to their deaths because of a mirage.

Probably had.

'Sorry, Mum,' he said later that night. 'I don't think the desert's going to give up its secrets.'

'There was no harm in hoping,' she said.

'Not after all this time,' he said.

'Your dad would have done what he thought was right at the time,' said Mrs Stubbings confidently.

'That's what you've always said,' said her son, nodding. 'All you can ever do, really, isn't it, if you've got to live with it afterwards?'

'Which is something he didn't have to do,' she reminded him, 'not coming back.'

'True.' It was something he hadn't thought about until now: the burden of living with military mistakes.

'Always knew his own mind, did your father,' she said.

'A complete mystery,' he announced to the East Calleshire Regimental Association at dinner on their last evening in Lasserta.

'We may never know what really happened.' He paused and gave a little, rather patronizing, smile. 'I'm afraid that war's like that – full of unsolved enigmas that have to be lived with.'

'And Anthony Eden?' enquired the Ambassador with genuine interest. 'What action did you say he should have taken at Suez?'

'Done a deal with Nasser,' said Colin Stubbings unhesitatingly.

'Reached a compromise?' translated Heber-Hibbs.

'Bought into the action more like,' cackled Stubbings. 'Saved a lot of trouble. If you can't beat 'em, join 'em.'

'Ah . . .' said the Ambassador.

'Costs less,' said the representative of the new

generation. 'Nothing wrong with a bit of baksheesh anyway, is there?'

'Well . . .' temporized the diplomat.

Stubbings smirked at Heber-Hibbs. 'As long as you keep it secret. That's what's important!' He winked and added, 'For more than thirty years, mind you . . .'

Handsel Monday

Sixteenth-century Scotland

The little girl lay motionless at the foot of the east turnpike stair. She was sprawled, head downwards, just where the bottom step fanned out into the great hall of the castle. How long she had been lying there, tumbling athwart the first three steps, the Sheriff of Fearnshire did not yet know. All he knew so far was that the child's cheek felt cold to the touch of his ungloved hand.

Quite cold. She was dead.

The air too was cold, bitterly cold, just as cold as it had been the last time that Sheriff Rhuaraidh Macmillan had come to Castle Balgalkin. To make matters worse – if they could be any worse than they already were, that is – it was snowing hard today as well. The cold, though, was the only thing that Sheriff Macmillan had so far found that was the same on this visit as it had been the last time he was at the castle.

Then – it had only been the Monday of last week, although now it seemed much longer ago – the whole of Fearnshire had been *en fête* for the feast of hogmanay. Or should, he mused as he took off his other glove, he start thinking of hogmanay by its French name of *hoguinane* now that everything in Scotland was being influenced by a queen from France?

That day – Hogmanay, he decided obstinately – there had been, as there was every year at Castle Balgalkin, a great ceilidh – and he wasn't going to change that good old Gaelic word for any French one – to celebrate the ending of the old year and the coming in of the new one. And that night, in the best Fearnshire tradition, the Laird of Balgalkin himself had answered the door to the first-footers.

Rhuaraidh Macmillan moved his hand from a cold cheek to the girl's outflung arms, the better to see her hands.

Today it was all very, very different. For one thing, when the Sheriff had arrived there had been no welcoming Laird at the door of the Castle Balgalkin. 'The ancient place of the stag with the white head' was what the desmesne had been called in olden times – Scottish times, not French ones. He wasn't surprised: this winter alone had been hard enough to bring any number of stags down off the hills in search of forage.

Macmillan lifted a limp little hand and started to examine small fingers with surprising tenderness.

On New Year's Eve, only the week before, Sheriff Macmillan and his lady wife had been acclaimed as they had arrived from Drummondreach by a piper who had taken up his bagpipes as soon as he saw the couple get near to the castle. There had been no piper at Castle Balgalkin today and no pibroch heralding his approach with ancient tune. Instead there had been only a distraught servant waiting at the gate, anxiously watching out for the coming of himself and his little entourage.

The child's fingers didn't seem broken to him. And the fingernails definitely weren't.

At the first sight of the Sheriff, the retainer had turned and run back inside the fortillage in a great hurry. Macmillan had heard quite clearly his urgent shout apprising his master of the Sheriff's arrival. His voice had echoed round the castle's sandstone walls with a diminishing resonance, but any sound made by the Laird as he crossed the great hall towards the Sheriff and his clerk had been muffled by the reeds and the rushes that were strewn about the floor.

Those same rushes, deep as they were, noted the Sheriff automatically, had not been deep and soft enough to save the girl as she fell. Even though her head was half covered by them, he could see from where he was standing that her face was badly discoloured by both blood and bruise on the left-hand side.

'It's a bad business, Rhuaraidh . . .' The servant's call had produced the man himself – Hector Leanaig, Laird of Balgalkin. He too had presented a very different picture from the genial host of the week before. A veritable giant of a man, he was sufficiently black-avised to have gone first-footing himself on New Year's Eve. He had come forward to meet the Sheriff, shaking his head sadly. 'A bad, bad business . . .'

'Tell me, Hector.' Macmillan had inclined his head attentively towards Hector Leanaig and waited. It would have been quite impossible to discern from the Sheriff's tone whether this was an invitation or a command.

'My Jeannie's dead,' the Laird had blurted out. Big and strong though he was, nevertheless the man looked shaken to his wattles now. There was an unhealthy pallor about him too, contrasting sharply with his raven-coloured hair. 'My poor, wee bairn.'

The Sheriff nodded. This was what he had been told.

'She's just where we found her,' Leanaig had struggled for speech but only achieved a rather tremulous croak. 'This way . . .'

Although at first the Laird had taken the lead through the castle, he fell back as soon as they neared the broken figure spread-eagled across the bottom three steps of the stair. The Sheriff had advanced alone, his clerk and the Laird lagging behind.

And now Rhuaraidh Macmillan was gently turning the girl's hands over and taking a long look at their outer aspects. There were grazes here and there on both and some dried blood over the back of the knuckles of her left hand.

'Poor wee Jeannie,' repeated the Laird brokenly.

'Aye, Hector,' agreed the Sheriff noncommittally. That, at least, was true enough, whatever had happened to her. He straightened up and changed his stance, the better to take a look at her head.

Seemingly Hector Leanaig could not bear to watch him going about his business, because he took a step back and averted his gaze from the sad scene.

The child was in her nightclothes, her gown rucked up on one side. A dreadful bruise disfigured the left-hand side of her face and, even without stooping, the Sheriff could see that her cheek was broken on that side. He dropped on one knee and, with great care, put his hand to her skull. That too might be broken. It was certainly cold to the touch and what blood was visible there was brown and dried: the girl, he concluded, must have been dead for several hours.

Hector Leanaig licked dry lips. 'She's just where we found her.'

'We?' queried Rhuaraidh Macmillan sharply. 'Who was it exactly who found her, then?'

'One of the women,' said Leanaig, jerking his head roughly over his shoulder but not turning round.

The Sheriff's gaze followed the direction of his gesture. In the far corner of the hall a buxom young woman was lurking in the shadows. She was weeping, stifling her sobs as best she could. Her face was almost invisible under a woven kirtle, but what he could see of her visage was swollen by tears. Here and there strands of blonde hair extruded from under the woollen garment. She would have been comely enough, he thought, had it not been for her obvious distress.

'Morag,' amplified the Laird, still not letting his gaze fall on her. 'Jeannie's nurse.'

Rhuaraidh Macmillan, though, took a good look at the weeping woman. Irony of ironies, she was standing under the traditional Christmas osier and evergreen kissing bough – the ivy and the holly there to ensure new growth in the spring to come. This had been suspended from a handy rafter – not too low to kiss under, not too high to be too difficult to secure. The apples and mistletoe in the kissing bough would have been an important part of the hogmanay festivities

until those had come to an end the night before –
Handsel Monday, as ever was. The kissing bough
would have been fixed firmly enough for sure: it was
considered very bad luck if it were to touch the ground,
because in nature the parasitic mistletoe plant always
hung downwards . . .

Perhaps, he thought, that was what had happened
at Castle Balgalkin, because there was 'nae luck aboot
this house, nae luck at a'. That was beyond doubt,
whatever had befallen the girl.

The young woman under the kissing bough let
forth a loud sob as she saw the Sheriff's eye rest upon
her. Wrapped tightly round her shapely shoulders was
a shawl; this she held with its edges closed together,
as if for greater protection against the outside world.
Rhuaraidh Macmillan, no amateur in these matters,
was well aware of how frightened she was. And no
wonder, if the dead child had been left in her charge.

'Morag Munro,' said Hector Leanaig roughly. 'She'll
tell you herself . . .'

'The bairn wasna' there in her bed when I woke
up,' said the young woman between chattering teeth.
'Handsel Monday or no'.' She stared wildly at the
Sheriff. 'And I'd warned her . . .'

'What about?' asked Macmillan mildly. No good
ever came of frightening witnesses too soon. He'd
learned that a long time ago.

'Handsel Monday, of course,' said Morag, visibly
surprised. 'Did ye not mind that yestre'en was Handsel
Monday?'

'Tell me,' he invited her. Nothing was to be assumed
when Sheriff Macmillan was going about his business

of law and justice, nothing taken for granted. Not even the ancient customs attached to Handsel Monday.

' "When all people are to stay in bed until after sunrise",' she quoted, ' "so as not to be meeting fairies or witches".'

Hector Leanaig said dully, 'The first Monday in January, that's Handsel Monday. You know that, Rhuaraidh Macmillan, as well as I do.'

'Jeannie knew it,' Morag Munro gulped. 'And I told her she wasna' to leave her bed until I came for her in the morning.' The young woman dissolved into tears again. 'And when I did, her bed was empty.' Her shoulders shook as her sobs rang round the hall. 'She was gone.'

'And Mistress Leanaig?' asked Sheriff Macmillan, suddenly realizing what it was that was missing from the *mise-en-scène* and what it was that he had been subconsciously expecting as a backdrop to this tragedy: the unique and quite dreadful wailing of a mother suddenly bereft of one of her children.

'She's away over at Alcaig's,' said Leanaig thickly. He jerked a shoulder northwards in the direction of the firth. 'They say her father's a-dying.'

Macmillan nodded his ready comprehension. Mistress Leanaig, he knew, was the only daughter of the Lord of Alcaig's Isle.

'Her brothers came for her yesterday afternoon,' said Hector. 'She went at once.'

'In her condition?' asked Macmillan. If he remembered rightly, Mistress Leanaig was in the 'interesting condition' that the French called *enceinte*. At least, that was the reason the other guests had been given for

Hector Leanaig spending most of New Year's Eve dancing with a high-spirited young woman called Jemima from Balblair. There had been a memorable Orcadian version of Strip the Willow which no pregnant woman could have danced with safety. And which he, Rhuaraidh Macmillan, for one, wouldn't forget in a hurry – even though he himself had danced it featly with his own lady wife. Nor, he thought judiciously, would the fair-haired young woman from Balblair called Jemima, with whom Hector Leanaig had danced most of that evening, be likely to forget it soon either.

'Old man Alcaig was asking for her.' The Laird pointed up through a gun loop at the leaden sky. 'We could see that there was snow on the way and they were anxious to be well beyond Torgorm in daylight.'

'So . . .' invited the Sheriff, bringing his gaze back to the pathetic little form at his feet. He had no need to ask why Leanaig hadn't gone with his wife to her dying father's the day before. It was no secret in Fearnshire that old Alcaig and his fine sons didn't like the Laird of Balgalkin. And never had.

'So she went with them,' said Leanaig.

'Leaving the bairn with you . . .' If the Sheriff had remembered rightly, old Alcaig had quibbled for a long time over his daughter's tocher going with her to Leanaig. That it had gone there in the end was a triumph of tradition and usage over personal inclination.

'She said Jeannie was too young to be crossing the water on a night like last night.' Hector Leanaig ran a hand over his eyes. 'God!' he said distractedly, 'she'd have been safer with her mother . . .'

The Sheriff didn't answer this. Instead he started to examine the child's clothing. Though her nightgown was caught up under one knee, it did not look to him as if it had been really disarranged other than by the tumble down the stairs. Then he started to pull it to one side, lifting it clear of her piteous body.

A hectic choler took over Hector Leanaig's pale visage. 'Rhuaraidh, I swear by all that's holy that if there's a man in this place who's laid so much as a finger on her, I'll kill him myself with my bare hands, kinsman or not.'

'Whisht, man,' said the Sheriff soothingly. 'There's no call for that. No one's been near her in that way. Her goonie's quite clean and there's no sign of interference.'

A low moan escaped Morag, the nurse. 'The poor mite . . .'

'And there's no sign of a struggle,' added Rhuaraidh Macmillan, turning his attention to the turnpike stair, which curled up clock-wise from the hall on their left. He put his foot on the bottom step and peered up. The stone steps curled away out of his sight in an endless spiral. Above them, the turret tower was capped by a conical wooden roof. The stonework and wood of the turret, he noted, looked in reasonable condition. Some of the dowry which had come with Alcaig's daughter in the end had no doubt been spent on her new home, the castle at Balgalkin.

'Wait you here,' the Sheriff commanded, motioning to his clerk to keep everyone where they were. 'All of you,' he added firmly as Leanaig started forward to join him.

The Sheriff stepped delicately round the inert

figure on the lower steps and started to climb the round stair tower. In the first instance it took him up from the great hall to the second floor of the castle, but he could see that it went further up and beyond still. As he mounted the stair, he ran his left hand over the wall, but only a fine red sandstone dust marked his fingers.

He took his bearings afresh when he stepped off the stair at the first landing and reached the rooms above.

He came first to a little room hung about with fine linens and women's things which he took to be Mistress Leanaig's retiring room. The French fashion these days was to call a lady's place something quite different – by a new French word which he couldn't call to mind just this minute. His wife would know the name of it – and would be wanting one herself at Drummond-reach soon too, he'd be bound.

He came next to the nursery. Here, against the longest wall of the room, was the child's bed and, over in the corner, a little truckle bed where he supposed the nurse, Morag Munro, slept. Macmillan took a careful look at both. Neither showed any sign of great disturbance. The bedding on the child's bed had been turned back as by its occupant slipping out of it quite normally.

There was nothing unusual about the other one either. He put a hand in the child's bed and then did the same between the rugs on the servant's one. There was no residual warmth to be felt now in either sleeping place.

Leaving the nursery he went to the master

bedroom, where the Laird and his lady slept – when she was at Balgalkin, that is. He paused on the threshold, the French name of Mistress Leanaig's own room having suddenly come to him after all. Boudoir – that was it.

The room here was a much grander affair than the others. Not only were there a great bed against the further wall and a garderobe, but there were hangings on all the walls and in the corner a small privy stair which did not climb to the upper floors like the turnpike one. Instead, it descended in a clock-wise spiral from the main bedroom to the great hall. This west turret, he deduced, was the Laird and his lady's stair and theirs alone.

The Sheriff advanced on the bed and pulled aside the curtains hanging from the tester – and found another bed covered in thick rugs from which all interior heat had gone. This one, though, did show signs of someone in it having had a rude awakening. To him, the bed coverings had all the look of having been thrust aside in great haste by its occupant.

Rhuaraidh Macmillan walked across to the window. To the north, under a lowering sky, lay a snow-clad Fearnshire and somewhere in that wilderness was a woman whose young daughter was unaccountably dead at the foot of the other stair with her skull broken.

Unaccountably to him, that is.

So far.

Taking his time, Rhuaraidh Macmillan went round the second floor all over again, and then climbed up to the top level by the turnpike stair. Here, without any refinements at all, slept the other retainers of

Castle Balgalkin. A persistent curious flapping sound he traced not to pigeons but to an old flagstaff from which was already flying the flag of the Leanaigs at half-mast.

He felt a spasm of pity for Mistress Leanaig, who from all accounts would be leaving one deathbed only to find another. And unless Hector had sent a messenger to Alcaig's Isle, she would read the flag's message as she neared Torgorm but not know for whom it was flying so low.

Macmillan came down to the main bedroom again and stood there thoughtfully before making for the privy stair. Again he put his left hand out and ran it over the wall, this time as he went down rather than up the stair. This time too a fine red sandstone dust marked his fingers.

But so did something else.

He paused and considered his hand. There was no doubt about it. He was looking at blood. Not a lot, but blood for all that. Macmillan stood for a long quiet minute on a step just above the last turn of the stair but still out of sight of those waiting at the foot of the other stair at the east end of the great hall.

Where the body lay.

Then the Sheriff put his hand down again on the wall of the privy stair.

Low down.

The sandstone felt slightly damp to his touch. He would have been the first to admit that the walls of Castle Balgalkin probably always felt slightly damp to the touch in winter – it was no wonder that the Queen from France was finding Scotland not to her liking after warmer climes. But this dampness was different. He crouched down to consider the patch. Unless he was very much mistaken, someone had taken a wet cloutie to the stone and rubbed it as clean as they could before he reached the castle.

Rhuaraidh Macmillan straightened up and turned silently back up the privy stair. He then walked through the master bedroom, and past the nursery and Mistress Leanaig's boudoir to the main east turnpike stair. He descended this and rejoined the dejected group waiting beside the distressful body at the bottom of the stairway.

Hector Leanaig was standing where he had left him, although his head was now sunk on his chest as if he was afraid to look up. The child's nurse, Morag Munro, was still standing under the kissing bough, well away from the others. As the Sheriff appeared down the turnpike stair, her weeping changed to a more primitive keening.

'It wasn't only me,' she said when she managed to speak. 'The mistress warned her about Handsel Monday too. She told her that on Handsel Monday night everyone has to keep to their beds until sunrise. Made her promise her mother she would stay there.' She gulped. 'I heard her say that myself.'

'I wonder why the child didn't stay in her own bed then,' mused Sheriff Macmillan aloud, addressing nobody in the great hall in particular.

'It's a dangerous night, Handsel Monday,' growled Hector Leanaig.

'I ken that right enough, Hector,' agreed Macmillan.

'But I don't believe in the fairies and witches myself, that's all.'

'Not believe?' echoed the Laird of Balgalkin, astonished.

'No, Hector.' The Sheriff shook his head. 'I'm afraid Handsel Monday is just an ancient way of putting an end to the feasting of hogmanay, that's all.'

Hector Leanaig said obstinately, 'Jeannie believed in it.'

'The English,' remarked the Sheriff, ignoring this, 'call the time when the kissing has to stop by the name of Twelfth Night.'

'Oh, the English,' said Leanaig dismissively. 'They're not right-minded folk at all.'

'But it's still when the kissing has to stop,' said the Sheriff, adding meaningfully, 'all the kissing, Hector . . .'

The Laird of Balgalkin stared at him, a flush mounting his cheek.

Rhuaraidh Macmillan stared down at the pitiable figure on the floor. 'What, Hector, do you think it could be that would make a wee girlie like this so disobedient?'

'I canna' think, man, of anything at all.'

'And I can only think of one thing myself,' said the Sheriff.

The Laird jerked his head up, the flush suffusing his whole face now. He searched the Sheriff's face. 'You can?'

'I'm afraid so,' said Macmillan very quietly. 'I think that Jeannie woke up in the night and found her nurse gone from her bed.'

Hector Leanaig said nothing while Morag Munro clutched her kirtle round her head even more tightly.

'And,' said the Sheriff evenly, 'I think when that happened, Jeannie was naturally frightened that the fairies or the witches must have spirited away her nurse, Morag.'

The wailing under the kissing bough stopped abruptly and a palpable silence fell in the great hall of Castle Balgalkin.

'But,' continued Rhuaraidh Macmillan in a steely voice, 'I don't think they had.'

'No?' said the Laird hoarsely.

'No, Hector. I think that something much worse than fairies or witches had taken Jeannie's nurse away from her bed in Jeannie's room.'

The Laird moistened his lips. 'Something much worse?'

'You, Hector,' said the Sheriff.

'Me?' spluttered the Laird of Balgalkin.

'I think,' maintained Macmillan unperturbed, 'that when little Jeannie woke up and saw Morag Munro was not in her bed in the nursery, her next thought – her very natural thought – was to find you, her father.'

'Well, that would be understandable, right enough,' responded Leanaig non-committally. 'If she did,' he added lamely.

'Don't forget,' carried on the Sheriff ineluctably, 'that last night – Handsel Monday – was one your daughter had been told on all sides by people she trusted to be very afraid of indeed.'

'Aye,' admitted Leanaig, 'that's true.'

'I think,' resumed Macmillan, 'Jeannie was very

frightened and did come looking for you – after all, you were only in your own bed in the next room, weren't you, Hector?'

Hector Leanaig said nothing.

'You either were or you weren't in your own bed, Hector,' said Rhuaraidh Macmillan without impatience. 'Which was it?'

'I was,' said Hector Leanaig gruffly.

'The trouble was,' said the Sheriff almost conversationally, 'that though you were in your own bed, I think you were not alone in it.'

Hector Leanaig's face told its own story. The flush on it slowly drained away before the Sheriff's eyes, to be replaced by a marked pallor. The man of law pointed to the pathetic bundle at their feet and said, 'Your Jeannie was young all right, but not too young to know what makes the beast with two backs . . .'

The woman under the kissing bough screamed. 'We didna' kill her. I tell you, we didna' kill her. She ran away.'

'And her father ran after her,' said the Sheriff calmly.

'To try to explain,' jerked out Hector. 'I swear that's all I did . . . I swear.'

'I know,' said Rhuaraidh Macmillan imperturbably. 'But Jeannie ran away down the stair before you could catch up with her.'

'She fell,' said Hector. 'Before I could catch her and explain.'

Morag Munro ran across the great hall and flung herself at the Sheriff's feet. 'Believe us,' she pleaded. 'We didna' touch her. It's true.'

'Partly true,' responded Macmillan. He pointed diagonally across the hall. 'But it was the other stair that she ran down. You didn't want anyone to guess she'd come from your room.'

Leanaig brushed his hair away from his eyes. 'How do you know that?'

'How else do you account for the crack on her head being on the left of her skull? This is a clockwise stair going up and a left-hand one coming down. If she'd tumbled down this turnpike stair here, her head would have hit the right-hand side of the stairway.' He looked down at the child and then at the step tapering to the apex of its triangle as it became the central pillar of the stair. 'There's nothing to catch her head on coming down on the left in this turnpike. She would have fallen to the right . . . and it's the left of her head that's stove in.'

The only sound in the great hall now was the heavy breathing of the Laird of Balgalkin as he struggled to control himself.

'And the privy stair,' whispered Hector Leanaig, as one making a great discovery, 'comes down the other way.'

'Clockwise from the top,' agreed the Sheriff.

'It's a stair that could be defended by a left-handed swordsman,' said the Laird almost absently.

'Jeannie hit her head on the left-hand side of the privy stair as she ran down it, away from you.' The Sheriff looked across at Morag Munro. 'From you both. And the pair of you hoped to get away with blaming Handsel Monday.'

Hector Leanaig sagged like a man stuffed with

straw reeling from a punch in the solar plexus. 'I may have killed my daughter, Rhuariadh, but I didn't murder her.'

'But she's as dead,' said the Sheriff bleakly, 'as if you had.'

The Laird made a visible effort to straighten himself up. 'What are you going to do?'

'Me?' Rhuariadh Macmillan gave a mirthless laugh. 'I'm not going to do anything, Hector Leanaig. No, I'm going to leave that to poor wee Jeannie here . . .'

'Jeannie?'

'Aye, man. She's going to haunt you here for the rest of your life.'

Preyed in Aid

'You're wanted, Seedy.' Inspector Harpe greeted his old friend Detective Inspector C. D. Sloan with the unwelcome message as he crossed the threshold of Berebury police station ready to report for duty.

'Who by?' asked Sloan cautiously. He was head of the tiny Criminal Intelligence Department of 'F' Division of the Calleshire force and a naturally careful man. Actually he thought he could guess who wanted him.

'Him upstairs, of course,' replied Harpe.

Sloan's step very nearly faltered. A request for attendance from his superior officer, Superintendent Leeyes, was never a good sign. Least of all did it cheer first thing in the morning on a dreary January day, the more especially when it was a day which fell at that low point towards the end of the month when memories of festive cheer had faded and the office Christmas decorations had been taken down but not yet decently put away for another year.

'How is he today?' he asked Harpe warily. The barometer outside the police station measured the ambient temperature and pressure of the county of Calleshire. The atmosphere inside the police station, on the other hand, tended to be calibrated against the current state of the Superintendent's temper.

Inspector Harpe gave this question some thought before he replied. 'Quiet.'

That, thought Sloan, could be good or bad.

'Very quiet,' added Harpe judiciously.

'Too quiet?'

'Could be.'

'Did he say what . . .'

'He wants to know all that you can tell him about the Reverend Christopher Carstairs.'

'The Vicar of St Leonard's?'

'None other.'

Detective Inspector Sloan drew breath and tried his best not to damn with faint praise. 'I should say he's well meaning, always trying to do his best, but more than a bit on the naïve side.'

'Gullible,' translated Harpe.

'And too compassionate by half,' finished Sloan.

'Always takes the side of the underdog.'

'That's exactly what I told the Super too.'

'And?'

'He wants you to see if there's anything known against.'

Sloan raised his eyebrows. 'Wouldn't have thought so myself for a moment, but I'll run a check.'

A few minutes later he was in his superior's office and saying, 'No, sir. Not a thing. Nothing known at all against Mr Carstairs. I've double-checked.' He coughed and enquired delicately, 'Were you expecting there to have been, then?'

'There was always the off chance,' said Superintendent Leeyes, not lifting his eyes from a sheet of paper on his desk, 'that the man might have plenty of previous and it's always just as well to make sure first.'

'No form of any sort,' insisted Detective Inspector Sloan firmly.

'It was just a thought, Sloan, that's all.' The Superintendent sounded almost wistful.

'Clean as a whistle,' said the Inspector, mystified.

The Superintendent essayed a little laugh. 'We can't say the same about Matthew Steele, though, can we?'

'Matthew Steele?' echoed Sloan, even more puzzled. Actually, he would have said that Matthew Steele didn't have one single thing in common with the Vicar of St Leonard's Church in Berebury, except, perhaps now he came to think about it, a well-developed way with words. 'No, sir. Record as long as your arm. You name it and Steele's done it. Done quite a lot of time for some of it too.' He paused. 'But not for all of it,' he added with heavy significance. 'Oh, no, not for all of it by any means.'

'And more talkative than a murmuration of starlings,' groaned Leeyes.

'But never a canary, sir,' pointed out Sloan.

'Steele never sings about anything,' snorted Leeyes. 'You don't have to tell me.'

'Always plenty to say for himself, though, when we take him in, has our Matthew Steele . . .'

'Talk the hind leg off a donkey.'

'He'll argue the toss with anyone,' agreed Sloan, 'but it doesn't usually amount to much.'

'That's not going to be a lot of help to me,' complained Leeyes.

'Should have been a lawyer,' said Sloan, wondering where all this was leading.

'Or in the pulpit,' suggested Leeyes unexpectedly.

'Not with his lack of principles,' said Sloan, realizing too late that, in standing up for men of the cloth, he'd inadvertently impugned the whole legal profession in passing.

With wholly uncharacteristic passivity, Superintendent Leeyes let this go by. Instead he went off at a tangent and asked if Sloan could tell him exactly when Ash Wednesday was.

'Not offhand, sir, but I'll look it up for you,' promised the Detective Inspector, even more puzzled.

'Do.' The Superintendent waved his hand. 'It's quite soon, isn't it?'

'A couple of weeks, at least . . .' Sloan's mother would know. She was a great churchwoman and would have the date at her fingertips. Bound to . . .

'That's what I meant, Sloan. Soon . . .'

'Easter's a movable feast, of course, sir, which is why the date varies from year to year,' murmured Sloan, mentally trying to connect Matthew Steele, con man and common thief, with any religious festival at all. He found it was just as difficult to equate 'a couple of weeks' with 'soon'. In Superintendent Leeyes's terminology, 'soon' usually meant within the hour at the very latest.

'Of course,' said Leeyes humbly. 'I'd quite forgotten that the date isn't always the same.'

'That's why, sir, I can't tell you straight away when

it will be.' On the other hand, unlike Matthew Steele, the Reverend Christopher Carstairs would obviously have a simple and straightforward link with Ash Wednesday on whatever date it happened to fall this year.

'Yes, of course,' said Leeyes, again unnaturally in agreement.

Sloan cleared his throat and asked, 'Has Steele been up to something again, then, sir?'

'Not that I know of,' said Leeyes.

Detective Inspector Sloan took a deep breath and said, 'Actually, sir, we think he may have been on the Tilson Street job.'

'The Calleshire and Counties Bank one?'

Detective Inspector Sloan nodded.

Superintendent Leeyes cocked his head to one side. 'Robbery with violence, wasn't it?'

'One of the girl tellers was hit over the head and the Bank Manager threatened. But it's only a hunch, sir, that Steele was involved. There's no way we can prove it. Not yet, anyway. Probably not until we can find the proceeds. We're doing all we can, of course, but it hasn't amounted to much so far. Is that the problem?'

The Superintendent shook his head. 'No, no, Sloan, it's not that. It's just that he and I are both in this church business at St Leonard's together.'

Sloan raised his eyebrows. 'You and Steele, sir?' Privately he was absolutely certain that Matthew Steele had orchestrated the Tilson Street bank job. All the Berebury CID needed now was hard evidence to prove it, but Sloan didn't want to say so. Not just now. Not until he knew what all this peculiar prevarication was about.

'Him and me,' said his superior officer regretfully.

'Sir?' If he couldn't finger Steele, then finding what had been stolen would be the next best thing . . .

'The two of us.' Leeyes grimaced. 'That's the trouble – or, rather, part of the trouble.'

Sloan frowned. This could be serious. In the police book, the Superintendent's consorting with known criminals would be considered a bad thing. Having anything to do with the likes of Matthew Steele – as opposed to actually having him on a charge for anything that could be considered wrong doing – would be a risky business for any policeman, let alone a full-blown Superintendent. 'Where, sir,' he asked tentatively, 'does Mr Carstairs come in, then?'

'It was all the Vicar's idea in the first place,' said Leeyes, his eyes still cast down on the paper lying on his desk. 'He's asked Steele too – not that he wanted to do it either, I gather, but the Vicar's a persuasive sort.'

'And what's Steele got to do with the Vicar?' asked Sloan pertinently.

'Steele's been repairing the church tower of St Leonard's for weeks now,' said Leeyes.

'He has, has he? I didn't know that.'

'I expect that's how the Vicar got to know him – and, come to that, it's probably why Steele didn't like to refuse to do it.'

'And does the Vicar know that Steele's got a bad record?' asked Sloan, still in a verbal fog.

'I shouldn't think so for a moment,' said Leeyes.

'But they've got trouble in their belfry. And before you ask, not bats.'

'At least there's not a lot Steele can nick in a church tower,' said Sloan, 'though we decided long ago that you couldn't ask for better cover for burglary than a builder's business. A covered van, ladders and a good excuse for going equipped with as many tools as you like . . .'

'And for parking in odd places,' contributed Leeyes.

Sloan hesitated. 'But I still don't see where you come in, sir.'

'I think,' the Superintendent grunted, 'that my wife may have had a hand in it.'

'Ah . . .' Sloan made a non-committal sound deep down in his throat.

'Only,' put in Leeyes with haste, 'because she was trying to be helpful, of course.'

'Of course,' agreed Sloan guardedly. By all accounts, the Superintendent's wife was a force to be reckoned with. Both at home and away, so to speak.

'You see, Sloan,' said the Superintendent, waving a hand, 'she's one of Mr Carstairs's flock – that's what you call it, isn't it?'

'A member of his congregation,' translated Sloan.

'That's it, Sloan, exactly. Mrs Leeyes attends St Leonard's Church every Sunday without fail.'

'And?' Sloan still couldn't see yet where all this was getting them.

'And,' said Leeyes hollowly, 'she went and volunteered me to take part in one of their Lent debates at the church.'

Sloan smothered a promising remark about it being

very good for the Superintendent's sins. This was only partly because his superior officer had never been known to admit to having transgressed in any way. Self-preservation came into it too. He said instead, 'I think I'm beginning to get the picture, sir.'

'I knew you would,' Leeyes said, seizing on this and pushing the sheet of paper on his desk over in Sloan's direction. 'Look. It's all here on this.'

Detective Inspector Sloan picked the paper up and read it. It was a letter from the Reverend Christopher Carstairs, Vicar of St Leonard's Church, Berebury, saying how much they were all looking forward to the participation of Police Superintendent Leeyes in an active debate with Matthew Steele at the church as part of their Lent Awareness Programme and enclosing a copy of a poster advertising it.

The Superintendent pointed a stubby finger at this. 'Have you got to the bottom line yet, Sloan?'

'Yes, sir,' said Sloan, hoping his lips hadn't been visibly twitching as he read that the subject of the debate was 'Original Sin'. 'I see what you mean now, sir.'

'But have you got to the very bottom, Sloan?'

Sloan ran his eye further down the poster until it lit upon the debate's subtitle: 'Would You Adam and Eve It?' This example of Cockney rhyming slang was displayed in eye-catching capital letters.

'What do you think of that, Sloan, eh?'

'Very trendy, sir.'

The Superintendent nodded dispiritedly. 'That's what I thought too.'

'And you, sir, I take it,' murmured Sloan, 'will be

there to put forward one view . . .' He scanned the rest of the letter, struggling not to let his voice quaver.

'That's part of the trouble.'

'And – ' Sloan took a very firm hold too of his facial expression, reducing it to the deadpan rigidity required of a public servant on distasteful duty – 'sir, have I got this right? Matthew Steele will be taking the opposite one.'

'Exactly, Sloan.'

'For or against original sin existing?'

'That's what it's all about,' said Leeyes tightly.

'Did you get to choose which, sir?' enquired Sloan diplomatically.

'The Vicar,' ground out Leeyes between clenched teeth, 'decided that I would want to take the orthodox police view.'

'Well, that's all right, then, sir, isn't it?' said Sloan.

'No, it isn't!' howled Leeyes.

'Sir?' Sloan decided he really should have paid more attention at his Sunday School classes. He hadn't known at the time, of course, that he was going to be a policeman.

'I've got to argue that man is equally ready to do either good or evil and has the freedom of will to choose between the two,' said the Superintendent.

'Ye-es,' said Sloan uncertainly. 'Well . . .'

'And Matthew Steele,' snarled Leeyes, 'gets to take the Vicar's personal theological stance. He's even given him a text.' He looked down. 'Romans chapter 7, verse 19: "For the good that I would I do not: but the evil which I would not, that I do." ' He snorted. 'I ask you, Matthew Steele!'

'That must be a first,' said Sloan sourly.

'It means that he's going to be able to argue that he doesn't have any choice whether he commits crimes . . .'

'Now I've heard everything,' said Sloan.

'Me too.'

'It's a new way of a villain saying he's got right on his side, sir,' observed Sloan after a moment's thought.

'It's what defence counsel are always on about,' said Leeyes grimly. 'The Vicar, you see, says that in the beginning – that is, when all this business about original sin first cropped up . . .'

'In the Garden of Eden?' suggested Sloan helpfully.

'No, no, Sloan. The Vicar says it was in AD four hundred and something when there was a famous dialogue on the subject with a man called Pelagius.'

'Pelagius?' Sloan sat up. 'Wait a minute, sir, wait a minute . . .'

'An English monk who got done for heresy when he went to Rome,' sniffed Leeyes. 'Makes a change that, for a God-botherer, doesn't it? Going from England to Rome.'

'The traffic's usually all the other way,' conceded Sloan. He frowned. 'But I do remember learning something about a man called Pelagius at school.'

'More than I ever did,' said Leeyes robustly.

'And a bishop called Germanus . . .'

'You've always had a police memory for names, Sloan,' admitted Leeyes grudgingly.

'In Religious Education, it was.' Detective Inspector Sloan metaphorically scratched his head. 'The teacher thought verses might stick in our minds better than talk.'

'And did they?' asked Superintendent Leeyes, never one to beat about the bush.

'I know it was someone called Hilaire Belloc who wrote them,'* said Sloan obliquely, giving himself time to think, 'because we all thought Hilaire was a funny name for a man.' The class comic, he remembered, had famously gone on a bit about it being very 'hilarious'. They'd all laughed uproariously at this, prolonged amusement being one of the tried and tested ways of cutting down teaching time.

'French, I expect, a name like that,' said Leeyes dismissively.

Sloan shut his eyes and concentrated hard. 'I don't know if I can remember the poem now.'

'Try,' commanded Leeyes.

' "Pelagius lived in Kardanoel," ' quoted the Detective Inspector, quondam schoolboy,

> ' "And taught a doctrine there,
> How whether you went to Heaven or Hell,
> It was your own affair."

'I don't know where Kardanoel is, sir,' added Sloan, aware that this was unimportant. If it wasn't in 'F' Division in the county of Calleshire, the Superintendent didn't care.

'What matters more,' said Leeyes grandly, 'is that the Vicar of St Leonard's has asked me to argue the toss with Matthew Steele of all people.'

---

* Hilaire Belloc, *The Four Men: A Farrago* (London: Nelson, 1912).

'On the side of law and order, though,' offered Sloan by way of comfort.

'Naturally,' snapped Leeyes.

Greatly daring, Sloan went on, 'Against there being original sin, though, sir.' His own old Station Sergeant had believed that original sin was always there, lurking in the woodwork, so to speak. Their tutor at the police training college, on the other hand, had made them write down a quotation from someone called Clive Kluckholm: 'Nature provides potentialities which culture neglects or elaborates.' He wasn't sure if he understood that either.

Leeyes looked pained. 'It's not as easy as that, Sloan.'

'No, sir.' Sloan hadn't thought for one moment that it would be. Outside of the Ten Commandments, theology was never that simple.

'The Vicar – are you sure the Vicar's straight up, Sloan?'

'Quite sure, sir . . . except that he believes the best of everyone.' This, he appreciated, was a considerable failing in the Superintendent's book.

'The Vicar tells me that Steele is going to argue that he is as he is – he called him Common Man – because of there being such a thing as original sin . . . it being in the genes and all that.'

'I can see that he might want to argue that way,' said Sloan moderately.

'And that the world therefore has him as it made him.'

'Then all I can say,' said Sloan warmly, 'is that the world didn't make a very good job of him.'

'What I want to know,' said Leeyes belligerently, 'is how come Matthew Steele gets to argue on the side of the angels and I don't?'

'Perhaps,' suggested Sloan, one at least of his Sunday School lessons coming back to him, 'the Vicar did it on the principle that there is more joy in Heaven over one sinner who has repented than over ninety-nine who haven't sinned.' He was going to get Steele for leading the Tilson Street job if it was the last thing he did, debate or no debate. In his canon, hitting young women bank clerks over the head with baseball bats was just not on.

'And has he repented,' enquired Leeyes with real interest, 'since we're sure he's sinned?'

'Not that I know of, sir.'

'But the Vicar's still going to let him have his twopenn'orth on the subject.' Leeyes sighed. 'And I've been landed with having to argue the other way – for there being no such thing as original sin.'

'Only free will,' said Sloan thoughtfully.

'I don't like it, Sloan. Not one little bit.'

'It's only for the sake of argument, sir. Don't forget that.'

'It's all very well, Sloan, but I don't believe that people such as Steele can stay on the straight and narrow if they just put their minds to it, but this old monk Pelagius did.'

Since the view of most magistrates and all the do-gooders Sloan had ever known was that all malefactors and most recidivists could do just that, the detective inspector nodded not unsympathetically. 'The Devil's got the best tune there, all right.'

'And Steele's a proper limb of Satan to match,' the Superintendent came back smartly.

'I'm not sure you should be bringing Satan into this, sir.'

'Enemy territory, eh?' said Leeyes unexpectedly. 'You could be right.'

'Confusing the issue was what I had meant,' murmured Sloan.

'What I want, Sloan, are solid arguments,' said Leeyes, not listening.

'Did the Vicar give you any to be going on with?' asked Sloan, playing for time.

'No.' Superintendent Leeyes consulted a tattered notebook which, from the look of its cover, hadn't been produced in evidence since he had last been walking the beat. 'But he did warn me about one of their clever old churchwardens who likes catching speakers out with a trick question.'

'Forewarned is forearmed,' said Sloan sententiously.

Leeyes squinted down at his notebook. 'Something to do with St Thomas Aquinas and the number of angels who can dance on the head of a pin. That mean anything to you, Sloan?'

Sloan struggled with his memory. 'I think it's as many as want to, sir, seeing as angels don't take up any room.'

'So where's the trick, then?' asked Leeyes suspiciously.

'If you were to say a specific number, sir, it would have meant that you didn't know that angels were – er – I think it's called "non-corporeal".'

'I never thought they weren't,' said Leeyes indignantly. 'And I've never thought Steele was an angel either.'

'Nor me, sir,' said Sloan. The bank robbers had worn Mickey Mouse headpieces and carried something that might at first sight have been charity collecting boxes on poles but weren't. 'The Vicar might, of course.'

'Oh, and the Vicar said,' went on Leeyes, suddenly recollecting something else, 'to leave the Manichaeans and St Augustine out of it, because another couple of his parishioners were going to debate the struggle between Good and Evil the week after us.'

'Pity, that,' said Sloan reflectively. 'I should have said that that was much more our line of country than whether or not what you made of yourself is your own affair or in-built. After all, sir, we're part of the good versus evil struggle here, aren't we?'

'We're here to uphold the law, Sloan,' declared Leeyes heavily, 'and that's all. And we know, don't we, which side Steele would be on in that one. How much did they get away with at Tilson Street?'

'Best part of half a million pounds in used small-denomination notes – they made the staff give them the safe keys or else.' It was the 'or else' that had lifted the Calleshire and Counties Bank job out of the ordinary ruck of robberies and made Sloan so determined to catch the perpetrators. 'And a load of boxes from their safe deposit, although no one knows what's in them.'

Leeyes grunted. 'Ill-gotten gains, I expect.'

'Take a bit of stashing away, that lot, sir. But none

of it's at Steele's house or his yard, because we got a warrant and had a look-see.'

Superintendent Leeyes jerked his head. 'We'll get the whole crew somehow.'

'Yes, sir. In time.' They weren't talking about a nice ethical and theoretical discussion now. This was proper police business, not about scoring debating points for the edification of the converted.

'Sooner or later one of the gang will slip up,' he forecast.

'Like Adam and Eve,' ventured Sloan.

'That's what the ACC thinks too.' Leeyes waved the poster in his hand. 'I happened to mention this debate to him, in case there was any comeback . . .'

'One can't be too careful.'

'And seeing how he was a college man and would understand.'

'Ah . . .' The Assistant Chief Constable had had a classical education and had a reputation for being able to put a scholarly slant on most police problems.

'He said that we are all sons of Adam . . .'

'Especially Matthew Steele,' said Sloan.

'And daughters of Adam too, I suppose,' said Leeyes, who much disliked the recent rise in female convictions. 'The ACC did say, though, to watch out for Steele talking *digitis evidenter traiectis*.' The Superintendent grimaced. 'Taking the mickey, that's what he was doing. As usual.'

'He's always a great one for the Latin, the ACC.'

'I had to ask him what it meant,' admitted Leeyes unwillingly.

Detective Inspector Sloan decided against saying

anything to this. He had his pension to think of. Besides, the ACC was the only person at Berebury police station capable of cutting the Superintendent down to size.

'I suppose I ought to have guessed,' sniffed Leeyes.

'Sir?'

'I don't know where he went to school . . .'

'Eton.'

'It means that when you keep your fingers crossed you don't mean to keep a promise.'

Sloan said that he knew that even though he hadn't been to Eton.

'But it's only if people can't see that they're crossed that it's not cricket.'

Sloan said that he knew that too, but that he didn't think Matthew Steele or his associates played any of their little games according to the rules of cricket. 'Poker, more like.'

'The ACC also mentioned something about some people called the Prelapsarians as well,' went on Leeyes, adding shamelessly, 'but I didn't quite catch what he said. Mean anything to you?'

'No, sir. 'Fraid not.' He brightened. 'But I do know a joke about the Garden of Eden and evidence which might be useful.' All they needed to arrest Matthew Steele was evidence. The bank robbers hadn't left a shred of it behind at Tilson Street. They'd worn gloves as well as Mickey Mouse masks and had touched nothing in passing. Their getaway car had been stolen minutes before the robbery and left abandoned minutes afterwards. Of the money and the safe-deposit boxes, there was no sign at all.

'Let's be having it, then, Sloan,' said Leeyes sourly. 'You never know what'll come in handy when you're on your feet. Especially a joke.'

'It goes like this, sir. God said to Adam, "Adam, did you eat that there apple?" and Adam said, "No, God." '

'I've just worked it out,' Leeyes interrupted him. 'Prelapsarian must mean before the Fall of Man.'

'Quite so, sir. Anyway, then God said to Eve, "Eve, did you eat that there apple?" and Eve said, "No, God." '

'Have a word with the serpent, after that, did he?' enquired Leeyes. 'If you ask me, that's when the trouble started.'

'No, sir.' Sloan drew breath and heroically carried on. He was going to finish his story, come what may. 'So God said, "What about them two cores, then?" '

'And I take it what you haven't got at Tilson Street, Sloan, are any cores?'

'Not a thing, sir,' said Sloan bitterly. 'Not a single scrap of anything that the Crown Prosecution Service would call reliable evidence.'

'Or even what we would call evidence,' said Leeyes magisterially, having no very high opinion of the CPS. 'That matters too.'

'I know, sir,' murmured Sloan.

'What about the bank's security cameras?'

'One Mickey Mouse looks very like another.'

'And in the meantime,' he snorted, 'the Vicar wants me to debate original sin with Matthew Steele . . .'

'The Vicar doesn't know it's in the meantime,' pointed out Sloan. 'Doesn't even know he's got a record, I dare say. He's probably just chosen Steele because he's been around doing some building work in the church and because he's got a good debating manner.'

'Plausible is what I would call it . . .'

'That's what the Judge said too, when we got him last time.' Sloan paused. 'I suppose he thinks that appearing in public against you would be a bit of a lark.'

'Unless the Vicar has fed him some nonsense about sanctuary.'

'If you ask me, sir, what it does is confirm either that Steele is as cocky as ever and doesn't think we're going to make a charge stick or that for some reason he doesn't want to upset the Vicar. Or both.'

'Huh . . .' Police Superintendent Leeyes, Berebury's thief taker-in-chief, gave it as his considered opinion that Matthew Steele shouldn't be allowed to get away with a child's lolly, let alone a king's ransom.

'If it's not bats in the belfry, sir,' asked Sloan suddenly, 'what exactly is the trouble up there?'

'Search me, Sloan.'

'I was wondering, sir,' said Sloan slowly, 'whether we should search the church tower instead . . .'

Leeyes shot him a look.

'Anyone could bang about up there opening safe-deposit boxes without being heard.' Sloan got out his own notebook. 'I bet you he's been hauling bucket-loads of cement and anything else you care to name up there too.'

'If you ask me,' said Leeyes, 'that Vicar is daft enough to have given him a key to the tower.'

'I shouldn't be surprised, sir. Ingenuous is the word that comes to mind as far as Mr Carstairs is concerned.'

'The Vicar did say something about original sin and the Age of Enlightenment and as well,' began the Superintendent, but Sloan was already on his feet.

'I've gone in for a bit of enlightenment on my own, sir,' he said. 'If what's in the church tower is what I think might be hidden up there, then you may just be off the hook in Lent.' He got to the door and turned. 'Keep your fingers crossed.'

A Different Cast of Mind

The moment he stepped inside the door of the inn, Christopher Helmsdale knew for certain that he was wrongly dressed for the place. In spite of conscientiously wearing his usual weekend clothes, he stood out like a sore thumb among the men there. His trousers and roll-neck jersey were neither old enough nor shabby enough to melt into the background at the Fisherman's Arms at Almstone. And his shoes were a mite too clean.

It wasn't that he hadn't suspected this before leaving London for rural Calleshire; he had recollected the ambience of the place well enough. The trouble was that any clothes he might once have had that would have been halfway suitable had been thrown away by his wife long ago. Strolling in Richmond Park on Sundays made different – though no less exacting – sartorial demands on a man.

He laid his overcoat on a dark wooden settle situated under an oil painting of dead fur and feather – a still life of the chase – and beside an ancient metal spring balance that measured weight only in pounds and ounces. He'd almost forgotten that, but he remembered the stuffed champion trout in its glass case fixed to the opposite wall well enough. As far as Christopher was concerned, it had been there for ever. Caught by Sir Coningsby Falconer in 1865, it was still the heaviest trout to come out of the River Alm to date – and that in spite of the best efforts of the present baronet (another Sir Coningsby Falconer), Christopher Helmsdale's own father and all his cronies to do better.

Under the trout was the hotel's game book, in which the day's catches were duly recorded before being hastened – the way of all flesh – to the kitchen.

Christopher made a move to open the game book, but suddenly changed his mind and made for the bar instead. Although the bar was crowded, he was instantly recognized by an elderly man and offered a drink.

'Come away in, man,' said Peter Heath hospitably. 'Good to see you. Now, what'll you have?'

Sitting comfortably in a corner of the bar, Christopher searched his memory for the right questions to ask an old angler. 'The Alm running well?'

'Not too badly,' said Peter Heath, sipping slowly. 'Not too badly at all, all things considered.'

'And are the fish taking just now?'

'Aye, sometimes.' The fisherman gave a small smile. 'Not often enough, of course.'

'They never do,' agreed Christopher.

The two men drank companionably in silence for a while and then the older man asked which part of the river he proposed to visit the next morning.

'I haven't decided yet,' said Christopher. 'I came here straight from the office and Fridays are always too busy to think of anything else, more's the pity.'

'Of course.' The countryman nodded. 'I quite understand.'

'London's like that,' said the man from the City, sounding apologetic.

'Not to worry. Plenty of good places to choose from,' observed Peter Heath, who had been retired long enough for all the days of the week to feel the same. 'And there'll be no problem with the light at this time of year.'

Christopher took another taste of his whisky. 'I plan to have a look at one or two possible spots before I really make up my mind.'

'Good idea,' nodded the old fisherman, adding, 'we'll make a fisherman of you yet.'

In the event Christopher Helmsdale realized it hadn't been such a good idea after all. The trouble was that he wasn't nearly as skilled a fisherman as his father. And having a case of hand-tied dry flies in one pocket and a small screw-topped flask in the other wasn't going to turn him into one overnight either.

He paused first by the humpbacked bridge near the hotel, because, although his father had specified the River Alm, he hadn't said exactly which pool he was supposed to be heading for now. As he rested his elbows on the parapet, he considered three distinct possibilities, just as at his work he would have carefully listed all the possible alternatives before taking any action.

The first of these was the deep pool just below the bridge. This was the spot where, years and years ago, his father had caught his best-ever brown trout. That trout, whose exact weight was lost in the mists of time – his mother had always declared it gained an ounce a year – had entered into family legend. In the way of fishermen, all his father's subsequent catches had been measured against 'the trout from the pool below the bridge'.

He dallied there for a few more minutes, though, before he turned and walked along the south bank, heading downstream. He was making for that stretch of the River Alm which had always been his father's favourite place for the dry fly – the hand-tied dry fly. This was known as the Ornum Stretch and it was here, before his arthritic hip had started to give trouble, that his father had spent most of his fishing time.

Christopher grinned to himself and decided that this was probably the place on the Alm that his father had had in mind when he had written his instructions out for him.

It was therefore only an innate conscientiousness that made Christopher turn his steps still further downstream. He tramped along the river bank until he got to that stretch of water known as Almstone Reach. It was a goodish walk but one that Helmsdale *père* had taken often enough until his health had begun to fail.

The Almstone Reach had never been his father's favourite place for fishing – on the contrary, he was wont to refer to it as 'The Challenge of the Alm'. The challenge arose because his father had never ever succeeded in landing a trout from this stretch of the river – and that certainly wasn't for want of trying either.

Christopher Helmsdale stood now beside the Alm

and tried to decide which of the three places on the river would be the best: the Bridge Pool, the Ornum Stretch or the Almstone Reach . . . He could have tossed a coin to decide if there had been only two alternatives. Having three put that out of court. He would just have to make up his own mind . . .

He put his hand into his pocket, took out the flask and grinned to himself.

The Almstone Reach – challenge and all – it would be. He'd see that his father got to the fish there in the end.

He unscrewed the top of the flask and slowly tipped his father's cremated ashes into the water. Out of his other pocket he took his father's little case of home-tied flies that he had intended to cast into the river after the ashes – but something stayed his hand.

Perhaps he'd just see what he could do with them there himself one day . . .

Examination Results

'What you need to do, Sloan,' said Superintendent Leeyes testily, 'is to teach that young Constable of yours exactly what constitutes evidence and what doesn't.'

'Yes, sir,' responded Detective Inspector C. D. Sloan in as neutral tones as he could manage.

'Hard evidence,' emphasized the Superintendent. He was still smarting from having the police case against one of their most persistent offenders dismissed at the Berebury magistrates' court for lack of evidence. 'Your Detective Constable Crosby needs to get into that thick head of his the difference between hearsay and a signed witness statement.'

'Yes, sir,' said Detective Inspector Sloan, heroically resisting the temptation to disclaim Crosby as his Detective Constable. Had he, Sloan, been given the slightest choice in the matter – which he hadn't – Detective Constable William Edward Crosby would not have been the man by his side in any police investigation whatsoever, let alone one brought against the most plausible rogue in the whole county of Calleshire.

'Telling the Bench what someone else had said about the accused as if that would do instead of finding out for himself,' snorted Leeyes. 'The very idea . . . quite apart from the fact that it showed to all and sundry that he didn't know the first thing about what constituted inadmissible evidence.'

'Yes, sir.' Come to that, thought Sloan to himself, Crosby wasn't someone you'd want with you in an open boat after a shipwreck either . . .

'The magistrates aren't all that bright,' grumbled Leeyes, 'but even they can tell the difference between reported speech and recorded speech. First thing they were taught, I expect.'

'Yes, sir.' Sloan wouldn't have wanted Superintendent Leeyes with him in an open boat instead of Crosby, but for quite different reasons. Ten to one, if shipwrecked, the Superintendent would be following his usual practice of making waves rather than calming the waters – and as for going with the flow, well, that had never ever been his way.

Quite the contrary, in fact.

'If there's one thing I don't ever like to see,' rumbled on his superior officer, still disgruntled, 'it's a real villain getting off a charge on a mere technicality.'

'No, sir.' Sloan was with him there.

'Doesn't do the force any good at all, that.' Leeyes sniffed. 'The only people who enjoy it are those who read certain newspapers.'

'I take your point, sir,' said Sloan, even though the Superintendent's description of what had constituted a mere technicality enshrined one of the most fundamental principles of English criminal law. From where he stood, that meant that neither the Superintendent nor the errant Crosby had understood the enormity, and that the Bench did, but he wasn't going to say this. He, Sloan, had his pension to think of.

Superintendent Leeyes was still worrying at the same bone. 'Next time, Sloan, I want nothing but hard evidence presented in court. Is that understood?'

'Yes, sir.' He suppressed a sigh. 'I'll have a word . . .'

'Do that,' said Leeyes. 'And you can start over at the Ornum Arms at Almstone.'

'Sir?'

'Thief in the place,' said the Superintendent. 'Or so the landlord says.'

'Johnny Hedger,' supplied Sloan.

'Oh, you know him, do you?'

'Been there since Nelson lost his eye,' said Sloan.

'But nothing known?'

'No, sir.' This was police-speak for having a criminal record and Sloan knew that Johnny Hedger didn't have one. 'Clean as a whistle. He doesn't stand any nonsense from anyone in his house either.'

'If what the landlord is saying is true,' prophesied Leeyes, 'someone at the Ornum Arms is going to have a police record sooner or later. Sooner, I hope,' he added meaningfully.

Detective Inspector Sloan took out his notebook.

'And the sooner or later bit,' added Leeyes waspishly, 'depends on whether your Detective Constable can make a better fist of producing his evidence next time than he did yesterday.'

Sloan suppressed a strong temptation to say something about Crosby first having to find the aforementioned evidence before he could present it, like that famous lady cook saying 'First catch your hare' when advising on the making of hare pie. Instead, he murmured that he and the Detective Constable would start their investigation out at Almstone first thing Monday morning.

The Ornum Arms in the village of Almstone was an old public house that had begun life as a coaching inn – a hostelry in the true meaning of the term. The old courtyard into which the daily stagecoach from Calleford used to be driven had been glassed over now and the ostlers' quarters turned into residents' bedrooms, but there was still that about the place redolent of journey's end after a hard ride.

The two detectives found Johnny Hedger behind his bar but far from his usual self. There was no trace in his manner today of the customary professional bonhomie for which the landlord was celebrated along the whole Alm valley. Instead, the normally jovial man looked pale and shaken, and when he moved, he did so with exquisite care. He seemed too to be needing the public bar for physical support – something quite at odds with his large frame and renowned vigour.

'I'm glad you've come, gentlemen,' he said, waving them to a table, 'though I'm afraid, as you can see, you've caught us at rather a bad moment.' He grimaced as he pointed at a white-coated woman who was striding purposefully about the public bar with some glass specimen bottles and a clinical-looking case.

'Don't say that forensics have beaten us to it, Johnny,' said Sloan, puzzled. 'Or has something else happened that we haven't been told about?'

'We've got the food police here,' sighed the publican. 'They're swarming all over the place . . .'

Detective Constable Crosby said, 'Are they looking for a thief too?'

The burly landlord shook his head. 'Nay, lad. I only wish they were. They're here because we had a right disaster at the place on Saturday afternoon.' He straightened up painfully. 'That is, it must have happened on Saturday afternoon but we didn't know it was a disaster until early Sunday morning.' He shuddered at the memory. 'Or how big a one . . .'

Detective Inspector Sloan murmured something anodyne but sympathetic about troubles never coming singly.

'Singly!' echoed Johnny Hedger bitterly. 'If only they'd come singly it would have been all right.'

'Battalions?' suggested Sloan, a latent memory of his schoolday Shakespeare lessons coming back to him.

Johnny Hedger looked puzzled. 'No. It was a cricket club party that we had in the functions room.'

'Ah . . .'

'We catered for a hundred and fifty – popular local team, you know. Valuable booking too, but I wish now we'd never taken it. So does the wife . . .' He glanced in the direction of the stairs. 'I had to get the doctor to her in the night. It didn't surprise him, because he'd been called out a dozen times already by other people who'd eaten here. And he said he was sorry but that he would have to tell the authorities about it because food poisoning is a notifiable medical condition under some Public Health Act or other.'

'Bad luck,' said Sloan sympathetically.

'She's still proper poorly. Says she doesn't want to face food or drink ever again.'

'Food poisoning,' opined Sloan, 'leaves you like that.'

'Too right, Inspector.' Hedger acknowledged this with a jerk of his head in the direction of the kitchen. 'They say it was the Queen of Puddings that did it.' He passed a hand over his damp brow. 'Don't ask me to tell you how they found that out, but everyone who chose it was ill.'

'They have their methods,' said Sloan. He very nearly brought in a neat reference to Sherlock Holmes and Dr Watson but thought better of it. Johnny Hedger was in no mood today for light relief.

The landlord glanced down at something written on the back of an envelope and frowned. 'The pathologist called it *Typhimurium*, if that makes any sense to you.'

'No,' said Sloan comfortably, 'but doctors like to use words that no one else understands. Makes them feel more in control.'

'One of our lecturers,' offered Detective Constable Crosby, not long out of the police training college, 'called the using of words that only an in-group could understand "Badges of Belonging".'

Johnny Hedger was not interested in either psychology or semantics. 'These people say they think whatever it was that did it was in the duck eggs used in the pudding topping. We get the eggs from the farm up the road, you know . . .'

'Ah . . .'

'They gave the soup and the turkey salad a clean

bill of health – which is more,' added Hedger spiritedly, 'than the Health and Safety people will give the Ornum Arms until we've been practically taken to pieces and fumigated.'

'Dangerous things, duck eggs,' observed Sloan sapiently. 'Salmonella bacilli like living in them.'

'You're telling me,' said Johnny Hedger.

'Especially when they're not hard-boiled . . .' The working knowledge required by a Detective Inspector had always bordered on the arcane, but there was one thing he did remember about Queen of Puddings from his childhood that might be relevant. 'Meringue, made from white of egg, whipped on top?'

'And raspberry jam,' put in Detective Constable Crosby, anxious to help.

'But not in the oven for very long?' There was the rub, Sloan thought.

'That's the one,' sighed the landlord heavily. 'Not that we can do anything about it now. The Health and Safety people have closed us down until further notice.'

'There's no arguing with that lot,' said Crosby, still a little unsure of his own authority as an officer of the law but aware of others in the wider world who had even greater powers – powers against which there was no appeal.

Hedger winced as he shifted his bulk in response to a twinge of pain. 'I've had to send all the domestic staff home this morning.'

'You wouldn't have had many customers anyway,' said Sloan, 'not with Environmental Health around.'

'They've been crawling everywhere since first thing.' Hedger gave a melancholy smile. 'It's just as well that the chef's off sick too. He wouldn't like to see them there, poking into everything. Very territorial about his kitchen is our Melvyn.'

'It's your kitchen we've come about,' Sloan reminded him. 'Or, rather, goods continually stolen therefrom . . .'

'I could wish now that someone had taken those duck eggs,' said the landlord feelingly, 'never mind the ham and cheese that's always going missing.'

'The high-value items,' observed Sloan.

'To say nothing of the meat,' said Mine Host.

Detective Inspector Sloan pointed to the array of bottles behind the bar. 'But not the wines and spirits?'

'Not a drop,' said Johnny Hedger. 'Mind you, it's under lock and key when the bar's closed and there's always someone here when it isn't.'

'But kitchen's aren't usually secure,' murmured Sloan.

'No, and my accountant says that, according to the figures for the provisions we buy in, we should be making much more profit on the catering side than we do.' Hedger sighed. 'How he knows beats me, but there you are.'

'Clever chaps, accountants,' said Sloan. It was a view endorsed time and time again by his colleagues in the Fraud Squad.

'I suppose they know all the wrinkles,' said Detective Constable Crosby naïvely.

'Nearly all of them,' remarked Sloan. The Fraud Squad had one or two up their sleeves too, but this wasn't the time or place to say so. He got back to the matter in hand. 'What does your chef say – assuming it isn't him that's half-inching the goods, of course.'

Johnny Hedger frowned. 'Melvyn says it could be any of the kitchen staff. Or all of them. And that *I* can look into their handbags when they go home if I like, but he's not going to.'

'Chicken, isn't he!' pronounced Crosby, who had yet to encounter a really cross middle-aged woman with a genuine grievance.

'He says he's too young to die,' said the landlord.

'They'd take umbrage as quickly as they'd take a joint of beef, I suppose?' said Sloan more realistically.

'Quicker,' said the landlord gloomily. 'And take themselves off too, I dare say.'

'As good cooks go,' murmured Sloan.

Hedger rolled his eyes. 'They very nearly walked out on me when I stopped them eating when they were working here.'

'Even the leftovers?' asked Crosby.

'What's a leftover?' demanded Hedger rhetorically.

'Ah . . .' said Sloan, a man who in his day had spent a lot of time in court listening to lawyers splitting hairs. 'That's a point.'

'At least the accountant saved me from that one,' said Hedger. He sniffed. 'Makes a change from him costing me, which he does. An arm and a leg, usually.'

'How come?' enquired Crosby, evincing some interest at last.

'Said if I fed the staff here – that is, allowed them to eat my food on my premises while they were working here without charging them the going rate – then it would have to show in the books.'

'Which shut them up pretty quickly, I expect,' said Sloan, who knew a thing or two about mixing human nature with money both not in hand and taxable to boot.

'I'll say,' said Johnny, with something of his old energy returning. 'They didn't like that one little bit.'

'So if they want it, the staff have to steal the food rather than eat it here,' concluded Crosby simply.

'But it doesn't apply to you,' pointed out Sloan to the landlord. 'You must have eaten some of the pudding . . .'

'The accountant allows in the books for the wife and me consuming the restaurant food whether we do or not,' agreed Johnny, 'it not being considered natural that it should be otherwise.'

'Or,' persisted Sloan, 'you wouldn't both have been ill too.'

'That's true,' said Johnny uneasily.

'There's a thief in the house, all the same,' said Crosby.

'You find him, then,' said the landlord wearily. 'Or her. You're the detectives. Not me.'

'Someone must be taking the goods,' said Sloan, briskly, 'if there's food missing from the place on a regular basis.' Somewhere at the back of his mind was lurking the proper distinction between groceries and provisions, but this was not the moment either for such verbal niceties. The all-embracing word 'goods' would have to do.

'But how to find out who?' asked Hedger.

'And how to prove it,' added Detective Inspector Sloan. The trouble with all the animadversions of

Superintendent Leeyes was that they stuck in the mind. As he had said, identifying the guilty was only half the problem these days . . . Evidence – preferably of the watertight variety – came into it as well.

'I just want the losses stopped.' Hedger shrugged. 'It's quite difficult enough making a place like this pay without having the ground cut from under your feet by thieves in the night.'

'Not in the night,' put in Detective Constable Crosby, who was of a literal turn of mind. 'In the day.'

'You're right there,' admitted Johnny Hedger. 'It must be in the day. The deep freezers and the refrigerator are all locked when Melvyn goes home to Luston. He gives me the keys.'

'Melvyn's off sick too, you said,' remarked Sloan casually.

'Can't keep a thing down, his family say,' said Hedger with patent sympathy. 'None of them can. They've had to have the doctor to him. Just like me and the wife . . .' His voice trailed away as he was struck by the significance of the words he had uttered.

'Just so,' said Detective Inspector Sloan sedately.

'I think I see your drift,' Hedger went on lamely.

'I don't,' began Crosby, then he stopped. 'Oh, yes, I do.'

'Good,' said Sloan drily.

The Detective Constable said, 'Your chef could be suffering from half-baked duck eggs too, Johnny.'

Sloan pointed to the envelope which Hedger had shown them. 'Yes, or more accurately what the doctors have called whatever it is that caused the food poisoning. *Typhimurium*, did you say it was?'

'Which he must have got from pinching the duck eggs,' deduced the Detective Constable, a trifle belatedly.

'Well, I can tell you he didn't buy them from the farmer,' said Johnny Hedger. 'The Health and Safety people have checked on all the customers who've bought eggs from him. First thing they did.'

'Though whether Melvyn got his food poisoning from pinching the duck eggs,' amended Sloan. 'is something which remains to be proved . . .'

'Beyond reasonable doubt,' put in Johnny Hedger, veteran of the odd pub fracas and therefore no stranger to the magistrates' court. He looked up as a pleasant-faced middle-aged woman came in, her coat over her arm. 'Thank goodness you've arrived, Margaret,' he said to her. 'You can take over the bar – drinks only to be served today – and I can put my feet up for a bit.' He gave the two policemen a strained smile. 'Excuse me, gentlemen, I must take a look at the wife too.'

Detective Constable Crosby turned to Sloan and said, 'Can we go over to Luston now, sir, and finger the chef – this Melvyn fellow?'

'On what charge?' asked Sloan mildly. Luston was right over the other side of the county and he was well aware that the constable liked driving fast cars fast.

'Theft,' said Crosby promptly. 'He didn't just take a bite while he was here, because his whole family is ill. He must have taken either a load of the eggs or enough of the pudding for the lot of them.'

'Very probably. But what are you going to use for evidence? Real evidence, Crosby – the sort that the Superintendent likes, not the circumstantial variety.'

'The eggshells?'

'Gone long ago, I'll be bound.'

He frowned. 'What you said, sir? The *Typhimurium*?'

'And how are you going to prove that?'

Crosby's face fell.

'Think, man,' adjured Sloan. 'Think.'

Crosby scratched his head. 'Send in the food police?'

'Better than that. Try again.'

The Detective Constable's face looked quite blank.

'Shall we assume,' said Sloan patiently, 'that Melvyn's doctor has also diagnosed food poisoning and . . .'

'And notified it!' Crosby's hand smacked down on the table. 'Like the doctor here did.'

'Exactly. A different doctor in a different part of the county certifying that Melvyn and his family are suffering from the identical strain of the bacillus present in the food causing the trouble here should help your case no end.'

'My case, sir?' the Detective Constable's face turned pink with pleasure. 'Thank you, sir.'

'After all,' said Sloan, since food was the essence of the case here, 'dog doesn't eat dog.'

Child's Play

Henry Tyler wouldn't admit it, even to himself, but he was – there was no doubt about it – panting ever so slightly as he approached the Beacon Hotel. But he wasn't disappointed with what he found. He'd been drawn to the place in the first instance by its address – the sound of Tea Garden Lane had an attractive ring to any walker. So did the name of the area where it was situated – Happy Valley.

And then he'd spotted the building itself from halfway across the opposite hillside and immediately realized that the view from its terrace would be well worth the climb up. In theory, visiting High Rocks had been next on his agenda, but the hotel and luncheon called. High Rocks would have to wait.

He paused on the hill just below the hotel itself, ostensibly to admire that selfsame view but actually to get his breath back properly before he presented himself at the bar. A walking tour was all very well in its way, but it came hard to a civil servant who normally spent his working days at a desk in Whitehall.

Henry had passed the weekend before with his married sister, her husband and their two children in the small market town of Berebury, in rural Calleshire, by way of both winding down from the cares of state and limbering up for his break from routine. This plan had worked up to a point, even though the children had clamoured for his attention almost all the time they were awake. But meeting their demands had not exactly been preparation for striding through the steep lanes of the delightful border country of Kent and Sussex round Tunbridge Wells in high summer.

His nephew and niece, after all, had only required him to play pen and paper games with them. As far as more active pastimes were concerned, they were united in being against them, smacking as they did, they insisted, of compulsory games at school. Their doting uncle had ruefully concluded that the children of today were totally opposed to any activity that involved them in making any move that required more physical effort than tearing open a packet of crisps.

His breath recovered, Henry clambered up onto the hotel terrace and acknowledged that the view was memorable. He stood looking south until a more urgent need made itself felt. After all, even Goethe had said that no man could enjoy a view for more than fifteen minutes. As far as Henry was concerned at this moment, the bodily requirement of a long cold drink displaced the soul's drinking in of beauty in less than five.

He made his way inside what must have once served as the ground floor of a rather grand private house and was now a welcoming bar. A Foreign Office man himself, he was naturally interested in architecture. The place must be late Victorian, he decided, but nicely shorn of Victorian excess. There was already the feel of forthcoming Edwardian comfort and amplitude about it.

Henry collected something with which to slake his immediate thirst but resisted pausing overlong at the bar on the illogical grounds that he was too hungry and too thirsty. He'd need to forgo wine with his meal if he was to tackle High Rocks that afternoon.

He climbed a flight of stairs and found himself faced with a choice of rooms in which to eat. There was a dining room on his right set for a formal luncheon which he shied away from like a nervous horse. Formal luncheons were the bane of his working life in the Foreign Office. Some important guest invariably said something very undiplomatic, no matter how much time had been spent on the *placement*. Attempting to retrieve the situation usually spoilt Henry's afternoon and evening.

Beyond that he spotted a small room, ideal for the intimate exchange, but long experience had taught Henry to be as wary of private encounters as of formal luncheons. These were the rooms that were the first to be bugged. They were also the ones whose comings and goings were the first to be noted by interested observers. Moreover, who could say afterwards with any certainty what had or had not been said in a private room? In an uncertain world, civil servants liked certainty.

He moved forward carefully, spotting an inviting table in the window which must enjoy a splendid view, but he stopped when he saw that there was already someone sitting there. In a way this was a help, as his first instinct – being a Foriegn Office man to his fingertips – would have been to avoid such an exposed position. He was just reminding himself that he was off duty and it didn't matter where he sat when the figure at the table turned and said, 'Hello, Tyler.'

'Good Lord, Venables . . . What on earth are you doing here?'

'You wouldn't believe me if I told you,' said the other man morosely. He was sitting with his shoulders hunched forward, his hands cradling the bowl of a wine glass.

'Perhaps not,' agreed Henry.

He had some justification for this response. Malcolm Venables was known to work for one of the obscurer branches of what used to be called – before the advent of tabloid newspapers and their investigative journalism – as the secret service.

'I'm damned if I believe it myself,' said Venables testily. 'Never thought I'd find myself in Tunbridge Wells of all places.'

'In the way of work, you mean?' asked Henry cautiously, taking a second look at the man. Downcast was the only way of describing those drooping shoulders and sunken head.

Always alert on behalf of the needs of his own great department of state, Henry Tyler started to run through in his mind the circumstances that might have brought Venables to these parts in such a state of obvious depression.

'Yes, worse luck,' grumbled Venables.

'I see,' said Henry. This could be serious. The interaction between the Foreign Office and Malcolm Venables's own particular division of the secret service (which rejoiced in the name of Mercantile and Persuasion) was a very delicate matter indeed; so delicate, in fact, that otherwise honourable – and sometimes even Right Honourable – gentlemen had been known to stand up in high places and declare that no links existed.

Venables indicated the chair opposite him. 'Are you going to join me, Tyler? I'm alone. Absolutely alone,' he muttered. 'And likely to be out on a limb into the bargain before very long.'

'I don't suppose things are as bad as that,' said Henry, with the detachment of a man safely out of reach of his own office. He could see, though, that something had seriously upset Venables this Monday morning.

Henry cast his mind rapidly back over the news items in the papers. There had been nothing in them which had caught his attention today, and in spite of the pen and paper games with his nephew and niece, he had taken care to study the weekend papers as thoroughly as usual.

'They are,' said Venables, waving to the waiter to bring another glass. 'And I just must talk to somebody . . .'

'Problems?' Henry enquired delicately, taking the proffered chair and pulling it up at the table in the window opposite him.

'Just the one,' said Venables, taking a long sip from his glass. 'But it's a big one.'

'Swans singing before they die?' suggested Henry lightly, since this was an increasing problem in all government departments.

'No,' said Venables rather shortly. 'Not that.'

'Certain persons dying before they've sung?' This, thought Henry from long experience, was less of a worry, but you never knew ...

'It's not a laughing matter, Tyler. This is serious.'

'Matter of life and death, then?' hazarded Henry a little unfairly. Unfairly, because he already knew that it wouldn't be death that worried the man from the Mercantile and Persuasion Division – an outfit known affectionately throughout the corridors of power as 'Markets and Perks'. Death was always the least of their troubles in that department – it was a number of other words beginning with 'D' which were the Four Horsemen of their particular Apocalypse. Henry was all too aware that Disclosure, Débâcle, Dishonour and Double-dealing ranked far higher on the danger list of M and P than mere death.

'Well, not quite life and death,' admitted Malcolm Venables grudgingly. 'Not for us, anyway. It might very well be for other people. Who can say?'

'Tell me what you can,' invited Tyler, mindful of constraints to do with the Official Secrets Act, D Notices, the need-to-know basis and plain common sense. There was, though, behind these the inviolable tradition of their respective services that that which was revealed between the two of them would not be spoken of to others. Ever.

Venables pointed to a row of venerable – if not yet quite antique – wireless receivers arrayed on a shelf above them by way of ornament. 'Would you say they were safe?'

'Valves worn out long ago,' said Henry briskly. 'Not a bug between them, I'm sure. Carry on . . .'

'I must say it'll be a relief to talk to somebody sane,' admitted Venables.

Tyler did his best to project sanity.

'Coming down to Tunbridge Wells has made me realize that there are no sane cryptographers. Did you know that, Tyler?'

'I've always had doubts about all experts,' said Henry Tyler mildly. 'Obsessive, conceited, compulsive, opinionated . . .'

'Paranoic . . . Oh, thank you.' This last was to the waiter who had brought more cutlery, a table mat and a napkin for Henry.

'Monomaniac too, most experts,' added Henry. 'Only about their own thing, of course.'

'Exactly,' agreed Venables, slightly more cheerfully. 'And that's the trouble. By the way, the wine here isn't at all bad . . .'

As he partook of an excellent white Macon Villages, Henry mentally struck High Rocks off his programme for the afternoon.

'Another thing about experts, Tyler . . .'

'Yes?'

'They just won't admit defeat.'

'Now that's your true specialist – totally unrealistic,' said Henry judicially. 'I've always found them more inclined to worry at problems long after the moment has passed.' Life at the Foreign Office could sometimes move on with surprising speed.

'They go on like a dog at a bone.' Malcolm Venables nodded and slid a piece of paper out of his pocket and slipped it inside the menu with a skill born of much practice at the ancient art of legerdemain. He handed the menu concealing the paper to Henry and said, 'What do you make of that, Tyler?'

It was a single sheet on which was written a series of apparently meaningless sentences.

'Well,' said Henry, after studying the paper for a long moment, 'I can see that there are – er – very definite overtones of *Alice in Wonderland* there.'

'That,' groaned Venables, 'is part of the problem. My boss thinks that my contact – I think we'd better call him my informant, my overseas informant, if you take my meaning – is having me on.'

'It has been known . . .'

'And our cryptographic department says it's one of the most interesting ciphers they've seen in many a long year and would I give them more time.'

'Which means they can't solve it,' Henry translated without difficulty.

'Exactly and, for reasons which I can't go into, I just can't give them more time . . .' He twisted in his seat and snatched the menu back as the waiter hove into view.

'Are you ready to order, gentlemen?' The man hovered, order pad in hand.

'We'll have the fish,' said Venables swiftly.

'Two fish . . .' The waiter melted away again.

'So urgent,' said Venables, handing the menu back to Henry, 'that if we fail, the problem'll probably end up on somebody's plate in your department, my friend, and nobody's going to like that.'

Henry, who could take a hint even better than the

next man – since hints, rather than plain English, were part of the currency of the Foreign Office – turned his attention back to the paper lurking inside the menu.

Venables leaned across the table and pointed to the words on the sheet. 'You'll see, Tyler, that each sentence contains a number incorporated in the text . . .'

'A written number,' murmured Henry, his eye running along a line which read, 'Beautiful Soup, so rich and green, Waiting in twelve hot tureens.' 'By the way, Venables,' he added plaintively, 'I mightn't have wanted the fish.'

The man from Mercantile and Persuasion ignored this last. 'What strikes you about those lines?'

Henry, who had been properly educated even at nursery level, searched for a childhood memory. 'Unless I am mistaken, the original text doesn't mention the exact number of tureens.'

'Precisely!' In his eagerness, Venables leaned across the table again and tapped the paper inside the menu. 'Here it says, "Who would not give all else for ten pennyworth only of beautiful soup?" '

'Soup?' The waiter materialized at their table. 'Do you want the soup as well?'

'No,' said Venables sharply.

The waiter put out a practised hand and started to tweak the menu from between Henry's fingers.

'I'm thinking about the soup,' said Henry with perfect truth, firmly hanging on to the menu.

'Very well, sir.' The man withdrew.

'What I'm thinking about the soup,' said Henry, as soon as he had gone, 'is that in Lewis Carroll's poem "Turtle Soup" it says two pennyworth not ten.'

'That's why I'm here in Tunbridge Wells,' said Malcolm Venables. 'I've been getting a world authority on the works of Lewis Carroll to take a look at it.'

'And?'

'And he says that while all the contexts on this paper here are textually correct, all the numbers that have been added or changed are meaningless to him.' Venables paused and added thoughtfully, 'Fancy devoting your working life to studying *Alice in Wonderland*..'

'No funnier than what you're doing,' said Henry.

'What do you mean?' responded Venables indignantly. 'I'm trying to save the nation from its actual and its commercial enemies...'

'One and the same from our perspective,' said Henry cynically.

'Could be,' admitted Venables. 'Well, this coded message is from one of our best men...'

'So..'

'And is meant to tell us the exact design of a new uranium-assisted gun hatched up behind the Net Curtain...'

Henry Tyler suddenly sat up very straight.

'... and moreover, one,' added Malcolm Venables meaningfully, 'which is remarkably like a new one of ours.'

'One of ours that no one was supposed to know about?' hazarded Henry intelligently. There, presumably, was the rub.

'Got it in one,' said Venables, his appetite reviving sufficiently for him to reach for a bread roll.

'And you need to know not only whether they –

whoever they are – have actually got it but who it was that gave it to them, if they did?'

'Precisely,' said the man from Mercantile and Persuasion, warming under this ready understanding. 'And preferably without anyone knowing that we know anything about anything at all.'

Henry Tyler was at one with him there. While, when there was cloak and dagger work about, he was quite content to leave the dagger side to the Ministry of Defence, he spent a lot of his own working life concentrating on keeping a number of cloaks tightly wrapped.

'But what forty-two walruses and seventy-two carpenters have to do with it, I can't begin to say,' the Foreign Office man admitted. Struck by a sudden thought, he said, 'Wasn't Lewis Carroll a mathematician in his private life?'

'He was and I've had one of them working on it as well,' said the man from Markets and Perks with a certain melancholy satisfaction, 'and all he said too was that it was interesting, very interesting.'

'Hang it all, Venables, it must mean something . . .'

'That's what my Minister thinks.'

'There's quite a lot hanging on it, isn't there?' deduced Henry realistically.

'You can say that again, Tyler. My 'K' for a start . . .'

'Quite, quite,' said Henry soothingly. Malcolm Venables was well known in the corridors of power to be suffering from 'Knight starvation'.

'Another odd thing about this message is that it's composed in words at all . . . Hang on, the waiter's coming back again.'

Henry exercised his own prestidigitatory skills by extricating the paper from the menu under cover of his napkin and slipping it beneath his table mat.

'Two fish,' announced the waiter, setting down a pair of substantial platters. 'Chef says to mind the plates. They're very hot.'

'They're not the only things at the table too hot to handle,' said Henry when the waiter had withdrawn to a safe distance and he'd retrieved the paper. 'I should think this *billet-doux* of yours is too.'

'What we were hoping for,' persisted Venables, 'was a drawing of the weaponry in question. We badly need to know if it's ours or theirs. A description wouldn't be half as good as a picture even if we could understand it, but we can't.'

'So the numbers aren't measurements?' said Henry, picking up his fish knife and fork.

'We've tried them every way we can – with and without computers – and no matter which way we hold them up to the light, they don't produce a measured drawing of any sort.'

'There is one thing about the numbers, though, isn't there,' observed Henry diffidently. 'Oh, yes, thank you, a little more of the Macon would go down very well.'

'What's that?' Venables paused, the bottle suspended over Henry's glass.

'There are no two the same.'

'Oh, that,' said Venables dismissively. 'Yes, the boffins.pointed that out first before they really got to work. All the numbers between one and eighty-seven, none recurring. It didn't help, actually . . .'

Henry took another look at the text. 'I wouldn't say that, old man. Lend me a pencil, will you?'

'Here you are.' Malcolm Venables produced one with a chewed end from about his person.

'Thanks. Now, give me a minute, will you? And don't you let your fish get cold. This'll take a minute or two . . .'

'I say, what are you doing, Tyler?'

Henry pushed his own fish to one side and laid the paper flat on the table. He began to apply the pencil to the message. 'Give me half a minute and I'll tell you.'

'I hope you know what you're doing,' said Venables anxiously. 'You do realize that I'll be done for if anything goes wrong with that message?'

'Would the barrel of this gun of yours happen to look like this?' enquired Henry, a design beginning to take shape under the pencil.

'Good God!' Venables sat up, his fish forgotten. 'How did you work that out?'

'And the sights like this?' What was even more clearly a very formidable piece of armoury emerged as Henry drew lightly over the written words.

'I don't believe it . . .' breathed Venables. 'I just don't believe it.'

'I think you'll just have to,' said Henry bracingly as the final details of a horrendous weapon grew before their eyes. Realism was prized very highly at the Foreign Office.

'That's it, all right,' said Venables with barely suppressed excitement. 'How did you do it, Tyler?'

'I joined up the full stops at the end of every sentence in order,' explained Henry modestly.

'You did what?' spluttered the man from Mercantile and Persuasion.

'Starting,' said Henry Tyler, 'with the one that mentioned the figure one and going on to the one which talked about eighty-seven lobsters.'

'I don't believe it,' said Venables.

'It's called "Dot-to-Dot" and my niece does it rather well. She's seven, you know.'

Malcolm Venables wasn't listening. He was gazing out of the window. 'Do you realize, Tyler, that we can come back here each year for the rest of time and sit at this table and spout Tennyson to each other?'

'Tennyson?'

Venables nodded 'You remember . . .'

'No,' said Henry, who was getting really hungry now.

' "And," ' quoted Venables dreamily, ' "gazing from this height alone, We spoke of what had been." '

Like to Die

'The law,' pronounced Superintendent Leeyes heavily, 'is an ass.'

'Sir?' Detective Inspector C. D. Sloan raised an enquiring eyebrow but didn't commit himself to the general proposition. However much he agreed privately with any sentiment of his superior officer's, he had always found it prudent to wait to hear first exactly what it was that had provoked the Superintendent into generalization. He wondered what it was going to be this time.

'A total ass,' repeated the Superintendent, pushing about some papers on his desk in a fretful manner. 'Doesn't the man know we've got better things to do?'

'Which man?' asked Sloan very tentatively. In Leeyes's present mood, it might even have been better not to have put the question at all.

'The Coroner, of course,' snarled Leeyes.

'Ah...' Now Sloan understood. Mr Locombe-Stableford, Her Majesty's Coroner for the town of Berebury in the county of Calleshire, was an old sparring partner – not to say arch-enemy – of the Superintendent. This was because he was one of the few people in the world whose authority exceeded his own.

'It isn't even as if he doesn't know that we've got more than enough other things on our plate,' carried on the Superintendent in aggrieved tones. 'Much more important ones than this potty little case . . .'

'What case might that be, sir?'

Leeyes ignored this. 'There's that road traffic fatality over at Cullingoak, for instance.'

'Hit-and-run killers are very hard to find,' put in Sloan by way of apology. 'Everyone's working on that one flat out.'

'Just what I mean, Sloan,' said Leeyes sturdily. 'And I told him so.'

'The Coroner, sir.' Sloan came back to the matter in hand. 'What exactly is it that he – er – wants us to do?' The Detective Inspector knew one thing about Mr Locombe-Stableford and that was – like it or not – his writ ran throughout the patch covered by 'F' Division of the county constabulary.

'The Coroner,' said Leeyes flatly, 'has decided for reasons best known to himself to hold an inquest on a Mr Thomas Lean, a wealthy retired businessman . . .'

Since this action was totally within that august official's prerogative, Sloan waited.

' . . . who died yesterday in a nursing home.' Leeyes tapped his desk and added meaningfully, 'The Bere-bury Nursing Home.'

'Ah . . .' said Sloan.

The Berebury Nursing Home was considered one of the best in the whole county. Only the well con-nected and the well off went there; Sloan promptly amended the thought – well, the well off anyway. It was no use being well connected unless you were also well off if you wanted to be treated at the Berebury Nursing Home. He'd heard that the fees were monstrously steep.

'And they don't like it,' said Leeyes.

'The nursing home, you mean, sir?'

'Naturally.'

'Not good for business,' agreed Sloan.

'The Matron's in a proper taking about there being a post-mortem. Dr Dabbe's doing it now.'

'I can see that she might be,' said Sloan, frowning at an elusive memory. 'Isn't that where the Earl of Ornum's dotty old aunt is? Lady Alice . . .'

'Shouldn't be surprised,' said Leeyes. 'Now, this Thomas Lean hadn't been in there very long. He'd been pretty dicky for months and just got too ill to be nursed at home.'

'So why the inquest?' Sloan was beginning to see why the Superintendent thought the Coroner was being perverse and making more work for the Consultant Pathologist at the Berebury District Hospital Trust, into the bargain.

'Because his illness didn't kill him,' came back Leeyes smartly, 'that's why.'

'I see, sir.' Sloan reached for his notebook. That did sound more like work for the head of Berebury's tiny Criminal Investigation Department.

'It was food poisoning. Or so the patient's doctor says.' The Superintendent sniffed. He didn't like giving medical opinion any more credence than was absolutely necessary.

'And what have the family got to say?' Their views, thought Sloan, might be just as relevant as those of the Matron.

'We don't know yet,' said Leeyes. 'They were away on holiday when Thomas Lean died. They're on their way home from France now.'

Detective Inspector Sloan opened his notebook at a new page. 'This old gentleman, sir . . .'

'He wasn't all that old,' said Leeyes briskly. The Superintendent was getting towards retirement age himself and had turned against ageism. 'He was just coming up to seventy-five and that's not old these days.'

'No, sir,' agreed Sloan hastily. 'No age at all.'

Leeyes pulled one of the pieces of paper on his desk towards him. 'That's right. Seventy-four and eleven months. His birthday . . . oh, his birthday would have been tomorrow.'

The Matron of the Berebury Nursing Home seemed as upset about that as she was about everything else. 'You see, gentlemen, we always try to celebrate the birthdays of all of our patients . . . poor dears. Nothing elaborate, naturally.'

'Naturally,' agreed Detective Inspector Sloan.

'Not in their state of health,' chimed in Detective Constable Crosby. Because they were so busy down at the police station, Sloan had taken the detective constable with him to the nursing home as being better than nobody. Now he wasn't so sure that Crosby was better than nobody.

The Matron, who looked more than a little wan

herself, waved a hand. 'You know the sort of thing, a glass of sherry and a special cake and so forth – not that poor Mr Lean would have been fit to join in anything approaching a celebration today.'

'No?'

'And, as it happened, none of us would have felt like eating. Not after yesterday.' She shook her head sadly. 'And this would have been his last birthday, you know. He wasn't going to get better.'

Detective Constable Crosby looked interested.

'He'd come in here to die,' explained the Matron. 'He'd been going slowly downhill with cancer for a long time, but the chemotherapy was keeping him going – and the painkillers, of course. Then it got that the family couldn't manage any more.'

'I see,' said Sloan carefully. There were some homes, the police knew only too well, where the pain-killers killed more than the pain, but this hadn't been what had alerted the Coroner about this death.

'And,' she said, 'they were certainly helping him to hold his own.' She made a gesture of despair with her hands. 'If it hadn't been for this terrible food poisoning, we might have had him with us yet for weeks – perhaps months . . .'

It began to sound as if the Coroner was being ped-antic to a fault and that the Superintendent was right after all. Mr Locombe-Stableford had dug his heels in over a legal nicety: a verdict of misadventure, perhaps, rather than natural causes.

'Tell me about yesterday,' invited Sloan.

'Everyone was very, very ill.' She shuddered at the memory. 'But everyone . . . staff and patients.'

'And especially Mr Lean . . .'

'Well, no . . . not at first anyway,' she said, drawing her brows together. 'That was the funny thing.'

'Funny peculiar or funny ha-ha?' asked Crosby.

She stared at him and said repressively, 'It was thought strange that he should appear to be less ill than everyone else and yet be the one to die.'

Detective Inspector Sloan leaned forward. He would deal with Crosby later, but all policemen were professionally interested in things that were funny peculiar. 'Go on . . .'

She winced. 'I – we – that is, everyone else started off with some dizziness and then abdominal pain . . .'

'Quite so,' said Sloan, making a note.

'And then there was nausea followed by severe vomiting.' The Matron obviously found reporting in the third person easier and went on in a more detached way: 'Several staff and patients collapsed and some of them then had diarrhoea . . .'

'But only Thomas Lean died,' said Crosby insouciantly.

She inclined her head.

'How did you manage?' asked Sloan. Perhaps the Coroner wasn't just being difficult . . .

'Dr Browne was very good. He came at once and saw everyone and took away specimens and so forth.'

Sloan nodded. He knew Dr Angus Browne – a family doctor of the old school. He was forthright but kind – and careful.

'He sent for the Environmental Health people or whatever it is they call themselves these days too.'

Very careful then, Dr Browne had been. Which was interesting.

'Food poisoning, you see, being a notifiable condition . . .'

'And then?'

'I can't really tell you that.' The Matron looked embarrassed and murmured apologetically, 'You see, I was one of the casualties myself at the time.'

'I understand.' Sloan turned over a page in his notebook. 'So . . .'

'So we had to call in extra staff.'

He looked up quizzically.

'Anyone,' she amplifed this, 'who hadn't eaten luncheon here on Thursday – night staff, people on stand-by and some agency nurses.'

'And then . . .'

'People started to recover later that night and by the next morning everyone was all right again.'

'Except Thomas Lean,' said Crosby mordantly.

'We – that is, the substitute staff alerted by Lady Alice – sent for Dr Browne again when they saw how poorly he had become.'

'Lady Alice . . .'

'She,' said the matron faintly, 'was the only person in the whole establishment not taken ill and spent her time wandering around, seeing how people were.'

'And she, I take it, was the only person not to have partaken of whatever it was that caused the food poisoning?' deduced Sloan, since not even *noblesse oblige* protected one against tainted food.

'Casseroled beef,' said the Matron with a certain melancholy. 'Dr Browne'll be here as soon as he's heard from the laboratory to explain to us exactly what was wrong with it. It was the only thing that everyone who was ill had eaten and everyone who had eaten it was ill.'

'But Mr Lean had it too,' said Crosby.

'Oh, yes,' said the Matron wearily, 'Mr Lean had the beef casserole.'

'He had his chips too,' said Crosby almost – but not quite – *sotto voce.*

The Matron, who still looked a trifle frayed at the edges, had too many other things on her mind to object to unseemly levity. 'By the time Dr Browne got back here, Mr Lean was having trembling convulsions and he died very soon after that.'

'We'll be talking to Dr Browne,' said Sloan, 'as soon as he arrives.'

'How long would the old boy have lasted otherwise?' enquired Crosby irrepressibly.

'Dr Browne wasn't sure and he didn't want to commit himself anyway. Not even when the family talked to him . . .'

'I was going to ask about them,' went on Sloan smoothly.

'Mr and Mrs Alan Lean – he's the son – had the chance of a few days' holiday in France.' She took a deep breath. 'I said to go if they wanted to. It wasn't as if there was anything more that anyone could do for his father and both he and his wife had been most attentive since Mr Lean had been here.'

Sloan made another note.

'We – that is, I – said they would have nothing to blame themselves for if he died while they were away.

Obviously,' the Matron expanded on what was clearly a well-worn theme, 'it is – er – more satisfactory if the family can take their farewells here, but – ' She paused for breath. Unwisely, as it turned out.

'All part of the service?' suggested Crosby, filling the conversational gap.

'But,' she rallied, 'I told them that if he were to die while they were away, we could always cope – do what was necessary and . . .'

'And put things on ice,' contributed Crosby helpfully.

'After all,' she said firmly, 'as Dr Browne has been kind enough to say more than once, some of our patients – like Lady Alice, for instance – come here and forget to die.'

'Except Thomas Lean,' remarked Crosby inevitably.

'We'd like to see Lady Alice,' said Sloan. What he would also like to do was to deal with Crosby. But not here and not now. Later, in the privacy of the police station.

Lady Alice might have forgotten to die; she hadn't forgotten Thursday's excitements. It seemed that people vomiting all over the place had brought back the dear old days during the war when she had served in the Women's Royal Naval Service. Until stemmed, she was inclined to reminiscence about the Bay of Biscay in winter in wartime.

'But you were all right,' said Sloan, getting a word in edgeways. 'Yesterday, I mean.' She had probably, he decided, been all right in the Bay of Biscay on a troop-ship too, submarines or no.

'Never have liked onions,' she cackled. 'They don't agree with me. So I don't eat 'em.'

'Very sensible,' said Sloan.

'They do me an omelette when there's onions about,' said the old lady.

'And I understand you saw Mr Thomas Lean . . .'

'He was like to die,' said Lady Alice.

'Like to die?' echoed Sloan.

'What they used to put first when they wrote their wills in the old days. They'd begin with "Like to die" and then you'd know they were making it on their deathbed.' She looked at him and said sadly, 'That's the worst of having ancestors . . . there's nothing new.'

'But Thomas Lean ate some of the casserole?' said the Detective Inspector, struggling back to the point.

'As to that,' responded Lady Alice, 'I couldn't say.'

'He was taken ill . . .'

'Oh, yes. But he hadn't been sick.' She looked at Sloan suspiciously. 'Did you say you were both police-men?'

'That's right, your ladyship.'

'St Michael types in disguise . . .'

'Not really.' It was Sloan's mother who was the churchgoer of the family; he didn't know the connec-tion. 'At least, I don't think so.'

'He saved three people from wrongful execution,' said Lady Alice. 'We had a painting at home of him doing it. Never liked it. It went for death duties.'

'I don't think that in this case there will be an execution.'

'Pity.' Lady Alice looked Crosby up and down. 'Did you know that one of my ancestors who was the Bishop of Calleford used to hang people in the days when he had temporal powers as well as spiritual ones?'

Sloan thought it was safe to say that things weren't what they used to be, while Crosby hastened to tell her that he'd always gone to Sunday School when a lad.

'You were very lucky to escape the outbreak, Lady Alice,' said Sloan, adding persuasively, 'Tell me, did you notice anything out of the ordinary yesterday?'

'Only in the kitchen,' she said. 'I went down there for more water jugs. Dash of salt and plenty of cold water's what you need when—'

'What was out of the ordinary?' asked Sloan.

'They weren't shallots,' she said.

'What weren't?'

'I may not like 'em,' she said enigmatically, giving a high laugh, 'but I know my alliaceous vegetables, all right.'

'I'm sure,' he said pacifically. 'So?'

'They were daffodil bulbs not onions. That dim girl who does the vegetables still had some on the sideboard. Saw 'em myself.'

Dr Angus Browne said the same thing but more scientifically twenty minutes later. 'The lab found the alkaloids narcissine – otherwise known as lycorine – and galantamine and scillotoxin – that's one of the glycoside scillamines – in the vomit and in the remains of the casserole.'

'And we found some *Narcissus pseudonarcissus* bulbs in the kitchen,' said Detective Inspector Sloan, not to be outdone in the matter of a 'little Latin and less Greek'.

'Easily enough mistaken, I suppose,' grunted the doctor, who was neither a gardener nor a cook.

'Animals seem to know the difference,' said Crosby, adding brightly, 'If they couldn't tell them apart, then they'd be dead, wouldn't they?'

'Just so.' The doctor looked at the constable and said, 'Anyway, the lab people have sent a copy of their findings over to Dabbe at the mortuary.'

'We've been on to the Environmental Health people and they tell us they've taken the wholesale green-grocers apart without finding anything wrong,' said Sloan, 'but we're going over there all the same.'

'They say they haven't found anything but onions in their onion sacks so far,' chimed in Crosby. 'They come in those string-bag affairs so you can see what you're getting.'

'There's one thing that's bothering me, doctor,' said Sloan. 'What I want to know is, if everyone else who had that casserole was promptly sick, why wasn't the deceased sick as well?'

'Easy,' the doctor said. 'He was on a whole raft of powerful anti-emetic tablets to stop him being sick. Vomiting is an established side effect of all his medication. He wasn't sick because he was on them and because he wasn't sick, he didn't get rid of the toxic substances as everyone else did.'

'It's a bit like a selective weedkiller, isn't it?' offered Crosby cheerfully.

Sloan stared at Crosby, struck by a new thought. 'I must say, Doctor, I find all that very interesting. Very interesting indeed. But not as interesting as something my constable has just said. Crosby, let us now go the way of all flesh . . '

'Sir?' The constable looked quite alarmed.

'To the kitchen.'

The vegetable cook, her colour still not quite returned to normal, did her best to be helpful. Her job was to take what was needed from the cold store outside, weigh up what was needed for the day, and wash and prepare it ready for the cook, who came in later.

And if she had done anything wrong yesterday she would like to know what it was, if they didn't mind, and they might like to know that they'd been asking her to come and work at the Red Lion Hotel if she ever felt like leaving the nursing home. Very friendly, they were, at the Red Lion. Not like some places she could mention.

'I'm sure they are,' said Sloan pleasantly. 'Now, will you just show us over the cold store again. There was something I forgot to look at before. The lock . . '

'A warrant?' echoed Leeyes back at the police station. 'Who for?'

'The son of the deceased,' said Sloan. 'On a charge of murder. Cleverest job I've come across in many a long day. Make everybody ill but just kill the one person who won't be sick when he's poisoned. All the son had to do was substitute the daffodil bulbs for the shallots in the cold store – you can see where he worked on the lock – and go away. I thought it was strange that he and his wife went abroad for the old boy's birthday.'

'What was so important about that? Couldn't it have waited?'

'Not if his father had written his pension funds in trust for him,' said Sloan. 'Thomas Lean would have had to die before he was seventy-five or take the pension himself. He left it as late as he dared because his father was so ill anyway.'

'I think,' said the Superintendent loftily, 'that I shall tell the Coroner that some new evidence came to light.'

Dead Letters

Sixteenth-century Scotland

The Sheriff of Fearnshire was definitely feeling his age. He was quite convinced too that winters were colder and lasting longer than they used to. And equally sure that summers were getting shorter and shorter every year. That Sheriff Rhuaraidh Macmillan's joints were a good deal stiffer than they had been when he was a young man was beyond doubt. There was, however, nothing at all wrong with his brain – even when he had just, as now, been abruptly awakened from a fitful doze in his chair.

This was why he was immediately alert when the youngest and smallest maid in his establishment suddenly staggered into his room heavily burdened with a pile of peats for the fire. For one thing, the fire was burning well and patently had no need at all of more peats until it was time to bank it up for the night. Another incongruity he noted was that it was not usually a maidservant who brought them into his sitting room, and certainly never this little one. Working at the peat hags and hauling their fuel about afterwards were considered to be man's work even though the peats did get lighter as they dried out.

The girl set the peats down by the fireside and came straight across to his side, standing close to his chair.

'There's a wee mannie that's after wanting to talk to you, sir,' she began timidly, sketching a token curtsy in his direction.

'Who are you?' he asked.

'Please, sir – ' the curtsy was deeper this time – 'I'm Elspeth from the kitchen.' That she was not familiar with the room was evident from the way in which she stared round at it.

'I didn't hear the pipes,' the Sheriff said. The house at Drummondreach had a hall-boy whose sole duty it was to herald equally the approach of friend and stranger with a fanfare of welcome on his uillean pipes. And set the bagpipes to sound the tocsin of warning too, should a known foe be sighted in the distance.

'Please, sir, the wee mannie wasn't at the door . . .' The girl was no height at all herself but she had a bright look. 'And I didn't see anyone coming up the brae either . . .'

One of the many things that being Sheriff of Fearnshire had taught Rhuaraidh Macmillan over the years was that a man could not be too careful to whom – and of whom – he spoke. Unknown men at his door very much came into this category: they could spell danger.

'He dinna' come by the high road, sir,' she said.

'So?' he barked crisply.

'Please, sir, he came out of the wood at the back.'

'Ah . . .' The Forest of Ard Meanach came right up to the very edge of the Drummondreach policies. A man could come out of the trees there without being observed from afar.

'I saw him in the steading when I was after getting the eggs from the nests.'

'You did, did you?' mused the Sheriff, thinking quickly. Back-door visitors could be very dangerous. It wasn't so much who came out of the wood that was a worry these days as what was liable to crawl out of the woodwork afterwards. And there was no knowing in the Scotland of today what exactly that might be – or where it might lead. He sighed and started to climb stiffly out of his chair. 'Well, then, Elspeth, you had better send my clerk to me at once and then go and bring the man in here.'

'He'd no' come in,' responded the girl. 'He said to say to you that he couldn'a.'

'He couldn'a?'

'And that he wouldn'a anyway, even if he could.'

The Sheriff, on his feet now, looked down at her. She was scarcely more than a child. But a bright child, for all that. 'Why not?'

'He says he needs must talk to the Sheriff privately.'

Rhuaraidh Macmillan frowned and said, 'I see.' These were difficult times in Scotland and a man in a position of authority such as the Sheriff of Fearnshire had to be careful, very careful. Actually, all men in Scotland now had to be very careful; and some women too, even more so. There was one woman in particular who should have been more so. A royal one, not noted for her wisdom . . .

'He's still outside,' she said, pointing over her shoulder in the direction of the wood behind the house.

'He called out to me on my way across the steading, but aye softly . . . and only after he'd seen I was alone.'

Sheriff Macmillan shot her a keen glance. 'And where exactly is he now?'

'In the little bothy behind the steading, sir.'

'Alone?' Men had been known to have been ambushed before now by messages such as these. Good men and true . . .

'Yes, sir.' She curtsied again. 'There's just himself.'

'How can you be so sure?'

'Please, sir, I looked specially when I went back to get the peats for the fire.'

'And did you ask him who he was?' If there was ever to be 'a chiel among them, taking notes' it had better not be this sharp-witted youngster or they would all be doomed.

'Yes, sir, but he wouldn't be after telling me his name.'

'Ah . . .' The Sheriff of Fearnshire was not totally surprised at this; only that whoever it was who wanted such secrecy had risked coming to Drummondreach in daylight in the first place. The burden of his spiel must be important, that was for sure. And urgent too.

'And he had his face hidden by his plaid,' she said, as if she had read his mind. 'But – ' she gave him a mischievous sideways glance – 'I ken't well enough who it was anyway.'

'Tell me,' he commanded her.

'It's Murdo Macrae from Balblair, sir.'

'And how did you know that?' Sheriff Macmillan knew Murdo Macrae all right. Murdo had always been a sound man, in favour of the rule of law and order even in distinctly shaky times: unhappy times, such as they were in just now, when no man knew who was his friend and who was his foe; and, more worryingly, knew who was a government spy – or, even worse, a double agent – whose aims and objects were not the administration of justice but the furtherance of the power of his political masters. He knew without being told that if Murdo Macrae had something to say then that something would be important, more important still if he deemed it to be a clandestine matter.

'Please, sir,' the girl was answering him, 'Dougal, the ferryman, brought Murdo Macrae over the firth last night.' Her gaze was resting in wonder on the wall hangings in the room as she spoke. She was looking at them as if she hadn't seen tapestries before. 'He'd come from the west . . .'

'Well?' Now that the Sheriff came to think of it, little Elspeth from the kitchen probably hadn't ever been in his private sanctum before, let alone seen a minor work from Angers. She might not have even been in this part of the house at all until now.

'Dougal, the ferryman, knew who he was and he told Fergus Macpherson and Fergus was at the house this morning with fish and Fergus told us . . .' She paused to take breath.

'It doesn't follow that Murdo Macrae is the man in the bothy,' objected the Sheriff sternly, quite forgetting that he was talking to a mere girl – and a kitchenmaid at that – and not addressing learned men in a court of law.

Quite unfazed by his words, Elspeth from the kitchen held out her own thin right hand. 'Dougal told

Fergus that his passenger had a bloody bandage on his right hand and Fergus, he told us in the kitchen.'

'So?'

'The man in the bothy has a wound on his right hand too, sir. I saw it when he was holding his plaid tight against his face.'

The Sheriff gave the girl a quizzical look. At this rate he would soon have to look to his own laurels – she hadn't missed a single thing that should be marked by a sheriff too.

Elspeth was still speaking. 'And the mannie outside said I wasna' to tell anyone but the Sheriff himself that he was there in the bothy. That was very important, he said.'

Rhuaraidh Macmillan gestured towards the hearth. 'So that's why you brought in the peats that the fire didn't need.'

She bobbed up and down. 'I don't ordinarily get to come in here, sir, and I thought if anyone saw me coming this way . . .'

'Quite right, Elspeth,' he said gravely. He would have to consider how he himself could best cross the steading to the bothy behind without causing comment. Scotland wasn't what it was. Or rather, perhaps, what it had been. And there might be men watching him too, as they watched others in these troubled times. He knew well enough that Drummond-reach was no safer than anywhere else in Fearnshire these days. He waved a hand. 'Now, away with you, lassie, while I think. Keep your tongue to yourself, mind.'

She didn't make any effort to take her leave.

Instead, she stood uncertainly between the fire and the door while the Sheriff looked up at the sky and tried to calculate how long it would be before the darkness was deep enough to allow him to slip out to Murdo Macrae unseen.

'Sir,' she began tentatively.

He turned. 'Yes?'

'Calum Beg will be after bringing the horses back soon from the fields.'

'What about it?' The girl should know that such mundane matters were outwith the concern of the Sheriff of Fearnshire.

'They have to go across the steading for their feed.'

'You're not wanting me to ride to the bothy, surely?'

'No, sir.' She bobbed again. 'But if we were to stop Calum on the road in front and you were to take the horses in instead of him . . .'

'Then I could lead the horses round towards the steading and into the bothy in his coat without being recognized,' finished Rhuaraidh Macmillan, appreciative of her use of the royal 'we'. If only the daughter of James V had had half as much sense – no, there was a better word for what he was thinking of, a Greek word 'nous', that was it – as this youngster had, then Scotland – and probably England too, for that matter – wouldn't be in half the turmoil that it was now.

Calum Beg's coat was old and dirty but it covered Rhuaraidh Macmillan well enough. The Sheriff didn't have Calum Beg's accomplished way with his equine team but somehow he got the pair round the front of the demesne and into the steading behind. He hitched the horses to their post and slipped first into the steading. He came out with an old bucket and then, thus laden with this unsavoury touch of verisimilitude, went into the bothy.

'Thank God you've come, Sheriff,' said a voice out of the darkness at the back of the unlit building. The bedraggled figure of Murdo Macrae emerged from the shadows. 'Macmillan, we need your help ower badly.'

'We?'

'There's a great trouble brewing over Loch a'Chroisg way.' Macrae didn't answer him directly. 'I got away yestre'en, but it was a near thing . . .'

'And sore wounded . . .' observed the Sheriff, pointing to Macrae's blood-caked hand.

The man winced as he moved forward. 'This wound, Sheriff, is why we need your help. I'm a marked man now.'

'And you can't go back without a working sword arm anyway,' observed the Sheriff, ever the realist. 'You'd no' be able to defend yoursel'. You'd be cut down in an instant.'

Macrae acknowledged the truth of this with a jerk of his head. 'You need to know that the blackguards are laying siege to the house by the loch.'

'The Rogart rebels?' Sheriff Macmillan didn't really, need to ask. That band was only one of those roaming the Highlands bent on causing trouble for the forces of law and order, but its men were the most prominent of the marauders presently terrorizing Fearnshire. And the best armed.

'Aye, and that's not the worst of it.' Murdo Macrae's

face twisted into a grimace of pain quite separate from that caused by his injured hand. 'There's women and children in the house without men there able enough to guard them. The doors'll no' last much longer. They've taken a deal of battering already.'

The Sheriff nodded. It was a tale he had heard many times before over the county.

Murdo Macrae's voice dropped to a whisper. 'And,' he said hollowly, 'a rowan tree by the track here has been set about.'

Rhuaraidh Macmillan acknowledged the seriousness of this. A rowan tree by the track roughly hacked down was an old Highland indication of trouble to come nearby and soon. 'They've taken the cattle, no doubt . . .'

'And torched the hay . . .' His shoulders sagged. 'Sheriff, I'm sure they're bent on laying waste to the whole strath and there'll be no stopping them unless we get help.'

Rhuaraidh Macmillan said in his measured way, 'There's no enemy like an auld enemy . . .' Highland memories went back a long way but he had no need to remind Murdo Macrae of Balblair of that. 'And the men of Rogart are auld enemies with the people from Loch a'Chroisg, right enough.'

'That's half the trouble,' said Macrae.

'And the other half?' asked the Sheriff, although he was sure he already knew the cause of the present troubles at Loch a'Chroisg.

Murdo Macrae lifted his shoulder in something like a shrug of despair. 'That there's still some for the Queen and some that are not.'

'That leddie'd not be wanting bairns starved out,' said the Sheriff firmly, 'whoever they're fighting for. She had one of her own, remember . . .'

'Not that she ever got to see him over much from all accounts.' Murdo Macrae grimaced. 'And that's not natural for a mother or her wean.'

'Aye.'

There was no denying that the Crown that had come in with a lass and was well on its way to going out with a lass – or even two, if rumours about the health of the Queen of England were true – was not what it had once been. Rhuaraidh Macmillan was profoundly grateful for one thing, though, and that was that the county of Fearnshire was a long way from Edinburgh and even further from Fotheringhay Castle, where he'd heard Mary Queen of Scots was presently imprisoned.

'So it is said,' he murmured noncommittally.

There was an even older Highland tradition than a savaged rowan tree: one that went, 'A silent tongue got no one hung.' He knew well enough that words could be as dangerous as swords; would that the Queen had known it too. But earlier.

Murdo Macrae said eagerly, 'If, Sheriff, we could get word to the Lord of Alcaig's Isle, I know he'd take up his men to Loch a'Chroisg and see the men from Rogart off . . .'

'Aye, Murdo, that's true. Old Duncan Alcaig would deal with them right enough,' agreed Rhuaraidh Macmillan, adding thoughtfully, 'And he has sons, too. Big men now.'

'But he's an aye careful body,' Macrae pointed out.

He sounded rueful. 'He'd no' trust any messenger, any more than I would myself . . . not these days.'

The Sheriff acknowledged the truth of this. Old Alcaig was nobody's fool. 'Messengers are not always what they seem,' he conceded.

Nothing, you could be sure, he thought to himself, was what it seemed these days. There had been those letters famously found in a casket first and now, he'd heard, letters concealed in a firkin of beer. None of those letters had been what they had seemed either. And all of them had caused a deal of trouble for a certain Queen – enough trouble to dissuade any man from trusting that any missive sent off into the blue would reach its destination without being tampered with and reported on to the man's – or the woman's – enemies. Moreover, no man could rest assured that, even if letters did reach the right reader, they would be seen only by the eyes of the man to whom they had been addressed. Not any longer.

Murdo Macrae struggled to get his good hand inside his torn jerkin. 'I have letters for the Lord of Alcaig's Isle here, but I'd need to know that they will get to him and him alone, mind you, otherwise . . .' His voice trailed away and there was a moment's silence in the bothy, broken only by the stamping of the hooves of one of the horses in the steading. 'Otherwise, Sheriff,' he went on hoarsely, 'I'm worse than a dead man.'

Rhuaraidh Macmillan did not attempt to contradict him. The slashed rowan tree was evidence enough that Macrae spoke the truth there.

'Wait you, man,' he said, 'while I think . . .'

The wounded fighter stood in front of him, anxiously scanning the Sheriff's face. 'There's men hiding up in the wood,' he said, 'who'll take letters to Alcaig, right enough, but he'll not know they're safe to act on and not a trap.'

Rhuaraidh Macmillan didn't need reminding of the dangers of a trap. Fearnshire might be a long way from London, but even they had heard about the uncovering of the Babington plot.

'I have a small chest indoors,' the Sheriff began slowly, 'with a good lock on it . . .'

Murdo Macrae's shoulders promptly sagged in despair. 'Locks need keys, Sheriff, and keys are no more safe than messengers these days.'

'Aye, man, I know that fine . . .' All Scotland knew that. The boy William Douglas had obtained the key to Loch Leven Castle when he had released Mary Queen of Scots. He had thrown the key into the loch as he rowed her and her maid across the water. 'But I wasn't thinking of your parting with the key of the casket . . .'

Murdo Macrae stared at him, nursing his blood-stained hand. 'Is Alcaig meant to break the casket open, then?' He looked even more weary now. 'And if so, how's Alcaig to know that that isn'a a trap too?'

Sheriff Macmillan stroked his chin. 'The messenger that takes the casket is to tell him to put his own lock on it too – a barrel padlock – and keep the key of that himsel'.'

The wounded man looked at him uncompre-hendingly. 'Why is that, Sheriff?'

'And when Alcaig has done that, he's to send the casket back to you.'

'Without his key?' asked Macrae dully, moving over to the bothy wall for support, clearly now beyond thought.

'That's right,' said the Sheriff briskly. 'Then all you have to do is to unlock your lock with your key and send the casket back to him with his own lock still on it . . .'

'So that he can open it with his own key,' said Murdo Macrae, his mud-bespattered face clearing and some of his weariness dropping from him.

'And only him,' said the Sheriff.

'I think I understand,' said the wounded man, passing his good hand over his brow. He was sweating now. 'But why . . .'

'Knowing that no one else can have got into it because only he has the key,' finished the Sheriff of Fearnshire. He stopped and picked up the noisome old bucket. 'Now, wait you while I send Elspeth from the kitchen and her egg basket out here. The casket and the key'll be in there under some food and drink.' He paused at the door and added drily, 'If you haven't got that business with the keys straight in your mind, Macrae, ask her to explain it to you. She'll tell you, right enough.'

Gold, Frankincense and Murder

'Christmas!' said Henry Tyler. 'Bah!'

'And we're expecting you on Christmas Eve as usual,' went on his sister Wendy placidly.

'But . . .' He was speaking on the telephone from London, 'but, Wen—'

'Now it's no use your pretending to be Ebenezer Scrooge in disguise, Henry.'

'Humbug,' exclaimed Henry more firmly.

'Nonsense,' declared his sister, quite unmoved. 'You enjoy Christmas just as much as the children. You know you do.'

'Ah, but this year I may just have to stay on in London over the holiday . . .' Henry Tyler spent his working days – and, in these troubled times, quite a lot of his working nights as well – at the Foreign Office in Whitehall.

What he was doing now to his sister would have been immediately recognized in ambassadorial circles as 'testing the reaction'. In the lower echelons of his department, it was known more simply as 'flying a kite'. Whatever you called it, Henry Tyler was an expert.

'And it's no use your saying there's trouble in the Baltic either,' countered Wendy Witherington warmly.

'Actually,' said Henry, 'it's the Balkans which are giving us a bit of a headache just now.'

'The children would never forgive you if you weren't there,' said Wendy, playing a trump card, although it wasn't really necessary. She knew that nothing short of an international crisis would keep Henry away from her home in the little market town of Berebury, in the heart of rural Calleshire, at Christmas time. The trouble was that these days international crises were not nearly so rare as they used to be.

'Ah, the children,' said their doting uncle. 'And what is it that they want Father Christmas to bring this year?'

'Edward wants a model railway engine for his set.'

'Does he indeed?'

'A Hornby LMS red engine called "Princess Elizabeth",' said Wendy Witherington readily. 'It's a 4–6–2.'

Henry made a note, marvelling that his sister, who seemed totally unable to differentiate between the Baltic and the Balkans – and quite probably the Balearics as well – had the details of a child's model train absolutely at her fingertips.

'And Jennifer?' he asked.

Wendy sighed. 'The Good Ship Lollipop jigsaw. Oh, and when you come, Henry, you'd better be able to explain to her how it is that while she could see Shirley Temple at the pictures – we took her last week – Shirley Temple couldn't see her.'

Henry, who had devoted a great deal of time in the last ten days trying to explain to a minister in His Majesty's Government exactly what Monsieur Pierre

Laval might have in mind for the future of France, said he would do his best.

'Who else will be staying, Wen?'

'Our old friends Peter and Dora Watkins – you remember them, don't you?'

'He's something in the bank, isn't he?' said Henry.

'Nearly a manager,' replied Wendy. 'Then there'll be Tom's old Uncle George.'

'I hope,' groaned Henry, 'that your barometer's up to it. It had a hard time last year.' Tom's Uncle George had been a renowned maker of scientific instruments in his day. 'He nearly tapped it to death.'

Wendy's mind was still on her house guests. 'Oh, and there'll be two refugees.'

'Two refugees?' Henry frowned even though he was alone in his room at the Foreign Office. They were beginning to be very careful there about some refugees.

'Yes, the Rector has asked us each to invite two refugees from the camp on the Calleford road to stay for Christmas this year. You remember our Mr Wallis, don't you, Henry?'

'Long sermons?' hazarded Henry.

'Then you do remember him,' said Wendy without irony. 'Well, he's arranged it all through some church organization. We've got to be very kind to them because they've lost everything.'

'Give them useful presents, you mean,' said Henry, decoding this last without difficulty.

'Warm socks and scarves and things,' agreed Wendy Witherington vaguely. 'And then we've got some people coming to dinner here on Christmas Eve.'

'Oh, yes?'

'Our doctor and his wife. Friar's their name. She's a bit heavy in the hand but he's quite good company. And,' said Wendy, drawing breath, 'our new next-door neighbours – they're called Steele – are coming too. He bought the pharmacy in the square last summer. We don't know them very well – I think he married one of his assistants – but it seemed the right thing to invite them at Christmas.'

'Quite so,' said Henry. 'That all?'

'Oh, and little Miss Hooper.'

'Sent her measurements, did she?'

'You know what I mean,' said his sister, unperturbed. 'She always comes then. Besides, I expect she'll know the refugees. She does a lot of church work.'

'What sort of refugees are they?' asked Henry cautiously.

But that Wendy did not know.

Henry himself wasn't sure, even after he'd first met them, and his brother-in-law was no help.

'Sorry, old man,' said that worthy as they foregathered in the drawing room, awaiting the arrival of the rest of the dinner guests on Christmas Eve. 'All I know is that this pair arrived from somewhere in Mitteleuropa last month with only what they stood up in.'

'Better out than in,' contributed Gordon Friar, the doctor, adding an old medical aphorism, 'like laudable pus.'

'I understand,' said Tom Witherington, 'that they only just got out too. Skin of their teeth and all that.'

'As the poet so wisely said,' murmured Henry, ' "The only certain freedom's in departure." '

'If you ask me,' said old Uncle George, a veteran of the Boer War, 'they did well to go while the going was good.'

'It's the sort of thing you can leave too late,' pronounced Dr Friar weightily. Leaving things too late was every doctor's nightmare.

'I don't envy 'em being where they are now,' said Tom. 'That camp they're in is pretty bleak, especially in the winter.'

This was immediately confirmed by Mrs Godiesky the moment she entered the room. She regarded the Witheringtons' glowing fire with deep appreciation. 'We 'ave been so cooald, so cooaald,' she said as she stared hungrily at the logs stacked by the open fireside. 'So very cooald . . .'

Her husband's English was slightly better, although also heavily accented. 'If we had not left when we did – ' he opened his hands expressively – 'then who knows what would have become of us?'

'Who, indeed?' echoed Henry, who actually had a very much better idea than anyone else present of what might have become of the Godieskys had they not left their native heath when they did. Reports reaching the Foreign Office were very, very discouraging.

'They closed my university department down overnight,' explained Professor Hans Godiesky. 'Without any warning at all.'

'It was very terrrrrible,' said Mrs Godiesky, holding

her hands out to the fire as if she could never be warm again.

'What sort of a department was it, sir?' enquired Henry casually of the professor.

'Chemistry,' said the refugee, just as the two Watkins came in and the hanging mistletoe was put to good use. They were followed fairly quickly by Robert and Lorraine Steele from next door. The introductions in their case were more formal. Robert Steele was a good bit older than his wife, who was dressed in a very becoming mixture of red and dark green, though with a skirt that was rather shorter than either Wendy's or Dora's and even more noticeably so than that of Marjorie Friar, who was clearly no dresser.

'We're so glad you could get away in time,' exclaimed Wendy, while Tom busied himself with furnishing everyone with sherry. 'It must be difficult if there's late dispensing to be done.'

'No trouble these days,' boomed Robert Steele. 'I've got a young assistant now. He's a great help.'

Then Miss Hooper, whose skirt was longest of all, was shown in. She was out of breath and full of apology for being late. 'Wendy, dear, I am so very sorry,' she fluttered. 'I'm afraid, the waits will be here in no time at all . . .'

'And they won't wait,' said Henry guilelessly, 'will they?'

'If you ask me,' opined Tom Witherington, 'they won't get past the Royal Oak in a hurry.'

'The children are coming down in their dressing gowns to listen to the carols,' said Wendy, rightly ignoring both remarks. 'And I don't mind how tired they get tonight.'

'Who's playing Father Christmas?' asked Robert Steele jovially. He was a plump fellow, whose gaze rested fondly on his young wife most of the time.

'Not me,' said Tom Witherington.

'I am,' declared Henry. 'For my sins.'

'Then when I am tackled on the matter,' said the children's father piously, 'I can put my hand on my heart and swear total innocence.'

'And how will you get out of giving an honest answer, Henry?' enquired Dora Watkins playfully.

'I shall hope,' replied Henry, 'to remain true to the traditions of the Foreign Service and give an answer that is at one and the same time absolutely correct and totally meaningless . . .'

At which moment the sound of the dinner gong being struck came from the hall and presently the whole party moved through to the dining room, Uncle George giving the barometer a surreptitious tap on the way.

Henry Tyler studied the members of the party under cover of a certain amount of merry chat. It was part and parcel of his training that he could at one and the same time discuss Christmas festivities in England with poor Mrs Godiesky while covertly observing the other guests. Lorraine Steele was clearly the apple of her husband's eye but he wasn't sure that the same could be said for Marjorie Friar, who emerged as a complainer and sounded – and looked – quite aggrieved with life.

Lorraine Steele, though, was anything but dowdy. Henry decided her choice of red and green – Christmas colours – was a sign of a new outfit for Yuletide.

He was also listening for useful clues about their homeland in the Professor's conversation, while becoming aware that Tom's old Uncle George really was getting quite senile now and learning that the latest of Mrs Friar's succession of housemaids had given in her notice.

'And at Christmas too,' she complained. 'So inconsiderate.'

Peter Watkins was displaying a modest pride in his Christmas present to his wife.

'Well,' he said in the measured tones of his profession of banking, 'personally, I'm sure that refrigerators are going to be the thing of the future.'

'There's nothing wrong with a good old-fashioned larder,' said Wendy stoutly, like the good wife she was. There was little chance of Tom Witherington being able to afford a luxury like a refrigerator for a very long time. 'Besides, I don't think Cook would want to change her ways now. She's quite set in them, you know.'

'But think of the food we'll save,' said Dora. 'It'll never go bad now.'

' "Use it up, wear it out." ' Something had stirred in old Uncle George's memory. ' "Make it do, do without or we'll send it to Belgium." '

'And you'll be more likely to avoid food poisoning too,' said Robert Steele earnestly. 'Won't they, Dr Friar?'

'Yes, indeed,' the medical man agreed at once. 'There's always too much of that about and it can be very dangerous.'

The pharmacist looked at both the Watkins and said gallantly, 'I can't think of a better present.'

'But you did, darling,' chipped in Lorraine Steele brightly, 'didn't you?'

Henry was aware of an unspoken communication passing between the two Steeles; and then Lorraine Steele allowed her left hand casually to appear above the table. Her fourth finger was adorned with both a broad gold wedding ring and a ring on which was set a beautiful solitaire diamond.

'Robert's present,' she said rather complacently, patting her blonde Marcel-waved hair and twisting the diamond ring round. 'Isn't it lovely?'

'I wanted her to wear it on her right hand,' put in Robert Steele, 'because she's left-handed, but she won't hear of it.'

'I should think not,' said Dora Watkins at once. 'The gold wedding ring sets it off so nicely.'

'That's what I say too,' said Mrs Steele prettily, lowering her beringed hand out of sight again.

'Listen!' cried Wendy suddenly. 'It's the waits. I can hear them now. Come along, everyone. It's mince pies and coffee all round in the hall afterwards.'

The Berebury carol singers parked their lanterns outside the front door and crowded round the Christmas tree in the Witheringtons' entrance hall, their sheets of music held at the ready.

'Right,' called out their leader, a young man with a

rather prominent Adam's apple. He began waving a little baton. 'All together now . . .'

The familiar words of 'Once in Royal David's City' soon rang out through the house, filling it with joyous sound. Henry caught a glimpse of a tear in Mrs Godiesky's eye and noted a look of great nostalgia in little Miss Hooper's earnest expression. There must have been ghosts of Christmases past in the scene for her too.

Afterwards, when it became important to re-create the scene in his mind for the police, Henry could place only the Steeles at the back of the entrance hall, with Dr Friar and Uncle George beside them. Peter and Dora Watkins had opted to stand a few steps up the stairs to the first-floor landing, slightly out of the press of people but giving them a good view. Mrs Friar was standing awkwardly in front of the leader of the choir. Of Professor Hans Godiesky there was no sign whatsoever while the carols were being sung.

Henry remembered noticing suppressed excitement in the faces of his niece and nephew perched at the top of the stairs and hoping it was the music that they had found entrancing and not the piles of mince pies awaiting them among the decorative smilax on the credenza at the back of the hall.

They – and everyone else – fell upon them nonetheless as soon as the last carol had been sung. There was a hot punch too, carefully mulled to just the right temperature by Tom Witherington for those old enough to partake of it, and homemade lemonade for the young.

Almost before the last choirboy had scoffed the last mince pie, the party at the Witheringtons' broke up.

The pharmacist and his wife were the first to leave. They shook hands all round.

'I know it's early,' said Lorraine Steele apologetically, 'but I'm afraid Robert's poor old tummy's playing him up again.'

Henry, who had been expecting a rather limp paw, was surprised to find how firm her handshake was.

'If you'll forgive us,' said Lorraine's husband to Wendy, 'I think we'd better be on our way now.'

Robert Steele essayed a glassy, strained smile, but to Henry's eye he looked more than a little white at the gills. Perhaps he too had spotted that the ring that was his Christmas present to his wife had got a nasty stain on the inner side of it.

The pair hurried off together in a flurry of farewells. Then the wispy Miss Hooper declared the evening a great success but said she wanted to check everything at St Faith's before the midnight service and she too slipped away.

'What I want to know,' said Dora Watkins provocatively when the rest of the guests had reassembled in the drawing room and Edward and Jennifer had been sent back – very unwillingly – to bed, 'is whether it's better to be an old man's darling or a young man's slave?'

A frown crossed Wendy's face. 'I'm not sure,' she said seriously.

'I reckon our Mrs Steele's got her husband where she wants him, all right,' said Peter Watkins, 'don't you?'

'Come back, William Wilberforce, there's more work on slavery still to be done,' said Tom Witherington lightly. 'What about a nightcap, anyone?'

But there were no takers and in a few moments the Friars too had left.

Wendy suddenly said she had decided against going to the midnight service after all and would see everyone in the morning. The rest of the household also opted for an early night and in the event Henry Tyler was the only one of the party to attend the midnight service at St Faith's Church that night.

The words of the last carol, 'We Three Kings of Orient are . . .', were still ringing in his ears as he crossed the market square to the church. Henry wished that the Foreign Office had only kings to deal with: life would be simpler then. Dictators – and Presidents, particularly one President not so very many miles from 'perfidious Albion' – were much more unpredictable.

He sang the words of the last verse of the carol as he climbed the church steps:

> 'Myrrh is mine; it's bitter perfume
> Breathes a life of gathering gloom;
> Sorrowing, sighing, bleeding, dying,
> Sealed in the stone-cold tomb.'

Perhaps, he thought, as he sought a back pew and his nostrils caught the inimical odour of a mixture of burning candles and church flowers, he should have been thinking of frankincense or even – when he saw the burnished candlesticks and altar cross – Melchior's gold . . .

His private orisons were interrupted a few minutes later by a sudden flurry of activity near the front of the church and he looked up in time to see little Miss Hooper being helped out by the two churchwardens.

'If I might just have a drink of water,' he heard her say before she was borne off to the vestry. 'I'll be all right in a minute. So sorry to make a fuss. So very sorry . . .'

The Rector's sermon was its usual interminable length and he was able to wish his congregation a happy Christmas as they left the church. As Henry walked back across the square he met Dr Friar coming out of the Steeles' house.

'Chap's collapsed,' he murmured. 'Severe epigastric pain and vomiting. Mrs Steele came round to ask me if I would go and see him. There was blood in the vomit and that frightened her.'

'It would,' said Henry.

'He's pretty ill,' said the doctor. 'I'm getting him into hospital as soon as possible.'

'Could it have been something he ate here?' said Henry, telling him about little Miss Hooper.

'Too soon to tell, but quite possible,' said the doctor gruffly. 'You'd better check how the others are when you get in. I rather think Wendy might be ill too, from the look of her when we left, and I must say my wife wasn't feeling too grand when I went out. Ring me if you need me.'

Henry came back to a very disturbed house indeed, with several bedroom lights on. No one was very ill, but Wendy and Mrs Godiesky were distinctly unwell. Dora Watkins was perfectly all right and was busy ministering to those who weren't.

Happily, there was no sound from the children's room and he crept in there to place a full stocking beside each of their beds. As he came back downstairs to the hall, he thought he heard an ambulance bell next door.

'The position will be clearer in the morning,' he said to himself, a Foreign Office man to the end of his fingertips.

It was.

Half the Witherington household had had a severe gastrointestinal upset during the night and Robert Steele had died in the Berebury Royal Infirmary at about two o'clock in the morning.

When Henry met his sister on Christmas morning she had a very wan face indeed.

'Oh, Henry,' she cried, 'isn't it terrible about Robert Steele? And the rector says half the young waits were ill in the night too, and poor little Miss Hooper as well!'

'That lets the punch out, doesn't it,' said Henry thoughtfully, 'seeing as the youngsters weren't supposed to have any.'

'Cook says—'

'Is she all right?' enquired Henry curiously.

'She hasn't been ill, if that's what you mean, but

she's very upset.' Wendy sounded quite nervous. 'Cook says nothing like this has ever happened to her before.'

'It hasn't happened to her now,' pointed out Henry unkindly, but Wendy wasn't listening.

'And Edward and Jennifer are all right, thank goodness,' said Wendy a little tearfully. 'Tom's beginning to feel better but I hear Mrs Friar's pretty ill still and poor Mrs Godiesky is feeling terrible. And as for Robert Steele . . . I just don't know what to think. Oh, Henry, I feel it's all my fault.'

'Well, it wasn't the lemonade,' deduced Henry. 'Both children had lots. I saw them drinking it.'

'They had a mince pie each too,' said their mother. 'I noticed. But some people who had them have been very ill since . . .'

'Exactly, my dear. Some, but not all.'

'But what could it have been, then?' quavered Wendy. 'Cook is quite sure she used only the best of everything. And it stands to reason it was something that they ate here.' She struggled to put her fears into words. 'Here was the only place they all were.'

'It stands to reason that it was something they were given here,' agreed Henry, whom more than one ambassador had accused of pedantry, 'which is not quite the same thing.'

She stared at him. 'Henry, what do you mean?'

Inspector Milsom knew what he meant.

It was the evening of Boxing Day when he and Constable Bewman came to the Witheringtons' house.

'A number of people would appear to have suffered

from the effects of ingesting a small quantity of a dangerous substance at this address,' Milsom announced to the company assembled at his behest. 'One with fatal results.'

Mrs Godiesky shuddered. 'Me, I suffer a lot.'

'Me too,' Peter Watkins chimed in.

'But not, I think, sir, your wife?' Inspector Milsom looked interrogatively at Dora Watkins.

'No, Inspector,' said Dora. 'I was quite all right.'

'Just as well,' said Tom Witherington. He still looked pale. 'We needed her to look after us.'

'Quite so,' said the Inspector.

'It wasn't food poisoning, then?' said Wendy eagerly. 'Cook will be very pleased . . .'

'It would be more accurate, madam,' said Inspector Milsom, who didn't have a cook to be in awe of, 'to say that there was poison in the food.'

Wendy paled. 'Oh . . .'

'This dangerous substance of which you speak,' enquired Professor Godiesky with interest, 'is its nature known?'

'In England,' said the Inspector, 'we call it corrosive sublimate . . .'

'Mercury? Ah . . .' The refugee nodded sagely. 'That would explain everything.'

'Not quite everything, sir,' said the Inspector mildly. 'Now, if we might see you one at a time, please.'

'This poison, Inspector,' said Henry after he had given his account of the carol-singing to the two policemen, 'I take it that it is not easily available?'

'That is correct, sir. But specific groups of people can obtain it.'

'Doctors and pharmacists?' hazarded Henry.

'And certain manufacturers . . .'

'Certain . . . Oh, Uncle George?' said Henry. 'Of course. There's plenty of mercury in thermometers.'

'The old gentleman is definitely a little confused, sir.'

'And professors of chemistry?' said Henry.

'In his position,' said the Inspector judiciously, 'I should myself have considered having something with me just in case.'

'There being a fate worse than death,' agreed Henry swiftly, 'such as life in some places in Europe today. Inspector, might I ask what form this poison takes?'

'It's a white crystalline substance.'

'Easily confused with sugar?'

'It would seem easily enough,' said the policeman drily.

'And what you don't know, Inspector,' deduced Henry intelligently, 'is whether it was scattered on the mince pies . . . I take it was on the mince pies?'

'They were the most likely vehicle,' conceded the policeman.

'By accident or whether it was meant to make a number of people slightly ill or . . .'

'Or,' put in Constable Bewman keenly, 'one person very ill indeed?'

'Or,' persisted Henry quietly, 'both.'

'That is so.' He gave a dry cough. 'As it happens, it did both make several people ill and one fatally so.'

'Which also might have been intended?' Nobody had ever called Henry slow.

'From all accounts,' said Milson obliquely, 'Mr

Steele had a weak tummy before he ingested the corrosive sublimate of mercury.'

'Uncle George wasn't ill, was he?'

'No, sir, nor Dr Friar.' He gave his dry cough. 'I am told that Dr Friar never partakes of pastry.'

'Mrs Steele?'

'Slightly ill. She says she just had one mince pie. Mrs Watkins didn't have any. Nor did the professor.'

' "The one without the parsley," ' quoted Henry, ' "is the one without the poison." '

'Just so, sir. It would appear at first sight from our immediate calculations quite possible that—'

'Inspector, if you can hedge your bets as well as that before you say anything, we could find you a job in the Foreign Office.'

'Thank you, sir. As I was saying, sir, it is possible that the poison was only in the mince pies furthest from the staircase. Bewman here has done a chart of where the victims took their pies from.'

'Which would explain why some people were unaffected,' said Henry.

'Which might explain it, sir.' The Inspector clearly rivalled Henry in his precision. 'The Professor just wasn't there to take one at all. He says he went to his room to finish a present for his wife. He was carving something for her out of a piece of old wood.'

'Needs must when the Devil drives,' responded Henry absently. He was still thinking. 'It's a pretty little problem, as they say.'

'Means and opportunity would seem to be present,' murmured Milsom.

'That leaves motive, doesn't it?' said Henry.

'The old gentleman mightn't have had one, seeing he's as he is, sir, if you take my meaning, and of course we don't know anything about the professor and his wife, do we sir? Not yet.'

'Not a thing.'

'That leaves the doctor . . .'

'I'd've murdered Mrs Friar years ago,' announced Henry cheerfully, 'if she had been my wife.'

'And Mrs Steele.' There was a little pause and then Inspector Milsom said, 'I understand the new young assistant at the pharmacy is more what you might call a contemporary of Mrs Steele.'

'Ah, so that's the way the wind's blowing, is it?'

'And then, sir,' said the policeman, 'after motive there's still what we always call down at the station the fourth dimension of crime . . .'

'And what might that be, Inspector?'

'Proof.' He got up to go. 'Thank you for your help, sir.'

Henry sat quite still after the two policemen had gone, his memory teasing him. Someone he knew had been poisoned with corrosive sublimate of mercury, served to him in tarts. By a tart too, if history was to be believed.

No, not someone he knew.

Someone he knew of.

Someone they knew about at the Foreign Office because it had been a political murder, a famous political murder set round an eternal triangle . . .

Henry Tyler sought out Professor Godiesky and explained.

'It was recorded by contemporary authors,' Henry

said, 'that when the tarts poisoned with mercury were delivered to the Tower of London for Sir Thomas Overbury, the fingernail of the woman delivering them had accidentally been poked through the pastry . . '

The Professor nodded sapiently. 'And it was stained black?'

'That's right,' said Henry. History did have some lessons to teach, in spite of what Henry Ford had said. 'But it would wash off?'

'Yes,' said Hans Godiesky simply.

'So I'm afraid that doesn't get us anywhere, does it?'

The academic leaned forward slightly, as if addressing a tutorial. 'There is, however, one substance on which mercury always leaves its mark.'

'There is?' said Henry.

'Its – how do you say it in English? – its ineradicable mark.'

'That's how we say it,' said Henry slowly. 'And which substance, sir, would that be?'

'Gold, Mr Tyler. Mercury stains gold.'

'For ever?'

'For ever.' He waved a hand. 'An amalgam is created.'

'And I,' Henry gave a faint smile, 'I was foolish enough to think it was diamonds that were for ever.'

'Pardon?'

'Nothing, Professor. Nothing at all. Forgive me, but I think I may be able to catch the Inspector and tell him to look to the lady. And her gold wedding ring.'

'Look to the lady?' The refugee was now totally bewildered. 'I do not understand . . '

'It's a quotation.'

'Ach, sir, I fear I am only a scientist.'

'There's a better quotation,' said Henry, 'about looking to science for the righting of wrongs. I rather think Mrs Steele may have looked to science too, to – er – improve her lot. And if she carefully scattered the corrosive sublimate over some mince pies and not others, it would have been with her left hand . . .'

'Because she was left-handed,' said the Professor immediately. 'That I remember. And you think one mince pie would have had – I know the English think this important – more than its fair share?'

'I do. Then all she had to do was to give her husband that one and Bob's your uncle. Clever of her to do it in someone else's house.'

Hans Godiesky looked totally mystified. 'And who was Bob?'

'Don't worry about Bob,' said Henry from the door. 'Think about Melchior and his gold instead.'

The Trouble and Strife

Detective Inspector C. D. Sloan sighed deeply and started to explain all over again to the woman sitting in front of him that people may go missing of their own accord at any time if they so wished. What they called it these days was 'dropping out', but he didn't suppose that the aggressive woman before him would want him to use the term about her daughter.

'Not my Susan,' declared Mrs Briggs firmly, 'whatever you're going to try to tell me about it being a free country.'

'Anyone,' stated the policeman, who hadn't been going to say anything about it being a free country. He also forbore to explain that Susan Cavendish wasn't 'her' Susan any more but had apparently been a married woman in her own right for nearly three years now. She should have been her own woman long ago.

'She's not been in touch for a full month,' said Mrs Briggs, ignoring this, 'and that's not right, is it?'

'She doesn't have to be in touch if she doesn't want to be,' repeated Sloan patiently. 'She is, after all, of full age.'

'And I may say, officer, she is also an English-woman born in wedlock and had her feet on dry land when I last saw her,' Mrs Briggs completed the adage tartly, 'but she's still missing.'

'Which she has every right to be if she so wishes,' pointed out the Detective Inspector. With a mother like Mrs Briggs, he might very well have opted to go missing himself.

'And that's never happened before,' insisted Susan's mother, ignoring this last remark of his too. 'They used to come in to see me every weekend without fail. Susan did my shopping while that no good husband of hers did any odd jobs about the house I needed doing.'

'I see.' Sloan had known a good few sons-in-law who never did a hand's turn in their wife's mother's house but this didn't seem the moment to say so.

'And I'm just not satisfied that she's all right,' said Mrs Briggs belligerently. 'So I'm reporting her missing here and now whatever you say.'

'Was your daughter all right when you last saw her?' parried Sloan.

'It depends what you mean by all right,' responded Mrs Briggs. 'Physically she was as fit as the butcher's dog . . .'

'That's something,' put in Detective Constable Crosby from the sidelines.

Mrs Briggs favoured him with a baleful stare and turned back to Sloan. 'But she wasn't happy in herself, even though she said the divorce was working its way through – and not before time too, if you ask me.'

'Divorce?' said Sloan, the policeman in him automatically pricking up his ears.

'She'd decided to leave him at last,' said Mrs Briggs.

'Nasty piece of work, I always said, that Christopher Cavendish, for all that he's done well at his job.'

'And what was that?' enquired Sloan, pulling a piece of paper towards him.

'He was one of those computer people,' she said, sniffing. 'You know – the sort who sit at home all day in front of a screen and call it working. How does anyone know whether you're working or not, that's what I want to know?'

'I dare say the usual yardsticks apply,' murmured Sloan.

'Come again?'

'The making of money,' said Sloan smoothly.

'He did that,' she admitted grudgingly. 'They had a lovely old house, though a bit on the small side if they'd wanted to start a family . . .'

'Ah, I was going to ask about—'

'Which mercifully, the way things have turned out, they hadn't done.' She sniffed. 'Susan wanted a baby – don't ask me why. Nothing but trouble, children. I was always telling her that.'

Detective Inspector Sloan made a note.

'Of course, half of the house will be my Susan's when they settle up – half of everything, come to that – so she won't come out of it too badly.' She glared at Sloan. 'If she's all right, that is.'

'Tell me, have you approached the husband . . .' Sloan paused and looked down at his notes. 'Yes, he is the husband still, isn't he, if the divorce hasn't come through yet? Have you asked him where she might be? He at least might have some idea, even if they have parted, as you say they have.'

'That's the trouble,' Mrs Briggs said instantly. 'I don't know where he is either.'

'So the husband is missing too, is he?' asked Sloan with interest.

'Well, I never,' remarked Detective Constable Crosby.

Mrs Briggs bridled. 'I wouldn't know about him being missing, but the house has been sold – I do know that – and he's gone too, but where I don't know. Good riddance for Susan, if you ask me.' She gave a self-satisfied smirk. 'I always said she should never have married him in the first place. If I told her that once, I told her so a dozen times.'

'Not good enough?' put in Detective Constable Crosby helpfully. He was still a bachelor himself.

'Not by a long chalk,' said Mrs Briggs, taking a deep breath preparatory to enlarging on this at length.

Detective Inspector Sloan forestalled her. 'And have you made enquiries at her place of work?'

'In a manner of speaking,' conceded Mrs Briggs. 'Not that I got very far.'

'How come?' asked Detective Constable Crosby, in whom his superiors had so far failed to instil any proper sense of formality when dealing with members of the public.

'Susan worked for a temping agency in Berebury and they say that someone just rang in one day to say she wouldn't be available for work any more.'

'Someone?' pounced Sloan.

'They couldn't swear it was her,' said Mrs Briggs. 'In fact, they couldn't even be sure that it was a woman who had rung.' She suddenly became a little more human and admitted, 'That's when I began to get really worried.'

'I see, madam.' He did too. 'You say their marital home has been sold?'

'The house agents' sale board has come down and Wetherspoons cleared the furniture at the end of last week.' She pursed her lips. 'Sid Wetherspoon wouldn't tell me where they were taking it. Commercially sensitive information, he called it.'

Detective Inspector Sloan made a note. He'd have a word with the house agents and the removal people himself.

'And their solicitors won't tell me either,' she went on in aggrieved tones. 'Client confidentiality was what they said.'

'Quite so,' murmured Sloan.

'There was something else.'

'What was that, madam?'

'All Susan's stuff was in that van that went along with Christopher's.'

'Not just his?' asked Detective Constable Crosby, patently puzzled.

'No, and I do know that because I watched it go.' She snorted gently. 'It was just as well she wasn't pregnant after all . . .'

'After all?' prompted Sloan, leaving aside for the time being the more germane matter of all the furniture going from the house together.

'She'd wanted a baby at first but one didn't come along,' said Mrs Briggs. 'And before you ask, the doctor wouldn't tell me anything either. Said he'd be struck off the register or something like that. Excuses,' she said richly, 'all of them.'

'That'd be because of that chap Hippocrates,' put in Crosby. 'He's the one the doctors swear by.' He frowned. 'Funny that, since he wasn't a Christian.'

'At least,' said Mrs Briggs, ignoring this, 'there being no baby on the way will have made the divorce simpler, which is something to be thankful for.'

'Quite so,' said Detective Inspector Sloan, rising to his feet. 'Well, thank you, Mrs Briggs. We'll be looking into the matter for you.'

'Then there's the question of her car,' said the woman, not making a move. 'That's worrying, too.'

Detective Constable Crosby's face brightened. 'Do you know the number?'

'Course, I do,' she came back at him on the instant. 'And the make.'

'What's so worrying about her car?' asked Detective Inspector Sloan quickly.

'She sold it before she disappeared. At least,' she said meaningfully, 'someone did. Took it into that big dealers down by the river and sold it.'

'For cash or a trade-in?' asked Crosby.

'Cash,' said Mrs Briggs promptly.

'How do you know that?' said Sloan.

'I saw it in their showroom.' She twisted her lips. 'Besides, car dealers don't have funny ideas about what's commercially sensitive information.'

'Except the real second-hand value,' muttered Crosby. 'They'll never tell you that about any car you're trading in.'

'That I wouldn't know, never having been a driver

myself,' she said, reminded of another grievance. 'At least their old house was on an easy bus route for me. It suited me nicely being where it was – I could get there whenever I wanted.'

'And what car does your son-in-law drive, madam?' enquired Sloan as casually as he could. These days owners of cars and their addresses could be traced by police authorities with the speed of light.

'Christopher?' she said scornfully. 'Oh, he didn't have a car. Only Susan did. Said he didn't need one, working from home like he did.' She screwed up her face. 'And anyway he'd got some potty idea about not adding to the world's pollution problems. What he thinks he could do about global warming beats me.'

'I think,' said Detective Inspector Sloan a trifle portentously, 'you'd better leave things as they are at present, madam. We'll be in touch in – er – in due course.'

'I'm sure I hope so,' said Mrs Briggs, 'but if you ask me, he's made away with her and made off with all the money.'

'Have you any particular basis for making these allegations, madam?' asked Sloan wearily. He was beginning to feel quite sorry for both her daughter and her son-in-law.

'I thought you'd never ask,' she said acidly.

'Well?'

Mrs Briggs dived into her handbag, retrieved a glossy sheet of paper and waved it before his eyes. 'This.'

'The estate agents' sale particulars of their house?' said Sloan.

'That's right,' she said.

'What about it?'

'Read it,' she commanded. 'Especially the bit about the garage.'

' "Detached garage, brick with slate roof," ' he quoted, ' "well equipped with workbench, tool cupboard and two electrical points." ' He lifted his gaze. 'Sounds very nice. What's wrong with it?'

'There's something missing from the description,' she said stubbornly.

'What?' asked Sloan.

'Inspection pit,' she said. 'There always used to be one there and it isn't mentioned in this.'

'And you think,' began Crosby incautiously.

'Yes,' she said. 'I do.'

Detective Inspector Sloan got rid of Mrs Briggs by falling back on an age-old police formula that comprised thanking her for coming in and promising to keep in touch with her to let her know how their enquiries were progressing.

He was nothing like as circumspect when talking to his Superintendent.

'I don't like it, sir. I've had a look at it and the inspection pit in the garage at the Cavendishs' old home has obviously been filled in very recently.'

'Go on,' said Superintendent Leeyes gruffly.

'The house agents say that they paid the cheque from the sale of the house direct to the bank as agreed. It was made out to both Christopher and Susan

Cavendish and their instructions were that it was to go into the couple's joint account there.'

'Which said joint account could still be functioning,' said the superintendent heavily, 'if either had power to draw on it.'

'Exactly, sir.' He cleared his throat. 'In fact, since then all the withdrawals have been made by Christopher Cavendish.'

'I don't like that,' said Leeyes.

'I also had a word with Sid Wetherspoon, the removals man,' continued Sloan. 'He took all the furniture over to a house right out in the country behind Almstone, but Christopher Cavendish had asked him particularly not to disclose where it was to anyone . . . He stressed that bit very heavily to Sid. Said there was woman trouble and he was sure Sid – man to man – would understand.'

'Well, then,' said Leeyes.

'Very nice place, actually, sir, that house, but empty except for the furniture that Sid had delivered there.'

'The neighbours?' Superintendent Leeyes always insisted that inquisitive neighbours were worth their weight in gold to an overworked police force.

'The woman next door had seen a man and a young woman arrive there a week or so ago. She'd offered them the proverbial cup of tea over the garden fence but they said they had a plane to catch and wouldn't be back until they'd had a long holiday.'

'That's a good one,' snorted Leeyes.

'The neighbour said the pair were collected by hire car and haven't been seen since.'

The Superintendent tapped his desk with his

pencil. 'I don't like it at all, Sloan. I'm afraid that in the first place you're going to have to open up that inspection pit.'

'That's what I thought too, sir.'

'Then get a warrant.'

It was half an hour before the spades of the sweating diggers who were working in the garage struck anything.

'It's metal from the sound of it,' called out Detective Constable Crosby.

'Keep going,' commanded Sloan.

'Looks like a small strong box,' said Crosby, while his fellow Constable scraped away the mixture of sand and aggregate that was covering a square metal edge.

'A little water and cement in there,' observed Sloan, 'and that lot would have set into concrete overnight.'

'Perhaps it was something he meant to do,' said Crosby, straightening up. 'And didn't get round to.' The Constable himself was a great procrastinator.

'Criminals usually make mistakes,' said Sloan. 'Can you get a grip on it?'

In the event the metal box came out quite easily.

'It's not even locked,' said Crosby, surprised and somehow disappointed.

Detective Inspector Sloan lifted the lid. The box contained nothing but a plastic bag. Inside it was a conventional Change of Address card of the variety bought at any stationer's shop. The details had been completed with a waterproof pen and spelled out the address of a house.

'But that's where Sid Wetherspoon delivered the furniture,' said Crosby.

'It is indeed,' agreed Sloan. 'Read on, Crosby.'

The Detective Constable peered over Sloan's shoulder and read out aloud, ' "To Whom It May Concern" . . . I don't get it, sir. Who does It concern?'

'Us,' said Sloan pithily. 'Keep going.'

'It says "Strictly Confidential",' said Crosby.

Detective Inspector Sloan tapped the card. 'Don't forget this last message.'

At the bottom of the card was written 'Important. We don't want Mum to know where we are until after the baby's arrived.'

'Christopher Cavendish was right when he told Sid Wetherspoon that he'd got woman trouble, sir,' explained Sloan to Superintendent Leeyes later. 'He had. We just thought of the wrong woman, that's all.'

Losing the Plot

'What a truly magnificent view!' exclaimed Marion Carstairs. Like everyone else who entered the sitting room
of the house on the hill at Almstone known as the Toft
for the first time, she had crossed straight to the bay
window and gazed out.

'It is indeed,' agreed Kenneth Marsden of Messrs
Crombie and Marsden, Estate Agents and Valuers, of
Berebury, 'although, as I am sure you already know,
Miss Carstairs, you don't own the view from your
windows unless, that is,' he added, 'you own that land
as well.'

'Like dukes,' murmured Marion absently. 'They
always made sure that they possessed all the land that
could be seen from their mansions. After all, Capability
Brown expected it of them.'

'Really?' said Kenneth Marsden politely. 'How
interesting.'

'But this panorama is quite exceptional.'

'That's what everyone to whom I've shown the
property says,' murmured the estate agent, finding
that there was something about this lean, intelligent
woman that made him pay more than usual attention
to his grammar.

'You know, Mr Marsden, I do believe you can see the whole of the Alm valley from here.' Marion scanned the horizon. 'Isn't that Billing Bridge over there? I'm sure I came over the river that way.'

'It is,' said the estate agent, adding with professional caution, 'I am told that on a clear day you can see the spire of Calleford Minster.' He was well aware that those now following his calling had to be so much more circumspect in what they said in these days of rules and regulation than hitherto.

She was still looking eagerly out of the window. 'South, south-west – the sunsets must be a real joy up here too.'

'I'm sure,' said Kenneth Marsden quickly, 'but as it happens I haven't ever been here in the evening to see.'

She smiled. 'And I am hoping that I shall be here quite soon to do just that. You've got the address of my solicitors, haven't you?'

'There are, of course, other prospective purchasers who wish to see over the property.' He said this quite automatically, although in fact there had been very few and none of those were local. Miss Carstairs had come from London.

'Naturally. I quite understand that.' She turned back and said, 'Tell me, how could Mr and Mrs Boness have borne to move away from here?'

'Well, in a manner of speaking they haven't.' Kenneth Marsden pointed out of the window. 'Do you see that little building down there to the left under the slope? It's called the Croft . . .'

'Toft and Croft!' exclaimed Marion Carstairs, clapping her hands. 'Of course! Toft and croft – that means the house and land on a hill in both Old English and Old Norse.'

'Well, they just moved into the Croft,' said Marsden, skating over the etymology.

'Keeping the view.'

'Exactly.'

'But,' she observed, pointing out of the window, 'if that wire fence over there is anything to go by, they've also kept the land right up to just in front of the Toft.'

'I am given to understand,' said the estate agent carefully, 'that Mrs Boness is quite a gardener and wished to retain as much of the original ground as possible.'

'Ah, I see . . .' All she could actually see were a few straggly wallflowers and an old felled birch tree.

'In fact, Miss Carstairs, as you will note from the title deeds, they did move their boundary back a little for the previous owners – the Mullens, they were called.'

'Oh, was there some trouble over it, then?' she asked swiftly.

'Mr Boness told me that it was to oblige the Mullens over some trees,' said the estate agent. 'They wanted them in their garden, not his. I believe, though, that Mr Boness had them cut down himself after the Mullens left.'

'But – ' Marion Carstairs's eyebrows came up – 'I thought it was Mr Boness who is selling this house now. You hadn't told me that there had been someone else occupying it after them.'

'Oh, yes, but they were here only for four or five

years. Michael Boness actually bought the place back from the new people, thinking he and his wife would move in again themselves.'

'But they didn't?'

'No. I was advised that in the end Mrs Boness decided she was quite happy where she was down in the Croft, and that's why they put the property back on the market.'

'Some gardeners like making new gardens and some don't,' observed Marion Carstairs. From what she could see of it, the garden of the house below had little to commend it besides the wallflowers but she did not say so. 'We're all different. That's the joy of being a gardener.'

The estate agent nodded. 'And, as you will have seen on your way in, there is still plenty of land with the property. It's just that it's on both sides of the house rather than in the front of it.'

'Oh, it's quite enough for my wants, Mr Marsden, I do assure you,' responded Marion Carstairs truthfully. 'Quite enough. And it's an alkaline soil, which is exactly what I am looking for.'

'Good. Now, if you'd like to see the other rooms . . '

It was early autumn by the time Marion Carstairs moved in to the Toft and was able to explore the garden properly for the first time. It was then that she took a really good look at the stretch of ground on her side of the wire fence opposite the bay window. What she saw was a row of sawn-off tree stumps, their remains now hardly visible above the grass. This had lain unmown through the summer months that the house had been on the market and it was now long and untidy.

On Michael Boness's side of the fence was a row of newly planted small young trees that had not been there when she had agreed to buy the Toft. The bed of the new trees extended almost exactly the length of her bay window.

'Leyland cypress, unless I'm very much mistaken,' she said to herself.

She said nothing to Michael Boness, though, when she met him in the village store, accepting his welcome to the Toft and Almstone with her customary reserved politeness.

It's *Cupressocyparis leylandii*, Jean,' she told her sister later that week, when she telephoned her to report that she was settled in at the Toft. 'It'll grow a good three feet a year. What's that? Oh, yes, it'll be up to the level of the bay window in no time at all. And it's planted as densely as possible too. Just like the hedge that was here before. I reckon that he moved the boundary back when he got possession so that the stumps wouldn't be in the way of this new hedge.'

'Naughty,' said her sister.

'Clever,' said Marion.

She spent the winter preparing the ground for a spring planting of little Christmas trees. These she installed in the ground to the sides of the house and adjacent to the boundary fence, tending them carefully until they were properly established. A good horticultural specialist might have considered her a little unwise to put them in ground so very near a rapidly growing hedge of leylandii since this would all too soon take both light and moisture from the infant Christmas trees, but this factor did not seem to have occurred to Marion Carstairs.

Instead she seemed to be concentrating all her attention on the tree stumps.

'Now that I've had the stumps freshly cut I'll be able to kill them off before I have them taken out,' she called cheerfully across to Michael Boness when he appeared near her boundary one day when she was in the garden, carefully painting the fresh surface of each stump with a clear liquid. 'I'm sure they'll be so much easier to lift when they've died off completely, aren't you?'

'If anything you're using in the way of poison gets to the hedge on my side and damages it,' her neighbour began belligerently, 'you'll be in trouble, I can tell you.'

Marion Carstairs looked quite shocked. 'I shouldn't dream of letting that happen, Mr Boness. I promise you, I'll be very careful.'

'That's all very well,' Boness grunted, 'but I'll have you know that that hedge stays where it is, no matter what you say.'

'I shouldn't dream of saying anything, Mr Boness,' said Marion Carstairs in dulcet tones. 'Why should I? It's your hedge.'

'Because if,' he began heatedly and then fell suddenly silent.

'Your hedge is nothing to do with me,' went on Marion, still sweetly reasonable. 'The very idea . . .'

At the end of her first year at the house, the leylandii was growing fast and thickening up well. All that Marion Carstairs had seen of Mr and Mrs Boness had been when she had called with the church choir singing Christmas carols. 'God rest you merry,' she had sung with the rest of the choir at their door. 'Let nothing you dismay . . .'

By the end of Marion's second summer at the Toft Mike Boness's new leylandii hedge was beginning to show signs of interfering with the splendid view of the valley from her sitting room.

'I'm planning on having these old stumps out in the spring, Mr Boness,' she said one day when he was up near her boundary, examining his leylandii hedge.

'You'd better not disturb any roots on my side,' he said gruffly, 'or there'll be real trouble. That hedge stays.'

'Oh, I think we'll be able to get them out all right without doing any damage to your garden or mine,' she said.

'They're coming along very well now, these trees of mine are,' he said.

'They are indeed,' she said warmly.

'They're going to be fine, tall trees in no time at all.'

'I'm sure,' said Marion agreeably.

'Give me and the missus a bit of privacy in our old age, they will,' he went on, puzzled by her lack of reaction.

'They will indeed,' she said immediately. 'Just what you want as time goes by.'

'Doesn't help your view much though, does it?' Boness ventured slyly, watching her face.

'True,' admitted Marion Carstairs, 'but then I've always thought Goethe got it right.'

'Who?' he asked suspiciously.

'Goethe. A German poet.' Marion waved an arm over the valley. 'He said that no one could look at the view for more than fifteen minutes.'

'Did he?' Michael Boness sounded baffled. 'You do know these trees could get to more than a hundred feet if they're not trimmed?'

'Really? Do take care, won't you?' said Marion solicitously. 'You wouldn't want to fall off a ladder . . .'

'I'm not going to fall off a ladder,' he said crossly, 'because I'm not going to trim them.'

'Ah, then you won't need to worry about falling, will you?' she said.

She duly recounted the conversation to her sister, Jean, over the telephone that evening. 'Poor man,' she laughed. 'He doesn't know what to make of me.'

'Poor nothing,' snorted Jean. 'He's waiting for you to go down on bended knee and beg him to cut the leylandii down so that you can have your lovely view back.'

'He's going to be disappointed, then,' said Marion Carstairs. 'I will ask him, of course, but not just yet.'

'So how are your Christmas trees coming along?' asked her sister.

'Slowly but well,' said Marion. 'Another twelve months should see them just right.'

'And his leylandii?'

'Just wrong,' said Marion. 'For him, I mean. Fomes spreads underground along the roots at about a yard a year.'

'I'm very happy to hear it . . .' She stopped. 'But, Marion, won't it look very odd if the whole of his hedge is attacked by it at once?'

'Ah,' said Marion mysteriously, 'I've thought of that. And about what to do if he gets on to someone about the fomes, as I'm sure he will.'

'I hope you have. After all, dear, fungi – what did you say the Latin name for fomes was?'

'*Heterobasidin annosum* . . .'

'Even ones with outlandish names like – er – that don't usually travel in straight lines – and you know that, even if Mike Boness doesn't.'

'Ah,' she said, 'don't forget that the source of the infection – the old tree stumps – is in a straight line too.'

'But surely you don't want him ever to know that that's where it's come from.'

'No, of course not. That's why I had the stumps out and the ground grassed over . . . Nobody will know they were ever there and as sure as eggs Michael Boness isn't going to tell anyone.'

'Why not?'

'For one thing, when he's had it spelled out to him, his estate agent won't like to hear what his client has been up to.'

'Go on . . .'

'But it could be argued,' Marion said cogently, 'that

229

recently planted trees such as his leylandii are unusually susceptible to that sort of infestation.'

'I do hope,' said Jean piously, 'that you don't have to argue anything.'

The next winter passed. This Christmas-tide the church choir sang the carol 'The Holly and the Ivy' at the front door of the Croft. When the choir came to the line 'When they are both full-grown' Michael Boness managed not to meet Marion Carstairs's eye.

It was high summer when Marion started to see early signs of disease in the leylandii hedge, which was now both thick and tall. That was when Marion first asked Mike Boness if he would consider lowering his trees so that she could have her view back.

'I thought you'd ask one day,' he said, grinning unpleasantly. 'All that talk about not minding what you looked at was hot air.'

'It's making my sitting room quite dark too,' she said meekly.

'That's your problem,' he said.

'Oh, dear.' Marion gave what she hoped was a womanly sigh. 'I really don't know what to do next.'

'You can't do anything,' he said roughly. 'It's my hedge, not yours. I can plant it wherever I like and let it get as high as I like, and neither you nor anyone else can stop me, no matter what you say.'

'But . . .'

'And,' he added, 'since you've probably already

thought about asking him, neither can your solicitor. They're clever, all right, but not that clever.'

'No.' She sighed again. 'I suppose not . . .'

'So you might as well save your breath and your money.'

'And that's your last word, is it?' she asked.

Mike Boness paused and seemed to consider this. 'Well,' he drawled eventually, 'I dare say I could buy the Toft back from you if I had a mind to.'

'Buy it back?'

'That's if you were prepared to agree to my price, of course.'

'You mean you would really like to have it back again?'

'Only if the price was right, naturally.' He sniffed. 'It's not worth anything like what you gave for it, I can tell you.'

'Really?' she said.

'Not without the view.'

'I suppose you're right.'

He waved an arm over the valley. 'But with it . . . then, that's different, isn't it?'

'Very,' said Marion Carstairs drily.

'Think about it,' he said.

'I will,' she promised.

'Mind you, I won't pay a lot.' He twisted his lips. 'But you're not going to get too many people willing to take the Toft off your hands now.'

'Not without the view,' she conceded gravely.

*

She was highly amused, though, when she described the encounter to her sister. 'What? No, we didn't talk money. It's a bit soon.'

'Soon for what?' enquired Jean.

'My Christmas trees. I'm waiting for the valuable seasonal trade, remember . . .'

'Of course.'

'And for the damage from the fomes to be quite apparent.'

Marion Carstairs was all sympathy the next time she saw Mike Boness. 'Your poor hedge, Mr Boness. It has got something nasty, hasn't it? I do hope you weren't hoping to use it for timber.'

'I've got an expert coming to see it,' he said thickly, 'and if he tells me that it's anything you've done to it, then I'll be taking the matter further.'

'Me?' protested Marion. 'I haven't been near your hedge.'

'He's a proper tree specialist.'

'Just what you need,' she said.

'He'll know, and then watch out.'

'If I've done anything,' she corrected him.

'We'll see about that,' he said, storming away, red-faced. 'For my money, you'll be hearing more about this.'

Marion watched the arboriculturist come and go from behind her bedroom curtain. The one thing she didn't want at this stage was to be recognized. She was pleased, though, to see the expert look long and hard over the fence into her garden and then go over to peer equally hard at and dig round the remains of a felled birch tree on Mike Boness's land. That was after he had taken some samples of soil and of a fungus that had made its appearance on some of the leylandii roots. He took a core sample too from the stem of one of the dying leylandii trees.

'A textbook examination,' she reported to her sister, metaphorically rubbing her hands. 'Any minute now he'll be telling Boness about the fomes and that the spore could have come from that old birch of his. Birches are very susceptible to fomes too.'

'Like leylandii and Christmas trees,' observed her sister happily.

'Exactly. Now, I think our time has come . . . How much did you say you and Paul lost when you sold the house back to Boness, Jean?'

The sum of money named by Jean Mullen formed the basis of a claim by Marion Carstairs, the retired professor of plant biology at the Toft, against Michael Boness, the owner of the Croft, for damage to a substantial crop of *Picea abies* – otherwise known as Christmas tree – by a fungus called fomes, caught from his leylandii trees.

It was successful.

And without coming to court either.

A Soldier of the Queen

Private Saffery was quite surprised at the extent of his own fear. Nothing he had ever experienced in his time in the army so far had been quite as frightening as this. He shivered, clutched his gun even more tightly and nerved himself to a total and unnatural stillness.

Worst of all was the waiting.

His ordeal had begun on the Friday morning when the next week's roster had been pinned up in the barracks which were presently being occupied by the 2nd Battalion of the East Calleshire Regiment.

'Sentry duty?' said his oppo, Mike Clarkson. 'Nothing to it, mate. Did my stint last month and not a thing happened.'

'As I remember,' Saffery remarked sturdily, 'you didn't enjoy it and said so quite a lot.'

'No . . . Well, not at the time, maybe,' agreed Clarkson. 'But it was all right afterwards.'

'So's having a baby, my mother says,' retorted Saffery.

'I wouldn't know about that,' conceded Clarkson, 'but all I can say, Kev, is that though I admit sentry duty is no picnic at the time, it's no problem after you've done it once. Honest.'

'Like having a baby, I suppose,' said Kevin Saffery, who at the time hadn't known all that much about either process.

He did now.

About the preparations for sentry duty, anyway. And just at this moment Private Kevin Saffery heartily wished it was already afterwards for him too, just like it was for Mike Clarkson.

Even so, his friend Private Clarkson had been more encouraging than some of his other mates. They seemed inclined to regard a turn of sentry duty in this day and age, let alone in this place, as something of an initiation rite.

'After which I'll be a real soldier, I suppose,' Kevin had said bitterly in response to this. He came from an old army family where the expression 'being a real soldier' didn't just mean not crying when you grazed your knee falling off your bike. It meant the same as 'being blooded' in other fields – notably the hunting ones – as well as most probably literally becoming 'bloodied' into the bargain.

'Well, you'll be different anyway,' Clarkson had mumbled inarticulately. 'And you'll feel different somehow. Bit difficult to explain . . .'

Now, out of the barracks and – except for one other soldier in sight – to all intents and purposes entirely on his own, Kevin Saffery knew what Clarkson had meant. He shivered again. And not from cold.

'Watch out for the kids,' Clarkson had warned him too. 'They're worse than the adults. Much worse.'

It was something Private Saffery had already heard on all sides and he had said so.

'When I have kids,' said Private Clarkson feelingly, 'I shall lock 'em up indoors when they're not in school. All the time.'

On the other hand, Private Milligan's advice had been strictly practical. 'When you see them getting ready to shoot . . .'

'Yes?' he had asked urgently.

'Freeze, man, freeze, or you'll never hear the end of it.'

'Thanks a lot, mate.'

For nothing, he nearly added. Not being able to keep absolutely still was the one thing Private Kevin Saffery feared most of all.

As usual, the Corporal had managed to be his customary nasty little self at the same time as being strictly practical. 'Your main problem, all of you lot,' he had said, when addressing the next week's roster of raw duty men in the barrack room, 'will be cramp. Simple but painful. And sleeping with corks in your bed like your granny does won't help.'

There was a dutiful snigger.

'The 'uman body,' he went on, 'wasn't meant for keeping really still for as long as you've got to do it for.' He sneered. 'Now, if you was cats it would come easy. But you're not cats, are you?' He glared at them. 'Well, are you cats?'

'No, Corporal,' they had chorused. Kevin had heard some reservation about this on his left, but fortunately the words 'It's that ginger tom from next door' and a veiled reference to an overseas cathouse had not reached the Corporal. There would have been trouble if they had.

Big trouble.

'Cats can watch mice for hours without twitching a whisker,' declared the little corporal, 'and if I catch any of you shower twitching whiskers while you're on sentry go you're on a charge. Understood?'

'Understood,' they had all echoed dutifully, murder in their hearts. The name of the murder was 'fragging' and Private Saffery had learned the word at his grandfather's knee.

'Saw a bit of it done once,' the old man had once told him, still too much of an old soldier and thus too wise to say right out whether or not he'd been the one to do it. 'On the road to Mersa Matruh.'

'But what is it, Grandad?' a younger and more innocent Kevin had wanted to know. He'd been of an age then when new words – especially the dubious-sounding ones which his grandfather used – were suddenly interesting. He'd only just been clouted by his mother for saying 'frigging' and to a lad of his age the word 'fragging' seemed deliciously dangerous-sounding too.

'Dangerous?' his grandfather had growled. 'Of course it was dangerous. To both sides, you might say.'

'But what does "fragging" mean, Grandad?'

Any resemblance of the tableau the two of them made, talking at his grandfather's gate, to the famous picture of little Peterkin asking old Kaspar about a certain famous victory at Blenheim was purely coincidental.

'Theoretically,' said old grandfather Saffery, a faraway look in his rheumy eyes, 'fragging is when you kill the man who leads you into danger in war.'

'Yes, but what is it really?' The word 'theoretically' was one that a young Kevin already knew and did not like. 'Can't you give me a f'rinstance, Grandad? Please . . .'

The old man had gone on staring into the distance. 'It's when you take the opportunity to shoot some bastard of a Corporal in the back of his head on the only occasion when you've got half a chance of doing it without being caught in the act – which is when you're going into action behind him. Now, be off with you, boy, before it happens to you.'

Kevin had got halfway down the path before he heard his grandfather shout after him. He turned back. 'What is it, Grandad?'

'I said that corporals are dangerous and don't you ever forget it.'

'No, Grandad. I won't.'

'Especially little ones . . .'

The person who looked most dangerous of all while the Corporal was going through his spiel was Private 'Edge' Bates. Edge wasn't his real name. Private Bates was called this because of the time he spent sharpening his bayonet. No one, declared Edge Bates with monotonous frequency, was going to creep up behind him on a dark night without feeling the specially sharpened blade.

The Sergeant had been as full of dire warnings as the Corporal in what passed as his pep talk. 'And remember, all of you, that should you happen to fall while you're on sentry go – ' here he glared at them all in such a way as to make it quite clear that if they did fall to the ground it would be considered to be their own fault – 'we shan't come and get you.' The Sergeant's eye travelled balefully up and down the serried ranks of men. 'That clearly understood?'

Kevin's great-grandfather had been a stretcher bearer in France in 1915 at the bloody cock-up called Loos. He'd – if family legend was to be believed – always got his wounded man whatever the danger. It seemed a bit hard that, if Kevin was to fall at his post, he'd just be left there until the guard was changed.

Kevin didn't remember the stretcher bearer in the family himself because, although he'd survived the Battle of Loos, a German shell had had his name on it at the mudbath that became the bloodbath of Passchendaele.

Private Saffery's hands were already clammy now where he clutched his rifle. He concentrated on thinking about his name – their name. Saffery, his father said, came from the Arabic for sword – at least the first part, 'saifer', did. That meant 'sword of' and 'rey' was Spanish for 'king'.

'So Saffery means "sword of the king",' explained his father, whose own army service had been in the dull and disappointing years of peace. 'Only in our case, we have queens.'

'Yes, Dad.'

Saffery *père* had served his time in the army uneventfully and then taken a pub in the country. He was still a disappointed man, having learned to his cost that Mine Host cannot afford to voice opinions of his own, still less express them with real feeling – not and keep the inn's customers, anyway. He could – and would – though, presently tell all and sundry about his son's sentry duty.

And be proud of it.

The accent had been on pride too, when their officer had addressed them that morning, but Kevin, who had been up since before dawn ready for a full inspection and had not in any case slept well, scarcely listened to him. The officer had been talking about the Battle of Talavera, in which the alertness and devotion to duty of a sentry had apparently saved the East Calleshire Regiment from either the enemy or the wrath of the Duke of Wellington – Kevin wasn't sure which – and in any case thought those geese whose alarm call had saved Rome would probably have done the job just as well at the time.

And, whatever the officer had in his mind, talk of a soldier's duty conjured up only one picture in Kevin's mind. It was of an ancient painting, a copy of which had hung in the miserable church hall where he'd been sent to Sunday School as a child. The picture had been of a dismayed Roman soldier at Pompeii, watching the remorseless advance of burning lava from Mount Vesuvius heading in his direction. The caption had stayed with Kevin longer than any text or regulation. He could see it now: 'Faithful unto death'.

His fingers were too slippery now to work properly should they need to, but that worry was succeeded by an even greater horror – he wanted to cough. A tickle somewhere at the back of his throat became a real threat to his stillness. He clamped his jaws shut and soon felt his eyes begin to bulge like a frog's. He would choke to death if he didn't open his mouth and cough soon . . .

It was then that he heard a whisper from the sentry on his right. Strictly forbidden, of course. The man would have been put on a charge if anyone had heard his warning.

'Watch it. Here they come . . .'

And Private Kevin Saffery of the 2nd Battalion, the East Calleshire Regiment, froze as still as Niobe herself as the day's first coachload of foreign tourists spilled out into Whitehall, directly in front of the entrance to Horseguards' Parade, cameras at the ready.

Touch Not the Cat

They said, of course, that she should have had a dog.
Not a great big dog that she couldn't handle at her time
of life, nor one which needed long walks night and
morning whatever the weather, which she obviously
couldn't have managed, and certainly not the size of
dog that ate a lot, things being what they were.

Or, at least, as they thought things were.

No, what the old lady could have done with, they
said – afterwards, of course – was a small dog that
barked. A barking dog, they thought, would have protected her in a way that a cat never could. They said
– afterwards, of course – that having a dog might have
saved her.

Well, someone modified this, at the very least it
might have raised the alarm. That would have been
something. Somebody, they said, might just have heard
a dog barking in her cottage and gone to see what the
trouble was. A small dog like a chihuahua, say, or a
little terrier. Everyone else's small dogs always seemed
to be barking when anyone came to the door. Why
hadn't she had one too, just to be on the safe side?
After all, Almstone was a pretty remote little village

and there weren't all that many people about there after dark these days.

They all knew the answer to why she hadn't had a dog, of course. Mrs Doughty had a cat.

But a dog would have helped.

And Mr Mackenzie next door, although both very deaf and very Scottish, might have heard a dog barking. In the event – the sad event – it had been Mr Mackenzie who had found her afterwards. On account of the milk bottles not having been taken in, that was, and very upset about it, he had been.

Old Mrs Doughty hadn't had a dog not only because she had a cat but also because she had always insisted that her cat would take care of her.

'Pusskins will look after me,' the old lady had said time and again, stroking the rather bad-tempered black and white moggie. 'Won't you, my lovely?'

Pusskins, who never miaowed except at mealtimes, would arch his back and allow her to rub behind his good ear. (The other had come to grief in a memorable encounter with a ginger tom in the alley on the other side of the cottage.)

It was a great-nephew, full of undesirable book learning, who had first said that Pusskins was the old lady's familiar. He'd always thought of his great-aunt as a witch anyway, probably because she didn't wash overmuch.

His mother, who hadn't quite understood his meaning, told him not to be so forward. At the time she had had high hopes of a bracket clock that had stood on the cottage mantelpiece (without going) for as long as she could remember. As she was to tell the other relations again and again, the clock had been promised . . .

Familiar or not, Pusskins was therefore eyed warily while Mrs Doughty's relations consoled themselves in the way that relations will – afterwards, of course – with saying things to each other such as, 'You didn't get to her age and go on living alone without having a mind of your own,' and, 'If she didn't want a dog on account of having that mangy old cat, then that was that, wasn't it?'

That had certainly been that in the old lady's cottage when the burglar had come and gone. That is, the police were fairly sure that he had come only as a burglar. What was unfortunately undeniable was that, though he might have come only as burglar, he had indubitably left as a murderer as well.

What was equally obvious was that the cat had not been able to protect his mistress after all. The police as well as the relations knew Pusskins had done his best, of course, because not only was there the old lady's blood everywhere in the little cottage but, most interestingly, the police said, there was also blood – human blood, that wasn't hers – on Pusskins's claws as well.

It was a young detective constable from Berebury called Crosby, who manifestly hadn't enjoyed the sight of an elderly bludgeoned head, who had first turned his wayward attention to the cat and noticed some blood there. He had even managed to get a sample of it before Pusskins – a preternaturally clean member of his species, in spite of his battered appearance – could lick it off his paws.

Which the cat had promptly tried to do.

'Be careful, Crosby,' Detective Inspector C. D. Sloan had adjured, seeing him with the cat. 'It might turn nasty.' It was he who, for his sins, was in charge of the murder inquiry.

'Yes, sir,' the young Constable had said, promising to take every precaution, while remarking inconsequentially that Captain Hook had killed himself by scratching behind his ear with the wrong hand.

'Nature red in tooth and claw,' was what the clever great-nephew had said when he heard about it.

His mother hadn't liked that remark either.

'And when you've finished with the animal welfare side,' the senior policeman had said to Detective Constable Crosby with some asperity, 'you can come and give me a hand over here while we establish a common entrance.'

Common entrance, Detective Constable Crosby had learned early on, was not only an entrance examination for children going to public schools but a safe route established by the police at a murder scene for all those professionals in homicide who have to approach the body, and, having their lawful business there, mustn't accidentally destroy important evidence in the process.

'And you'd better look sharp, Crosby,' said Detective Inspector Sloan. 'The photograph boys'll be here any minute now and Dr Dabbe doesn't hang about when he's at the wheel either.'

*

Dr Dabbe, the Consultant Pathologist to the Berebury Hospitals Trust, readily gave it as his considered opinion that the cause of Mrs Doughty's death was a fracture of the base of the skull brought about by the application of a blunt instrument from above and behind.

'A heavy blunt instrument,' he added after a closer examination of Mrs Doughty's head.

'Anything you can tell us about the person who used it, doctor?' asked Detective Inspector Sloan carefully. When he was a lad, the use of heavy blunt instruments as murder weapons had been thought to be an exclusively male province, but you could never tell these days.

'Anyone with the ability to lift a club hammer,' said the pathologist briefly.

Sloan just managed not to remark that that narrowed the field nicely and asked the doctor a few questions on haematology instead.

But, as Detective Inspector Sloan presently explained to the family, who, though they might have been a bit slow to visit while the old lady was alive, had assembled quickly enough when they heard that she was dead, what help was a cat's scratch on a man unless it happened to be on his face and needed explaining away?

The blood sample, the Inspector explained to them and to a slightly crestfallen Detective Constable Crosby, would become important only if they were able to catch the man from whom it had come – and that, he had to remind them, was not necessarily going to be easy. Blood there was, and that in plenty; other clues there were not. Someone had come and robbed and killed and gone, and that was all anyone in authority could tell them at this stage.

As well as the relatives, there had also been the next-door neighbour, Mr Mackenzie, to question, comfort, inform, pacify . . . and take a statement from. Detective Inspector Sloan was never entirely clear about the actual role of a police officer in these circumstances. He knew the theoretical one backwards. Members of the Criminal Investigation Department of every constabulary were there to investigate criminal occurrences, but, like a lot of life, it seldom worked out quite as simply as that. He'd long ago come to terms with the fact that a policeman had nearly as many parts to play in life as the seven ages of Shakespeare's man.

And some of them were not so easy.

What did you say to an apparently rational neighbour at a murder scene whose main concern was an archaic, not to say primitive, belief that it portended misfortune if a cat were permitted to leap over a corpse?

'I think, sir,' he said to Mr Mackenzie as kindly as he could, 'that these days that is just felt to be superstition. I can't see what further injury a cat could possibly do to a dead body already damaged almost beyond recognition.'

Sloan knew, of course, as well as everyone else, of the hundred and one uses of a dead cat, but that was something quite different.

Mr Mackenzie insisted that this fear was a real one and not just what he had the honesty to call a 'fret' on his part. 'Why, man, do ye no' realize that a watch was kept over a corp' in Scotland in the old days expressly to stop something like that happening?'

'No, sir.'

'Funny things, cats,' mused Mr Mackenzie. 'You never know what they're thinking.'

'Just so,' agreed Sloan, meticulously making another point, 'but we don't know for certain whether – er – the animal in question did actually jump over the late Mrs Doughty, do we, sir?'

All Sloan hoped was that this subject never ever came up in Superintendent Leeyes's presence. Ever since the Superintendent had attended an evening class on 'Physics for Everyman' he had been trying to explain something called 'Dead Cat Bounce' to the entire constabulary.

Without success.

Pusskins, his paws now decently clean, was present at this family and friends conference. In fact, he stared at Mr Mackenzie as balefully as Detective Inspector Sloan would have liked to have done, but the latter had his pension to think of.

It soon emerged that Pusskins might have his pension to think of too.

Therefore the cat was also present at the subsequent meeting at which his own immediate future was decided. There was a surprising amount of competition to give him a new home. This had more to do with having an eye to the future than any concern for animal rights – it not yet being known how the old lady might have provided for him. There was a very real fear in the family that Pusskins might be the residuary legatee . . .

Something else that was troubling to the – by now very – extended family was whether Mrs Doughty had had money or not. (The bracket clock had been stolen but no one knew exactly what else.) Nobody else really knew what she had had in the way of assets, except perhaps now the burglar. The family, though, to be on the safe side, was taking a distinctly Morton's Fork view of her finances – she must have had money because she hadn't spent it – and, at least until the will was read, Pusskins was safe, not to say to be pampered.

In the end the old lady's niece took Pusskins home with her, her claim – as a blood relation – over that of a nephew on Mrs Doughty's late husband's side of the family being considered superior. This delicate matter was clinched by the said nephew's wife having in the past always used an allergy to cats as an excuse for not visiting the cottage at Almstone.

Once in the niece's home, Pusskins retreated to a south-facing windowsill, where he devoted his days to lying in the sun and attending to his personal hygiene in full view of the neighbours, which the old lady's niece didn't think was very nice.

The cat alternated his pose effortlessly between couchant and rampant as the fancy took him and, to the niece's despair, ate this but not that – and then that but not this. Moral ascendancy over the niece having thus been achieved, he just waited.

And waited.

He waited for exactly seventeen days.

Even when Detective Inspector Sloan and Detective

Constable Crosby – and a veterinary surgeon – came to the niece's house, Pusskins only evinced a rather languid interest in their tale of a man with some rather nasty scratches on his arms and legs who had had to consult his doctor because he had an indolent ulcer on his right leg and some very enlarged and suppurating lymph nodes.

'The doctor,' reported the police inspector with a pardonable touch of drama, it being something of a professional coup, 'diagnosed that the man was suffering from *Pasturella multicida*.'

The niece exclaimed, 'Lord, bless us, and whatever is that when it's at home?' having not yet caught up with the precise dangers of salmonella poisoning as presented by the popular press and vaguely associating the two.

'Moreover,' added Crosby, the detective constable accompanying Detective Inspector Sloan, who was determined to have his say too, 'the man had the same blood profile as the blood which the cat had on its claws.'

Even then Pusskins didn't stir. But when he heard the veterinary surgeon explain that a diagnosis of *Pasturella multicida* in the man meant that the old lady's murderer must have caught 'cat-scratch fever' from this particular member of the family *felix domesticus*, Pusskins twitched his whiskers in a very satisfied way indeed.

Exit Strategy

'There's nothing wrong with her heart,' said the doctor, folding his stethoscope and stuffing it back into his black bag. 'Sound as a bell.'

'Only her mind,' said Mrs Barker's daughter tightly.

'That means she could go on like this for a long time,' the doctor said. He paused. 'A very long time, I'm afraid.'

'I'm not so sure that I can,' said Mrs Barker's daughter, near to tears.

The doctor shot her a quick professional glance, taking in her slight tremor and quavering voice, as well as the imminence of a loss of self-control she might not welcome.

'I wouldn't mind so much, doctor,' she said with deep feeling, 'if it was her heart that was bad and her mind was all right.'

'The elderly mentally infirm are very difficult to deal with,' he said to her as he had said to so many adult sons and daughters in this painful situation in his time in general practice. 'There's no getting away from it. Very difficult indeed.'

'You don't need to tell me that,' she said, adding on a rising note of despair, 'Mother doesn't even know

251

who I am any more. She doesn't recognize me, her own daughter!'

'It's not at all uncommon.' He nodded, and waved to Mrs Barker's medical record on the table. 'We agreed, didn't we, that she's been suffering from senile dementia for quite a while.' In the doctor's book this was preferable to hiding the patient away from society, concealing incontinence and pretending to the neighbours that there was nothing wrong, but not everyone, he knew, would agree with this. 'What is sadder,' he went on, 'is that your mother doesn't know who she is either.'

'And I shall be going the same way quite soon, I'm sure.' She managed a little laugh. 'The other day I caught myself putting the cat's dry food in my own cereal bowl. I'd even poured milk over it before I realized what I'd done.'

He smiled. 'Happens easily enough. We all do that sort of thing.' He was a busy man and went straight back to the point of the consultation. 'I'm only sorry that I can't promise you an early place in the right sort of nursing home for her. There are very long waiting lists for the good ones and – ' he hesitated – 'they are rather expensive.' Mrs Barker, he knew, had sold her bungalow when she came to live with her daughter, and so there would then be nursing home fees to be clawed back from her assets to pay for her long-term care. But her exhausted daughter was his patient too and so he asked, 'Is there any chance of your sharing the care or are you the only one?'

'I've got a sister over Calleford way,' said Mrs

Barker's daughter slowly. 'I might ask her if she'd do her stint for a while to give me a bit of a rest.'

'A little respite care can be a great help,' said the doctor, going on his way. 'Try her.'

Mrs Barker's daughter didn't allow herself the merest smirk of self-congratulation after she'd shown the doctor out of the house. Instead, she picked up the telephone and dialled her son in Luston. 'No problem, Martin,' she said. 'I think the doctor imagines I might be going to lose my Elgins soon too.'

'Good. Now when?'

'I thought you said Sunday morning's the busiest time over there.'

'I did. That'll do fine.'

'I've got her a costume.'

'No labels?'

'I'm not the one who's demented,' said his mother sharply.

'Only teasing,' chuckled the voice at the other end of the line. 'There's no inscription inside her wedding ring, is there, by any chance? You know, her and grandad's name or anything like that?'

'I got the nurse to take it off her finger months ago,' said his mother, 'because of granny's arthritis.'

'Ah, I thought you might have done,' said Martin drily. 'What about her dentures?'

'I thought we'd leave those behind here just in case,' said Mrs Barker's daughter. 'You never know . . .'

'What about her teeth? Dentists are very good at keeping records these days.'

'She hadn't been near one in years – besides, she's only got a couple left now.'

'That's good,' said the voice at the other end. 'And no distinguishing scars, you said?'

'None,' said Mrs Barker's daughter, adding almost absently, 'In her way she's always been very healthy.'

'Good,' said the voice in matter-of-fact tones. 'I think that's everything, then.'

'I'll put the costume on under her ordinary clothes before we leave the house and I'll meet you in the car park there. When do you suggest?'

'Half past ten,' said her son briskly. 'Don't be late.'

'I won't,' promised Mrs Barker's daughter, putting down the telephone and heading to the kitchen to make some lunch. Nobody was going to be able to say that Mrs Barker wasn't well nourished or hadn't been properly looked after. She had. That was part of the trouble.

If old Mrs Barker thought there was anything out of the ordinary in being dressed in a swimming costume before putting on her outdoor clothes she did not say so. Indeed, she did no more than give her customary grunt and start to dribble. She trotted out to the car happily enough though – she liked being driven around. She even got out of the car when it stopped – which was something that did not always happen without a struggle.

Her daughter wiped Mrs Barker's face clean and took her by the arm. Her grandson sauntered across the swimming pool's car park and joined them. With the old lady between them, daughter and grandson strolled casually up to the entrance.

'You get the tickets, dear,' called out Mrs Barker's daughter cheerfully, 'and we'll see you in the water.'

'Righteo,' said Martin, approaching the booth, cash in hand.

He collected three tickets and handed two of them over to his mother. Much to her annoyance, the changing area at the swimming pool had recently become unisex. She had vociferously disapproved of this at the time but now she was grateful. It gave Martin a chance to be at his grandmother's other side, after she had been undressed, as they assisted her towards the swimming bath.

Martin had been right. On a Sunday morning the pool was indeed crowded. They helped Mrs Barker down the little flight of steps at the shallow end and stood with her there for a while. Then Martin swam away, while Mrs Barker's daughter gently folded her mother's stiff fingers round the safety bar. 'Stay there, Mother,' she said, 'and hold on until I come back. I'm just going for a swim.'

There was no change in Mrs Barker's customary expression of total bewilderment. It didn't noticeably alter when time went by; nor when one of the attendants came up to her to ask her if she was all right – or how long she had been there – or who she was – or where she lived – and, most importantly, who it was who had brought her there.

There was only one thing that was really certain

and that was that by nightfall Social Services had got her safely installed in a specialist care home in a strange town.

There, as a temporary measure, they named her Mary Celeste, because, as the care worker on duty that day said, 'She had been found adrift in the water and no one knew why.'

But they guessed.

The Wild Card

'Not another?'

'Two more actually, sir.'

'How many is that altogether now?'

'Six, sir.' Detective Inspector C. D. Sloan enjoyed practising what has come to be known as 'the discipline of curiosity' in its own right, but looking into this particular matter had been work: police work.

Superintendent Leeyes grunted. 'Doesn't make sense, Sloan, does it?'

'No, sir.'

'Who was it this time?'

'Gerald Ardingly . . .'

'Not the Chairman of our sainted bus outfit?' snorted the Superintendent.

'Him,' agreed Detective Inspector Sloan inelegantly.

'Can't be too sorry for either him or his Calleshire buses. Must be making a mint. And who else?'

'The editor of the *Luston News.*'

'Not he who will use his columns campaigning for a better police presence in the city?' said Leeyes sardonically.

'There's a mention of how ineffective we are most

weeks,' agreed Sloan uneasily, 'although I must say I didn't notice anything this week.'

'If I remember rightly,' said the Superintendent, 'he's always writing that we're wasting too much time these days on rural policing.'

'Crime does seem to have shifted out to the country and away from the city lately,' ventured Sloan tentatively. It was ironic that fictional crime seemed to have moved in the opposite direction at the same time. Country house robberies were for real these days.

'He will go on about what we haven't done rather than what we have,' persisted Leeyes.

Detective Inspector Sloan decided against saying anything about good news not selling newspapers.

'Who else?' asked Leeyes, coming back to the notes on his desk.

'Nigel Halesworth,' said Sloan.

'Huh.' Leeyes's snort was even more pronounced this time. 'He's the top bean counter over at United Mellemetics, isn't he?'

'Finance director,' said Sloan.

'Same thing,' said Leeyes robustly. 'He's a skinflint anyway. I heard that he wouldn't give the Mayoress anything at all for the charity of her choice for her year in office.'

'The children's hospice,' supplied Sloan, who had already made his own contribution. 'They need all the money that they can get.'

'He said, if I was told rightly,' growled Leeyes, 'that he didn't approve of handouts to help the health service.'

'Credit card stolen last week,' carried on Sloan stolidly, 'and the card company duly notified of the loss by Nigel Halesworth. Couldn't do it quickly enough actually. Tried to blame the police for not preventing the theft, let alone for not catching whoever took it, even though he'd been the one who'd been careless. Left it in his jacket pocket somewhere.'

'Wanted to know what he paid his taxes for, I dare say, as usual,' said the Superintendent placidly.

'Yes, sir.'

'Then?'

'Then the same evening his card was pushed back through the Halesworths' letter box.'

'Just like with all the others?'

'Yes, sir.' He cleared his throat. 'Wiped clean of fingerprints, of course.'

'It's not the wiping that matters,' barked Leeyes on the instant, 'it's the swiping that counts, let alone the skimming.'

Sloan frowned. 'There's no evidence of these cards being used to make counterfeits, sir. There's been only one withdrawal on each of them. And,' he added, 'you don't even need to have the card swiped these days, sir.'

'If you ask me, Sloan, there's far, far too much of that done over the telephone now – and without any checks.'

'And just as with all the others taken so far,' carried on Sloan, 'the credit card companies will confirm only that a large single withdrawal had been made just before the loss was notified and the account stopped.'

Superintendent Leeyes sat back in his chair and

stroked his chin in deep thought. 'We could be looking at a rather sophisticated form of blackmail, Sloan.'

'We could indeed, sir,' agreed Sloan warmly. 'No written demands, no muddled assignations, no handing over of actual cash – just a credit card stolen and returned to the owner's house almost immediately the unauthorized transaction has been made.'

'I don't like it,' said Leeyes.

'Just the one snag actually . . .'

'An audit trail,' said the Superintendent, simply.

'In theory the credit card company should be able to tell us where the payment has gone,' said Sloan, pausing.

'They should indeed,' Leeyes grunted. 'Save us a lot of bother.'

'And would be able to,' pointed out Detective Inspector Sloan, 'but they say they'll do it only if the customer queries the charge to the account and gives them their permission. They won't play ball otherwise. Not without a court order.'

Leeyes muttered something distinctly subversive about the Human Rights Act and its pernicious effect on the proper pursuit of enquiries by a beleaguered and overworked police force.

'And,' hurried on Sloan, 'I don't see us getting access to any of their accounts if the customers don't complain.'

'And you say the card holders won't do that?' said Leeyes. 'You're quite sure about that, Sloan, are you?'

'Not a single one of them,' insisted Sloan. 'Half a dozen of the richest businessmen in the town who have had a charge made on their account by the unauthorized use of their credit cards won't say a dicky bird about it . . . That's as far as we've got.'

'Large amounts,' declared Leeyes in a worldly-wise manner. 'Must be. We wouldn't have heard anything about it at all if it had been peanuts.'

'It seems,' said Sloan, 'that they all just say that nothing has been wrongly charged to them and pay up as if everything was hunky-dory and nothing out of the ordinary had happened.'

'Smells worse than dead fish,' pronounced the Superintendent.

'Even the chairman of the Chamber of Trade won't say a word,' said Sloan, 'and he's usually the first to make a fuss about anything.' He sniffed. 'Only, we are always given to understand, on behalf of one of his members, of course.'

'As usual.'

'Whenever he complains, he always insists it's never him personally.'

'Pompous ass,' said Leeyes succinctly.

'The head honcho at Calleshire Systems wouldn't even speak to us after his card came back. Made a terrific fuss to begin with when it was first stolen and then afterwards got his public relations lady to sweet-talk us into thinking that nothing noteworthy had happened and that everything in the garden was lovely.'

'Sounds like blackmail to me,' said Leeyes again. 'And now this business with the Dipper has come up.'

'Our Charlie, the town's lightest-fingered crook,' agreed Sloan.

'Now dead,' said the Superintendent without any noticeable regret.

'Totalled his car and himself on the Luston road last night,' said Sloan. 'Going faster than he should, of course, and then he hit a spot of black ice by the bridge and went into the river.'

'It's a tight corner at the best of times,' said the Superintendent.

'No one could've called last night the best of times on the road,' said Sloan. 'Car and Dipper both written off before any of the rescue services got there. Straightforward accident – Traffic Division are quite sure about that.'

'And after the Lord Mayor's Show, the dustcart,' observed the Superintendent.

'Beg pardon, sir . . . Oh, I see what you mean.' Sloan's face cleared. 'The Coroner's officer.'

'Constable Stuart,' agreed Leeyes. 'Go on.'

'He reported that a credit card was found on the Dipper's body that isn't – wasn't – the Dipper's,' said Sloan.

'Ah . . .' said Leeyes.

'It belongs to the chairman of the Luston Football Club.' He consulted his notebook. 'As well as finding the chairman's credit card,' he went on, 'Constable Stuart also reported that there was a note with it with the chairman's name and address on it and the exact time that the card had to be put through the owner's letter box last night.'

'Whose handwriting?' pounced Leeyes.

'The Dipper's,' replied Sloan regretfully. 'He must have been on his way over to Luston to deliver it when he hit the ice. The timing was quite tight – he'd have had to step on it.' He paused. 'Probably did, which would account for the skid.'

'We might get a "calls made" telephone printout,' said Leeyes who had lost interest in the Dipper's accident and was concentrating on the job in hand.

'But not calls received,' said Sloan pertinently. 'I think we would find that all the relevant calls were made to the Dipper and none by him.'

'Which means he might not have known who made them,' concluded Leeyes.

'I think that we'll find that will be the case,' said Sloan prosaically.

'That is,' growled Leeyes, 'when we find whoever made them.'

'If we ever do,' temporized Sloan. 'The Dipper might've been the best pickpocket in the business . . .'

'No doubt about that,' grunted Leeyes. 'Should have been on the stage.'

'But, although he certainly wasn't the brightest of the bright, even he wouldn't have been daft enough to ask questions when it was better not to do so.'

'It's all this new business of the "need-to-know" basis catching on,' grimaced the Superintendent, who resented being denied any information at all by anyone at any level at any time. 'It's all the fashion these days, more's the pity.'

'And the Dipper always knew what constituted evidence and what didn't,' sighed Sloan. 'I will say that for him.'

Superintendent Leeyes said something unflattering under his breath about wishing that the same could always be said of the Crown Prosecution Service.

'Quite so, sir,' he murmured. This, diplomatically, Sloan affected not to have heard. 'Petty crook the Dipper might have been, but he was no amateur at keeping out of real trouble.'

'And someone else knew that too,' said Leeyes.

'Oh, yes,' said Sloan at once. 'The Dipper'll have been hand-picked, you can be sure of that.'

'And paid in cash presumably.'

'Funny you should say that, sir . . .'

'Well?'

'PC Stuart's had a bit of a shufti round the Dipper's place, looking for relatives and so forth . . .'

'Loads of cash?'

'No, sir. Come to that, hardly any. All he found that could be called at all out of the ordinary was a cutting from this week's local paper . . .' He paused.

'Get on with it, man,' barked Leeyes.

'It was a published list of the latest donors to the Mayoress's appeal on behalf of the children's hospice.'

'Well, I never.' A beatific smile overtook Superintendent Leeyes's usually scowling features. 'And would, by any chance, any of the people on this list of ours here feature on it?'

'Prominently,' said Detective Inspector Sloan. 'All except the last one.'

'Which, I take it, will be on next week's list?'

'I shouldn't be at all surprised, sir.'

'Neither would I, Sloan.' He slapped the file on his desk shut and handed it back to the detective inspector. 'Neither would I.'

Coup de Grâce

'That you, Wendy? Henry here.' Henry Tyler, civil servant *extraordinaire*, was sitting at his desk in the Foreign Office in London. He was presently on the telephone to his sister in the little market town of Berebury. 'I thought you ought to know that I'm going to be coming down to Calleshire next weekend.'

'Darling, how lovely!'

'No, no . . .'

'But the children will be so pleased to see their favourite uncle again.'

'It's not quite like that . . .' He rattled the telephone cradle up and down. 'Operator! Operator! Don't cut us off, please . . . We haven't finished yet.'

'Henry,' he heard his sister say amidst crackles, 'this is a terrible line and I can't hear you properly. I said when may we expect you?'

'It's not quite like that, Wen,' he repeated hesitantly. 'I'm afraid I shan't be staying with you this time.'

'Work?'

'Only in a manner of speaking.'

Henry was staring out of his office window while he spoke to his sister. A busy London street scene was visible below, but he wasn't looking at the cabbies or the men and women hurrying along the pavements beneath him. It was the screaming headlines on the vendors' boards which had caught his attention. He could read the words 'Von Ribbentrop' and 'Herr Hitler' quite clearly even at a distance. One newspaper seller had obviously abandoned an attempt to fit in the name 'Chamberlain' as being too long a word for his newsstand.

Wendy Witherington said, 'I know I shouldn't ask . . .'

'I'm bidden to stay at Calle Castle for the weekend,' volunteered her brother. This statement could be fairly described as the truth but not by any means the whole truth.

'At the Duke of Calleshire's?' exclaimed his sister. 'How lovely for you, darling.'

'There's a hunt ball on the Saturday . . .'

He forbore to explain that he was going to Calle Castle because there would be others there who had also been invited on whom his political masters in Whitehall wished an eye kept. A wary eye. And those particular others were going to be there – and not perhaps, for instance, at Cliveden that weekend instead – because an invitation to Calle Castle from Her Grace, the Duchess of Calleshire, to stay there for the hunt ball was one that very few people would refuse. Actually, he mused, as he drew little pictures on his blotting paper, these particular others wouldn't have wanted to refuse the invitation anyway. Like himself, they would all have their own reasons for being at the castle, with European matters in the highly fragile state they were just now.

'Everybody'll be there, I suppose,' said his sister a little wistfully.

This, he knew, did not include Wendy and her husband, Tom Witherington, but did embrace everyone who was anyone in the mainly rural county of Calleshire and quite a number of luminaries from the outside world. The *haut-monde* as well as fashion and politics would be well represented there for sure and, more importantly, so would international affairs – which is where Henry Tyler's duties came in.

'Oh, how exciting for you,' continued Wendy.

'I very much hope not,' returned Henry Tyler vigorously, although he knew very well that some of the people who would be at Calle Castle at the weekend were not without a taste for danger and might not be too averse to a little action, as well – strictly in the interests of national security, of course. 'In my experience, my dear sister, a man can have a little too much excitement for his own good.'

'I'm sorry, darling,' said Wendy Witherington immediately. Apologetic she might be; deceived she was not. She was well aware that some of her brother's assignments on behalf of his employers had verged on the bizarre. 'I shouldn't have asked, I know, but do be extra careful, won't you?' She gave a sigh. 'Do you suppose it will be as splendid an occasion as the Duchess of Richmond's great ball before Waterloo?'

'I'll tell you whether it was next week,' Henry said lightly. The parallels were a mite too close for his liking – another war in Europe was undeniably in the offing, although with different enemies and different allies from those at Waterloo – but he did not say so. Wendy and her Tom would find that out for themselves soon enough. And be thankful that their son – his nephew – was too young for the coming conflict.

Wendy hesitated and then said, 'Of course you don't want anything to go wrong naturally, but if . . .'

'And neither does anyone else,' he finished firmly before she could say anything more, adding under his breath, 'especially my Minister.'

Henry's Minister was a man with so much on his mind at this defining moment in world history that he didn't need anything else to worry about. Which is where Henry Tyler and his watching brief came in.

'It won't go wrong if you've got anything to do with it,' Wendy said loyally, 'but I would like to know what the ball dresses are like, Henry. Especially if light green is still in – such a very flattering colour, I always think.'

'I'll make a note,' he promised gravely.

Not a hunting man himself – of foxes, that is – it was white tie and tails for him at Calle Castle, rather than hunting pink, when he ascended the magnificent staircase there on the night of the hunt ball.

He was received by the Duchess, resplendent in the famous Calleshire diamonds. 'I'm very glad you could come, Mr Tyler,' she murmured so graciously that Henry was quite left in the dark as to whether she knew there was a purpose to his visit. 'How nice to see you back in Calleshire,' she added, before handing him over to her husband at her side.

The Duke had probably guessed that he was here on duty.

'Good to see you, m'boy,' he boomed. 'Do you know the Ambassador here? Ambassador, this is Henry Tyler – an old friend. Henry, let me introduce His Excellency the Polish Ambassador to the sheikhdom of Lasserta . . .'

Henry bowed, concealing his inward amusement at the way in which the Duke – like everyone else – had ducked out of pronouncing the Ambassador's name. Fortunately an extensive training at the Foreign Office had encompassed practice with saying Polish titles out loud.

'Count Zeczenbroski,' said Henry, bowing again slightly whilst resisting the temptation to click his heels together as well. 'I don't know how long you've been in post there but I'm sure you'll know our man in Lasserta.'

'Indeed,' said the Count, shaking hands warmly. 'Your Mr Heber-Hibbs and I are old friends. In fact, his boy Anthony plays with my own son. A good man.'

'Who lies abroad for the good of his country,' Henry completed the definition of an Ambassador with practised ease. The sheikhdom of Lasserta was in theory not really big enough in size or history to merit an ambassador-in-residence from either Great Britain or Poland, or, for that matter, few of the other European countries who saw fit to be represented there at that diplomatic level. However, since the sheikhdom was sitting on the only known supply of queremitte ore on the planet outside the Soviet Union, they were all there all the same.

In strength.

This was understandable, since queremitte was an element of great value in the armaments world. It was thus much sought after by those nations who were arming – or rearming – as fast as they possibly could. Countries who had already put 'guns before butter', so to speak, had almost exhausted their stocks, while those nations that had only just come under starter's orders in the arms race were even more anxious to secure supplies of one of the hardest-wearing of all known metals to aid them in their hasty manufacture of new weapons.

'And you left the Sheikh well, I trust?' Henry enquired. Of one thing he could be quite sure and that was that the young son of Sheikh Ben Mugnal Mirza Ibrahim Hajal Kisra would not be mixing with the sons of any of the ambassadors at his court. The Sheikh played his cards far too close to his chest to risk anything being given away by childish babble. And there was also the very real fear of the kidnap and ransom of his heir.

'In great form, I assure you,' said the Count. He smiled politely as an overweight man with a red face overtook them on their way into the castle's ballroom.

'The Lord Lieutenant,' murmured Henry. 'A great man in the saddle in his day, I understand.'

The Count, whose own sport was duck-shooting on the Pripet Marshes, acknowledged this fact with a cursory nod before passing on to Henry some information of his own. 'I understand,' he said in a voice rather below that used in normal conversation, 'that your man in Lasserta has been beaten at the post by a very unfriendly power.'

Henry bent his head towards Count Zeczenbroski. 'Indeed?' he said, not showing by even the flicker of an eyelid that this fact was not only not news to him but the very reason for his own presence at the castle tonight.

'It is said that that young man over there – ' here the Count indicated a handsome blond man who was squiring a tall, elegant girl in a dress of deep electric blue – 'has obtained a verbal agreement to the assigning of the queremitte mining rights to his government.'

'He is their Military Attaché,' observed Henry mildly, 'so perhaps we shouldn't be too surprised.' The blond young man was one of the reasons that Henry was at the hunt ball, but he did not say so. Yet another reason was the well-built girl with whom the man was now starting to dance. She had a vaguely foreign look and a slightly old-fashioned evening bag on her arm. They were a well-matched pair – she was nearly as tall as the Military Attaché and was dancing with notable verve. 'Besides, what does a verbal agreement amount to in these modern times?'

'If it's from the Sheikh, everything,' the Polish Ambassador replied. 'It is said that the word of the Sheikh is his bond.'

'Tell me then, Count, how did that young man manage to persuade the Sheikh to part with his precious ore verbally?'

The Count raised his shoulders ever so slightly and opened his hands in an age-old gesture. 'My dear Mr

Tyler, who knows? There was some talk, I understand, of – what shall I call it? – leverage . . .'

'Really?' said Henry Tyler, feigning a well-bred astonishment. A man did not have to be a linguist to translate that word into the uglier one of 'blackmail'.

The Ambassador leaned forward and spoke in confidential tones. 'Something to do with a secret distillery having been found in the hills to the north was what I had heard,' volunteered Count Zeczenbroski after he had made sure no one was within earshot.

'A distillery,' concurred Henry Tyler, nodding sagely, 'would not have gone down very well in Gatt-el-Abbas.' In the capital of Lasserta, consumption of alcohol in any shape or form was deemed a flogging matter. If the Sheikh was known to have been guilty of this, then his throne would have been in very real danger.

The Count became even more confidential. 'I gather the Sheikh got quite fond of the stuff while a pupil at Sandhurst.'

'And that particular Military Attaché knew about it?' said Henry, looking across at the blond young man.

Had the Count had a fine waxed moustache he would undoubtedly have twirled the ends of it when he asked, 'About the fondness or the distillery?'

'Either, my dear Count,' said Henry smoothly, 'or both.'

There had been no need at all for him to pose the question since Henry already knew all about the Sheikh's weakness for a dram of whisky from His Britannic Majesty's Ambassador to the sheikhdom, Mr Godfrey Heber-Hibbs. His note to the Foreign Office had explained that there had been a batch of wild, hard-drinking Scots in the Sheikh's cohort during his terms at Sandhurst who had led him astray in the matter of that golden liquid which was so strictly forbidden in Lasserta. The distillery which had been 'discovered' many miles to the north of the Sheikh's palace at Bakhalla had, Henry also knew, been planted there by the aforementioned Military Attaché on behalf of his political masters. A promise to keep it secret in return for sole access to the queremitte would have been easy enough to extract from a Sheikh occupying a distinctly uncertain throne. Unlike the redoubtable Lion of Judah, Ben Mugnal Mirza Ibrahim Hajal Kisra did not, by any means, have all of his people behind him. And some of those who were behind him were there only for the purpose of trying to stab him in the back . . .

'I gather,' said the Polish Ambassador cautiously, 'that his having been led astray in the respect of alcohol at your military academy was not unknown among a certain group of his contemporaries.'

'Ah . . .' said Henry expressively.

What neither the Polish Ambassador nor, he hoped, anyone else knew was that the fake distillery in the desert had disappeared as secretly as it had arrived – thanks to the nifty overnight spadework of some active 'gardeners' temporarily on Mr Heber-Hibbs's staff in Lasserta. The odd mentions of the word 'mirages' in such local papers as there were had been dropped casually by the Ambassador's press attaché.

Henry looked up. 'You must excuse me now, Count. I see an old friend in need of a partner . . .'

Henry crossed the ballroom and soon was taking to the floor with the wife of the High Sheriff.

'George was never a dancer,' complained George's wife, Judy, allowing herself to be swept to her feet, 'and now he won't even try.'

'One of the delights of growing older,' said Henry diplomatically, 'is that one doesn't have to do what one doesn't like doing any longer.'

Judy, Henry knew, did like dancing and in a moment they were stepping it featly round the ballroom. This enabled Henry to keep an eye on the blond young man and his tall, elegant partner, who were doing much the same but considerably closer together.

This pattern was repeated after supper in the castle's famous dining room, a long saloon dedicated to trophies of the chase. To the outside observer, it seemed that a chase of an altogether different – but as old a – kind was going on between the Military Attaché and his lady companion. Their dancing was becoming wilder and wilder, and more and more intimate. The girl appeared almost abandoned in her gyrations, while the young man would seem to have too much drink taken.

After yet another turn of the ballroom, Henry saw him pulling the girl towards a door that Henry knew gave eventually on to a flight of stairs and thence to the upper storeys of the castle.

The girl appeared to stumble and then regained her balance. She let the man take her hand and they went off together through the door.

'What it is to be young!' said Judy, watching them go.

'I dare say they're going in search of a little night air,' murmured Henry. 'It's pretty warm in here.'

'It reminds me of the evening that George and I—'

'Judy, my dear,' he interrupted the Lord Lieutenant's wife suavely, steering her off the dance floor, 'I simply must return you to George now or he'll be after me for alienation of affection . . .'

This done, Henry began to make his way out of the ballroom himself.

Before he could do so, the girl from the dancing pair came rushing into the room in great distress, her electric blue dress all dishevelled. 'Monsieurs, help! Help!' she cried. 'Hans, he 'as gone and jumped out of the landing window . . .'

Henry strode towards the door.

'No, no, m'sieur,' she called out urgently, barring his way. 'Not up there. Down 'ere. He is lying outside on the ground.' She gave a great cry. 'He asked me to marry him, you see.'

'And?' barked the High Sheriff, who might not have been a dancer but was still quick on his feet. He had reached the girl nearly as quickly as Henry.

'And when I said I wouldn't, he opened the vindow and jumped out.' She gulped. 'It's all my fault. He always said 'e would kill himself if I wouldn't marry 'im.'

'He did, did he?' said the High Sheriff.

'But, moi, I didn't believe him.' She started to sob. 'He's dead! I know he's dead – it is such a long way down to the ground in this place.'

'This way,' said the Duke of Calleshire, making for

a different door, while Henry edged ahead of the Lord Lieutenant.

The girl continued her loud keening. 'Poor Hans, oh, poor Hans, but, m'sieur – ' this to the Lord Lieutenant, now an unhealthy shade of purple, and clearly wanting to follow the Duke – 'I can tell you, 'e was not ready for marriage. No, not yet, but 'e was much too young to die.'

Henry shot after the Duke, a man who presumably knew the quickest way to ground level. Spread-eagled on the drive before them lay the body of the blond young man. Even at a distance Henry could tell that the fellow was dead – it wasn't only vultures who could recognize absence of life from afar.

So could experienced men.

And women.

Henry reached the body and then turned and looked back at the castle.

There was something wrong, but he couldn't think for the moment what it was. He stood, taking in the scene as quickly as he could and concentrating furiously. Then it came to him.

He slipped quickly away from the men standing over the body of the blond young man and hastened back into the castle. As he shot up the stairs to the ballroom, he met the Lord Lieutenant, quite choleric now, hurrying down. 'I'm ringing for a doctor,' Henry said, dashing past the man.

He didn't do any such thing, but instead rushed up to the first-floor landing. There were three windows there, all closed, but only one unfastened. He flung it open just as the High Sheriff, nobody's fool, looked up. Henry waved at him. After the High Sheriff had turned his attention back to the body, Henry ran his finger along the underside of the sash window to make sure there was no blood there – the girl, well trained in unarmed combat as she had been, might, after all, have had to bring it down on the man's fingers before he would let go. What she had forgotten to do was open it again after she had pushed him out.

'And was it all very splendid?' asked his sister, Wendy, later when he did visit her. 'Apart from that poor young man's suicide, of course. Though I do understand if he was really in love ... He wasn't English, was he?'

'No.'

'Ah, that explains it,' she said, adding rather complacently, 'Tom was beside himself until I said I'd marry him.'

'I remember.' He smiled.

'But what about the girl?' Wendy recollected herself. 'She was foreign too, wasn't she?'

'So it was said,' agreed Henry. 'She left the country before the inquest – though she'd given the police a statement, of course.'

'And you?' asked his sister anxiously. 'How did you get on?'

'Oh, I just had a watching brief, that's all. You might say that I did a bit of light dusting – a woman's work is never done, is it? By the way, Wendy.'

'Yes?'

'Light green is out this year.'

'Oh . . .' Her face fell. 'So what colour is in, then?'

'Electric blue. I noticed specially . . .'

Dummy Run

'I'm sorry to trouble you, Inspector Sloan.' The voice of the Station Sergeant on the internal telephone at the police station at Berebury interrupted the Detective Inspector while he was working in his office. 'But I'm afraid we've got a bit of a problem down here in the custody suite.'

'Who with?' enquired Sloan immediately, since it was unlikely that any problem arising in what he still thought of as the charge room would be of a vegetable or mineral nature, and cars came under Traffic Division anyway. At any police station the most probable problem would be animal – human animal, that is.

'An old sparring partner of yours and mine,' replied the Sergeant.

Sloan sighed. He had been attempting to tackle some paperwork that was too sensitive to be put on any computer – which was saying something about the security of computers – and too important to be left to Detective Constable Crosby. This said quite a lot about the skills of that junior officer, who was at this very moment waiting outside his door while Sloan thought of a job for him to do that was within his slender capabilities. The paperwork was long overdue in its rightful place in his locked filing cabinet which didn't help.

'All right,' he said to the Station Sergeant. 'Tell me . . .'

'Larky Nolson.'

'Oh, not him again!' Sloan exclaimed in pure exasperation. Not for nothing was Larky Nolson known throughout 'F' Division of the county of Calleshire constabulary as the Prince of Recidivists.

'None other.' The Station Sergeant coughed. 'He's asking for you particularly, sir. He says he won't deal with anyone else.' He paused and added significantly. 'Not even the ACC.'

'Where does the ACC come in?' asked Sloan warily. The Assistant Chief Constable was of the old school, not so much out of this world as a cut above it. The likes of Larky Nolson were usually kept at a respectable distance from police officers as senior as the Assistant Chief Constable.

'He just happened to be passing through our entrance and heard all the fuss,' the Station Sergeant said. 'He couldn't help hearing it, of course. We all know that Larky can be noisy if he thinks he isn't getting his rights. And naturally once Larky caught sight of the ACC, he had to have his say, didn't he?'

'Who? Larky?'

'No, the ACC.'

Detective Inspector Sloan sighed again. 'And what did the ACC say?'

'As far as I can remember, sir,' the Station Sergeant said, 'it sounded like *deprendi miserum est.*'

'Latin,' divined Sloan. The ACC was long on old and

outmoded languages; equally, he was a little short on experience of the beat.

'That's right, sir. I thought at first he was calling Larky a miserable so and so. Which he is, of course.'

'But he wasn't?'

'No, sir. The ACC said it meant "getting caught is no fun at all".'

'And what' enquired Detective Inspector Sloan with interest, 'did our Larky have to say to that?'

The Station Sergeant coughed. 'I didn't quite catch it sufficiently clearly to put it in the report book, sir.'

'I see.' The Station Sergeant was long on common sense. That went with the territory.

'But the gist of it was that Larky wanted you to come down to see him yourself, sir, and not to be fobbed off with some toffee-nosed cleverclogs . . . or words to that effect.'

'He's making a big mistake,' said Sloan vigorously, 'if he thinks that sort of flattery will get him anywhere.'

'I've already told him that,' said the Station Sergeant stolidly.

'And what did he say?'

'I thought it better that time not to have heard his comments at all, sir,' the Sergeant replied, demonstrating that at least one policeman had good judgement too.

'Demanding his rights as usual, I suppose,' grumbled Sloan. 'With knobs on.'

'Demanding his rights, yes,' responded the Station Sergeant, 'but as usual, no.'

'Well, lock him up and tell the custody officer that I'll be down presently.' He would see Detective

Constable Crosby first. The lad would still be waiting outside the office for his marching orders for the day.

'I don't think I can do that, sir,' said the voice at the other end of the line, adding regretfully, 'not with the law as it stands.'

'Why not? What's the charge?'

'The charge that Larky has come in about,' said the Station Sergeant, picking his words with unusual care, 'is one of common assault . . .'

'Well, I grant you it's not in his line,' conceded Sloan promptly. 'I've never known him violent when he's been on a job, although as I remember he has been known to have a nasty attack of "dock asthma" when the prosecution starts to get to him.'

'Larky isn't being charged,' said the Station Sergeant gently.

'So what's all this about, then?' demanded the Detective Inspector irritably.

'It's him that's bringing the charge.'

'Larky?' exclaimed Sloan. 'Are you sure?'

Larky Nolson's very considerable criminal reputation rested on his success in keeping a low profile when on the job. His hallmarks were a capacity to remain totally unmemorable and the ability to keep his every illegal action as unobtrusive as possible. In the event, few of his victims even noticed him, still less suspected him of criminal propensities.

'Dead sure, sir,' said the Station Sergeant. 'He alleges that he was attacked without provocation at two o'clock this morning in Acacia Avenue.'

'And did he happen to say what he was doing in Acacia Avenue at two o'clock this morning?'

'Taking a walk with his wife.'

'Tell him to pull the other one,' said Sloan wearily. 'And that I've got better things to do than come down and listen to some cock-and-bull story . . .'

'I'm afraid that the time and place are not in dispute, sir,' said the Station Sergeant.

'Not even the bit about him taking a walk with his wife?' asked Sloan acidly.

'I'm afraid that's true too, sir.'

'Sergeant, have you ever encountered Mrs Nolson?'

'Many times, sir,' sighed the voice at the other end of the telephone. 'She always comes in when we nick him.'

'Love's young dream, she isn't,' said Sloan flatly.

'No, sir,' the man agreed. 'More like "ill met by moonlight", you might say.' He paused. 'Actually, now I come to think of it, ill met by moonlight would go for the whole of this business.'

'So what exactly is the problem, then?' enquired Sloan briskly, hanging on to his patience with an effort. 'In a nutshell, if you can . . . I've got work to do, and Crosby needing to see me before he gets going . . . although on what I don't know, as he's pretty useless.'

'The problem, sir,' said the Station Sergeant heavily, 'is seeing that we don't conspire to pervert the course of justice.'

'That is not usually a problem . . .'

'It is now.'

'You'd better explain.'

'Larky insists that he was assaulted by a man called Bates . . .'

'At two o'clock this morning in Acacia Avenue when he wasn't robbing him?'

'You've got it in one, sir. This Bates – Herbert, I think he's called . . .'

'Hang on, Sergeant, hang on. I know a man who lives in Acacia Avenue called Herbert Bates, but he's an elderly man . . .'

'That's him, sir.'

'Can't be,' declared Sloan confidently. 'The Herbert Bates I know is an ancient little fellow and quiet with it. Wouldn't say "Boo" to a goose, let alone tackle Larky and his missus in the middle of the night.'

'Him,' repeated the Station Sergeant.

'Retired clerk,' mused Sloan. 'Took on the secretary-ship of our horticultural society when the previous one died . . .'

'That's exactly what I meant by our having a problem, sir.'

'And a very good society secretary Herbert is . . . What did you say, Sergeant?'

'That's the problem, sir.'

'How come?'

'Herbert Bates did hit Larky and Larky wants Bates's guts for garters.'

'Herbert Bates? Are you trying to tell me that little old Herbert Bates fetched his fist to Larky Nolson? I don't believe it!'

'It's not me that's telling you, sir,' said the Station Sergeant, who had earned his spurs long ago in the magistrates' court and therefore knew all about the difference between the spoken word and reported speech. 'It's Larky that's telling us.'

'Then I definitely don't believe it.'

'No, sir.' The Station Sergeant coughed. 'I wouldn't have done so myself either, except that Mr Bates says not only that he did hit Larky but that given half a chance, he'd do it again.'

'See that he doesn't get half a chance,' Sloan instructed him automatically, his mind elsewhere. 'Tell me, Sergeant, what had Larky done?'

'Depends on who's telling you,' responded the Station Sergeant promptly.

'Frankly, I'd go for Herbert Bates's version first,' said Sloan. 'Any day. He's a good bloke. First-class secretary too . . . best we've ever had at the Horticultural society.'

'This case is all about gardens—' began the Sergeant.

'Herbert's a vegetable man,' Sloan interrupted him. The Detective Inspector himself was a noted rose grower. 'Prize vegetables,' he added with emphasis.

'That,' said the Sergeant drily, 'would appear to be the trouble.'

'But Larky Nolson isn't into flowers or vegetables.' He stopped. 'Unless he was trying to steal them, of course. I wouldn't put that past him, and old Herbert's cauliflowers would be worth stealing, no doubt about that.'

'That would seem to be Mr Bates's view too,' said the Sergeant. 'Beautiful, he said they were. The curd just right . . .'

'So,' divined Sloan, 'that was what Larky and his wife were up to, wasn't it?'

'Nearly, but not quite, sir.'

'Well, all I can say is that I don't blame Herbert if Larky was knocking off his vegetables . . .'

'I understand from Mr Bates,' reported the Station Sergeant cautiously, 'that some of his best cauliflowers had in fact been stolen from his garden by someone on three occasions in the past couple of weeks, one four days before.'

'Larky?'

'This has not yet been established,' said the voice down the telephone with even greater circumspection. 'It is, of course, a distinct possibility.'

'Vegetables don't come any better anywhere in Calleshire,' averred Sloan with all the enthusiasm of the true gardener.

'This is Mr Bates's opinion too,' said the Station Sergeant.

'And that of most show judges,' said Sloan warmly.

'Unfortunately, Larky was heard by Mr Bates to take another view . . .'

'At two o'clock in the morning?'

'Quite audible, Mr Bates says he was.'

'And what was Herbert Bates doing up and about then?' asked Sloan, although he thought now he could guess.

'Lying in wait for whoever was stealing his cauliflowers.'

'And who should come along but Larky and his missus?'

'That's right, sir. Mr Bates was hiding up in his shed for the third night running at the time.'

'And?' The old man must have been getting pretty tired and fractious by then.

'Larky and his wife came along and looked over Mr Bates's fence . . .'

'But didn't enter his garden?'

'Unfortunately not. I mean, no, sir.' The Station Sergeant hastily corrected himself on this important point of law. 'All Larky did was say very loudly and clearly that he didn't think Herbert Bates's cauliflowers were half as good as Stan Redden's down the road.'

'Stan is Herbert's great show rival,' said Sloan.

'Not worth stealing, were Larky's words, and I understand his wife agreed. Rather loudly, from what Mr Bates said.'

'Which, I take it,' concluded Sloan realistically, 'was why and when Herbert came out of his shed and went for Larky.'

'It was,' agreed the Station Sergeant. 'Mr Bates says that he was provoked beyond his powers of self-control.'

'I'm afraid, though, that Larky Nolson's a real barrack-room lawyer,' mused Sloan.

This sentiment was heartily endorsed. 'Everyone around here'll tell you that, sir.'

'Let me think this through, Sergeant. I'll come back to you as soon as I've sent Crosby on his way.'

Sloan put the telephone down and called the Detective Constable in. Before he could frame any orders for him, the telephone rang again. It was the Assistant Chief Constable.

'Ah, Sloan . . .'

'Sir?'

'This alleged assault case . . .'

'Yes, sir?'

'I don't like the sound of it at all.'

'No, sir.'

'Can't have grown men hitting each other like this in the middle of the night.'

'No, sir. Certainly not.'

'Gives the place a bad name.'

'Quite so, sir.'

'And we can't on any account be seen to condone that sort of behaviour.'

'No, sir,' agreed Sloan virtuously. 'Definitely not.'

'Nor, on the other hand, though,' said the ACC consideringly, 'does it do any good for a case to be laughed out of court. Or fail.'

'Never,' said Sloan with feeling.

'Can't have that, then, can we?'

'No, sir.'

'I ask you, Sloan, what sort of a *casus belli* are cauliflowers?'

'The press will like the cauliflowers,' forecast Sloan gloomily. 'Right up their street.'

'The Lord Chancellor won't,' responded the Assistant Chief Constable smartly.

'No.'

'Of course,' mused the ACC, 'the Crown Prosecution Service could always decide the case won't stand up in court.'

'The accused has admitted to the assault,' Sloan told him.

'Ah . . .' The ACC sounded as if he was tapping a pencil on his desk. 'I thought that might be the case. So we can't get away with *de minimus* . . .'

'Cabbages, perhaps, sir, assault no!' That the law did not concern itself with trifles was one of the ACC's favourite quotations. In Latin, of course. 'Although you never can tell with the CPS,' added Sloan feelingly.

'Very true, Inspector. Very true!' He coughed. 'It seems to me that their motto is "Evidence before justice".'

'Quite so, sir,' said Sloan, before the ACC put that into Latin too. 'Of course, sir, admitting guilt here and pleading guilty in court are not necessarily one and the same thing.' In his experience, nothing brought about a sea change in an accused person's stance quicker than a lawyer for the defence.

'Quite right, Sloan. Solicitors do have to earn their oats . . .'

'If you say so, sir.'

'So do policemen, Inspector.' The Assistant Chief Constable paused before adding, 'And young policemen have to learn their job first too, don't they?'

'Naturally, sir,' said Sloan stiffly, unsure of where this was leading.

'And they've all got to begin somewhere . . .'

'Of course . . .'

'Even the least promising.'

'Them, too,' said Sloan fervently.

Detective Constable Crosby, who was standing in front of him now, was a case in point. He was the least bright star in the detective firmament of 'F' Division, the police equivalent of being all fingers and thumbs in whatever he did.

'In my opinion,' said the ACC loftily, 'it's never a

bad idea for beginners to cut their teeth on something not too important.'

'Of course . . .'

'Cases where the outcome isn't vital to law and order.'

'I think I take your point, sir.'

'After all, he – I mean, any inexperienced young constable – could make mistakes in putting a case together.'

'Easily, sir.'

'And even accidentally let fall things he – or she, of course – shouldn't.'

'It has been known, sir.'

'And afterwards he – or she, of course – could be shown what he – or she, of course – had done shall we say less than well rather than wrong.'

'If they had,' pointed out Sloan.

'On the other hand, Inspector, no way must we fail to honour our obligations under paragraph forty of Magna Carta.'

'I can't quite recall . . .'

' "To no one will we sell, to no one deny or delay right or justice",' declared the ACC in ringing tones, thus clearing his own decks and handing the problem straight back to Sloan.

Sloan passed a modified version of this on to Detective Constable Crosby – jejune but eager – and sent him off to take statements all round and prepare the case against Herbert Bates.

'It's all yours, lad,' said Sloan basely. 'See how you get on for starters . . .'

Detective Inspector Sloan's highly confidential filing was almost finished by the time the young Detective Constable reported back the next day.

He looked crestfallen. 'I'm sorry, sir,' he mumbled, 'but there isn't going to be a case after all.'

'How come?'

'Larky Nolson has withdrawn the charge.'

'Tell me.'

'It's like this, sir,' said Crosby very apologetically, 'I took some of the soil off Larky's shoes and matched it with that in Mr Bates's garden, although I know that doesn't actually prove anything . . .'

'No.'

'And the shoe matched the footprints in Mr Bates's ground, although they are four days old and it's only circumstantial evidence anyway.'

An uneasy thought occurred to Sloan, as ever worried by possible allegations of police irregularities. 'How did you get Larky to take his shoe off?'

'I accidentally spilt some hot tea on his foot, sir. It didn't scald him,' he added hastily, on catching sight of his superior's expression.

'And?' Heroically, Sloan refrained from comment.

'I got the remains of some cooked cauliflower from Larky's dustbin.'

'Without his permission?'

'I got it from the corporation waste collection van. Yesterday was collection day.'

'You did, did you?'

'I understand, sir,' he said anxiously, 'that once the contents have been taken by the binmen, the owner has voluntarily surrendered his rights to them. I did check that with the council, sir.'

'That's not proof positive either.'

'No, sir. So I got a sample of the cauliflowers in the supermarket. It's the only place where you can buy them in the town.'

'Now that all the greengrocers have gone . . .' No shopper himself, Sloan knew this from his wife.

'You remember that bit in the local paper complaining that they mostly sell foreign greengrocery there, sir?'

'I'm beginning to get your drift, Crosby.'

'So I got Forensics to check, sir.'

'Different cauliflowers?' So vegetable as well as animal did come into the equation, after all.

'Very. And, sir, they could tell which had been treated with commercial chemicals and which hadn't.'

'Herbert Bates's?' Larky could have bought his cauliflowers outside the town, of course, but it wasn't all that likely.

'Yes, sir. He doesn't use chemicals.'

'Wonderful what scientists can do these days. Now, when I was first on the beat . . .' He stopped. The luxury of reminiscence could wait. 'Then what, Crosby?'

'I drew Larky Nolson's attention to my findings, sir, and he decided against proceeding with the charge against Herbert Bates.'

'And are we now faced with Herbert Bates bringing a counter-charge for theft against Larky Nolson?'

'No, sir.'

'How can you be so sure?'

'The Forensics people told me that Herbert Bates's cauliflowers were on the list of varieties that can no longer be marketed under European regulations, sir.' He looked at Sloan and asked anxiously, 'Do you want chapter and verse on that, sir?'

'Heaven forbid,' said Sloan speedily. 'But Herbert isn't into marketing, surely?'

'There was a board by his gate with a chalk message on it to the effect that cabbages could be bought . . .'

Sloan scratched his chin, a little puzzled. It was something he had never noticed himself.

Crosby put his notebook down on Sloan's desk. 'I'm very sorry, sir, but nobody seems to be charging anybody now. Is that all right?'